I0819116

EXTRA SAUCE

EXTRA SAUCE

The GOOD, the BAD, and the ONIONS

A MEMOIR

ZAHRA TANGORRA

THE DIAL PRESS
NEW YORK

The Dial Press
An imprint of Random House
A division of Penguin Random House LLC
1745 Broadway, New York, NY 10019
randomhousebooks.com
penguinrandomhouse.com

Hardcover ISBN 978-0-593-73337-0
Ebook ISBN 978-0-593-73339-4

Printed in the United States of America on acid-free paper

1st Printing

FIRST EDITION

BOOK TEAM: PRODUCTION EDITOR: *Cassie Gitkin*
MANAGING EDITOR: *Rebecca Berlant* • PRODUCTION MANAGER: *Ali Wagner*
COPY EDITOR: *Leda Scheintaub* • PROOFREADERS: *Anya Getschel, Andrea Gordon, Nicholas LoVecchio*

Title-page image by Adobe Stock/aura studio
Book design by Barbara M. Bachman

The authorized representative in the EU for product safety and compliance is Penguin Random House Ireland, Morrison Chambers, 32 Nassau Street, Dublin D02 YH68, Ireland. https://eu-contact.penguin.ie

Dearest Babes,

May there be fire in your hearts
and wind at your backs
Alla Nostra!

I have no idea where this will lead us,
but I have a definite feeling it will be
a place both wonderful and strange.

—SPECIAL AGENT DALE COOPER,
TWIN PEAKS

CONTENTS

EXTRA SAUCE

FIRE EVERYTHING

CUE LINK WRAY'S "FIRE AND BRIMSTONE."

There was the road, and then, in an instant, there was not.

Asphalt to air rearrangement, a seamless transition, with the exception of a few large thuds early on. I have often wished that I could have replayed this metamorphosis in slow motion, to have seen the exact moment when my face went from soft and supple to rigid with fear and, ultimately, smashed. To have seen all of us who were on this tour bus suspended in air, floating like amateur astronauts, untrained in the art of antigravity exploration and unbraced for impact.

It's safe to say that my face looked like many other faces at the turn of the twenty-first century: my eyebrows were tweezed so thin that they made Greta Garbo look like Groucho Marx, the lids beneath caked in shimmery shades of white and brown shadow. It is safe to say that my tongue ring was visible if I was screaming, and that my Monroe piercing, and the box-dyed jet black hair that I had cut myself with a tiny pair of scissors meant for snipping thread, made it clear that I was flying off a cliff in the early aughts.

On December 3, 2006, I was twenty-two years old. My parents had known me for twenty-two years, and at that point neither of them liked me very much, and the feeling was mutual. My father and I had not spoken in over a year, a chilly quietness originating from me missing a visit to his house where he had planned to tell me he had cancer. I had canceled because there was a storm that dropped three feet of snow on our town and all of the roads were closed. At the time of the bus crash, I was still not aware that he had been diagnosed with multiple myeloma, or that he had had a stem cell transplant that nearly killed him. Upon hearing that I had narrowly escaped death, he would not call, instead sending a Get Well card from the drugstore simply signed *—John*. A card with no message sent in response to one's child almost passing away tragically is cold, and signing it "John" in place of "Dad" is subzero. When it comes in the mail, I will make it soggy with my tears and then rip it up and throw it in the trash. John would hold a grudge like Kate Winslet at the end of *Titanic*, letting love sink to the silty, black ocean floor instead of just moving over a few inches.

The time between the first thump, indicating to us that the bus had gone off the road, and when I regained consciousness is mostly lost. I will never know what shapes my face made, how many times my body somersaulted before landing, or how beautiful and macabre we must have all looked for those strange few seconds, entangled with each other in the liminal space of the thirty-nine-and-a-half-foot bus as it soared off the arid Southern Californian cliffside. The tape restarts at what I imagine to be seconds after the crash. My body hurt in the way a body tends to when it is in shock, which is not at all. This is the calm before the storm, the smell of the first raindrops. I don't remember when I felt pain. It must have been in the UC San Diego Hospital between the stops and starts of the morphine drip. I try to remember feeling pain in those early moments, but to feel pain I think you have to believe you are hurt, which I wouldn't comprehend until my mother, Bobbie, arrived the next day. That was when I knew it was safe to be broken because she would make sure I got put back together; she may not have liked me very much at twenty-two, but she loved me, and that was the glue.

I lost time, I am not sure how much, but when I realized that I was still a part of the world, I was stuck underneath something, or rather someone, twice my size. I managed to slither out from under the man who was passed out on top of me, who thankfully also turned out to still be alive, with that elusive superhuman strength we hear of mothers using to lift cars when their child is trapped underneath. This strength is real. This strength is your will to live. It's Uma smashing her fist through the casket in *Kill Bill Volume 2* and pulling herself up through six feet of dirt for a breath of fresh air. It comes to us from a hidden spot deep within our animus, a powerful surge of adrenaline, divinity, or the third man even, depending on what texts you subscribe to, the voice that whispers into your soul: *not yet*.

Beyond the twisted burning metal and the man on top of me, I was also stuck beneath something else. Something with an unquantifiable metric that required a different type of strength to move. I was trapped beneath the belief that I was inherently no good and not worth loving.

When I spun off the edge of the canyon, I had been moving through the world in a chaotic gyration of indifference and a quiet desperation to belong. My parents had driven me over that particular cliff long ago, and while clawing my way up from it would take decades, it would begin in this moment, with the same snap of determination to survive. Not consciously, not an epiphany or a chat with God, more like a death or an earthquake that demands you grow around a new gash in your foundation. I was emotionally detached from my family, and myself, as I hung frozen in the sliver between life and death, facing the tribunal, waiting for the verdict. If I'd had the chance to act as my own counsel, I would have argued that despite my apathy toward my life at that exact moment, I did want my parents to know me for another twenty-two years, or at least ten, or until they liked me again. Until I knew how to truly like myself. Until I smelled New York City again on a freezing cold day, or felt prickling on my feet from stepping into a hot bubble bath. I fastened a strong grip around my life and pulled my way to safety, for the chance to fall a thousand more times. *Not yet.*

. . .

I FOUND MYSELF IN this burning bus because I had gone on tour to sell merchandise for my dear friend Jeffrey Haynes (aka the rapper Mr. Lif), as he embarked on a national and world tour with Boots Riley and The Coup, as a twenty-two-year-old's interpretation of finding herself, a first real attempt at adultness. I adored Jeffrey. I thought he was the kindest, most interesting person I had ever met, and although much of my hyperbolic thinking as a young woman turned out to be incorrect, this was an astute and wholeheartedly true opinion. He was and is a gentle, wonderfully nerdy, hilarious person who taught me to love the films of Charles Bronson, the perils of capitalism, and the value of living a life guided by feeding one's inherent creativity. I could have never known as an eighteen-year-old kid that the night we met at The Cop Shop in Smithtown, Long Island, would hold perhaps the most life-altering interactions of my life thus far, but these fateful chapters are so often written in invisible ink. I loved and admired Jeffrey so much that when he asked me to come along on the tour, I quit my job as a display artist at Urban Outfitters immediately, never for a second imagining a world where I did not return. It may have been considered rebellion had anyone cared that I was going in the first place.

At the time of the accident, I had been on the tour for about five days, and I was attempting to ward off the impending melancholia with beer and cigarette smoke. On the flight to San Francisco to meet up with Jeffrey and the twelve others on the tour, I had taken a Xanax and drank three Bloody Marys, and when I got up with my giant winter coat still on to prowl the plane for a fourth, I was escorted back to my seat, belted in, and warned to stay put until everyone else was off of the aircraft. I left my driver's license on the plane, in the seatback pocket next to the paper bag used for emergency vomiting, and had been desperately trying to have another one mailed to me in one of the many cities we were meant to be stopping in. My license would end up being mailed to Austin, Texas, where it would remain forever, as I was not going to make it to Austin, Texas, on this trip and have never been there since. Perhaps this was the source of my melancholy those first few days. Or maybe my brain was aware my soul had plans to break up with my body soon. Or it was the loneliness I felt. I missed my mother. I missed the cobalt blue water glasses in her kitchen cabinet, and the birthmark between her eyebrows. I missed how our hearts used to beat to the same rhythm before our relationship became a broken record. But every time she called to check in, I was standoffish, giving her only the bare minimum, even though what I really wanted to say was *Come get me.*

We had started the night at the House of Blues in San Diego, and Jeffrey and the tour manager had gotten into an argument about whether we should drive the six hours to Phoenix. Jeffrey said that he thought the bus driver looked tired, and suggested we stay parked and make the trip in the morning. The tour manager wanted to stay on schedule, so here we were, six of us watching *Anchorman* in the front of the tour bus, laughing and drinking beer, the other six listening to the recently released Clipse record *Hell Hath No Fury.* I had bought the DVD a week before we left, at the Tower Records in Union Square for ten dollars, which is even stronger affirmation that this was 2006 than the over-tweezed eyebrows.

There was a thud, and then another, and that quick and terrible feeling that electrifies you for a split second when you realize something awful and unstoppable is about to make head-on contact with your life. The DVD stopped, which stands out as the first sign something was wrong. Like the lights going out with the crack of a thunder clap. *Change has happened.*

I am the girl who peed in her pants at school in eighth grade from laughing too hard and had to walk around all day in damp jeans because my mother refused to pick me up, and now I am the girl flying off a cliff in a tour bus, almost certainly peeing again, but it will all be too bloody for anyone to notice. This is happening to every version of me that I have ever been, and none of us are ready for it, but that doesn't matter because chaos and gravity are not sentimental. There is nothing one can hold on to as a mortal being when the earth has plans to shake you loose. This is freedom, however unwelcome it may be.

I was weightless at this moment, moving from one piece to

many, healthy to injured. A terrible but important lesson that we are no more meaningful to the universe than branches being snapped off a tree in a storm. But I did not wish to be a branch, I wished to be a living person, and so I tried to hold on to anything that I could wrap my bloody fingers around. Specifically, a Red Stripe bottle, which exploded in my right hand like a firecracker, shearing all of the skin off and rendering it from this point on my *bad hand*.

We were on Route 8 in El Centro, California, the same strip of road where a very famous movie star I would rendezvous with six years later at the bar of my restaurant Brucie will tell me he filmed a blockbuster about the Iraq war. My response will be to make googly eyes at him and say, *What are the odds?* The odds are quite slim, and yet, this coincidence will not result in a steamy love affair, and eventual marriage, as I had expected.

This was not how I had wished to experience the desert for the first time. I had pictured something with a slightly more spiritual, less gory texture to it. Four years earlier, on a class trip to San Diego, I had been desert adjacent, spending a week in a youth hostel alongside twentysomethings dropping acid and having sex in their bunk beds. One day we took a drive about thirty minutes out of town to observe some nature. It was dry and brown, but lacked the haunted expansiveness of the real desert. I flicked the butt of my Marlboro Light into some bramble, which would have most certainly started a forest fire had a local not jumped into the thorny tangle and retrieved it. He screamed in my face, telling me that I had no idea how fucking stupid and careless I was, and he was correct. I had to assume that this was Mother Nature's way of seeking her revenge upon me, and who could blame her?

. . .

TODAY, DECEMBER 3, MY own mother is visiting her mother, my grandma Violet, in Boca Raton for her birthday. Violet, who lived through the Holocaust, while I won't make it out of this stupid trip to California. She is eighty-six to my twenty-two, and had the bus driver closed his eyes to sleep for fifteen seconds instead of ten, I may have stayed twenty-two forever. I would have never seen Violet again. She would have never been at the friends and family party for Brucie where I shook up a bottle of champagne and sprayed it into the crowd to kick things off, accidentally soaking her with the majority of the contents. I wouldn't have felt the thin, soft, spotted skin on her hands when I held them for the last time before she passed in 2012. I would not have the soul-satisfying career that I have now. I would not have smoked a blunt of chronic with Flava Flav, cooked for Parker Posey, or been violently electrocuted by a walk-in freezer. My mother would have had photos of me around the house with seven-day candles burning beneath them that would make her wince to look at. *That was my daughter,* she would have had to say. *Was. Is. Was. Is.* The seconds, the decisions, the micro universes between she *is* and she *was,* between alchemy and elegy, between dead and chef, are so liquidy, I've still not figured out how to keep them from slipping through the space between my fingers.

It has been scientifically proven that our brains reference collected memories from our lives before we die, thousands of profound moments condensed into one phrenetic epilogue. Why particular memories make the edit, I do not know, but I believe that they must be the ones that are so impossibly tender they can be filleted with a feather.

I do not recall a slideshow, but if I had, I'd have seen myself at age seven with Violet at the pool at her condo in Boca, sunburned nose, goggle marks, and pruney fingers. Showering off the chlorine in her elegant gray and white bathroom, under a stream of water so powerful it felt sharp. Getting lost in her walk-in closet, trying on her high heels and Chanel dresses. I'd have seen us later that day having cocktail hour, her drinking a scotch and soda, my mother tanned and perfect, standing on the balcony looking at the sun setting over the manatee-rich Intracoastal Waterway. Me shoveling shrimp cocktail and peanuts into my mouth with the voracity of someone who has been lost at sea for six months. I'd have seen my mother's dark eyes illuminated in the moonlight as I snuck under the covers with her on the mattress she had propped against the open sliding glass balcony door of Violet's apartment, listening to the silence and the crashing waves.

I'd have seen my father sitting on a bench in the Smith Haven Mall, waiting for me while I bought my biweekly Troll Doll from Spencer Gifts, smirking under his orange mustache. I'd see him awake in the middle of the night watching *Star Trek* reruns and eating puffed Cheetos, in the cottage he rented when my parents first split. I'd see his pea soup and his chocolate chip cookies, and my mother's chicken strudel and chocolate mousse pie and the fabulous corn pudding with sharp cheddar cheese that she makes for Thanksgiving.

I'd see the tomatoes in my grandfather's garden, and his giant, rock-hard belly and ears the size of a baby elephant's. And Violet's sweet and sour meatballs, the sauce made from jarred marinara and a can of jellied cranberries, and a turkey sandwich with American cheese, lettuce, tomato, and extra mustard and mayo from the Northport Deli. And nectarines, corn on the cob, juicy lobsters, and green mint chip ice cream in the summertime after a long day bobbing in the surf at Robert Moses beach.

I'd see burning hot pizza rolls and raw cookie dough from the package being devoured at middle school sleepovers on the ivy green couch in my living room with my then best friends Jen and Madi, taking shots of Sprite, pretending to be drunk, watching *Faces of Death* between the cracks in our fingers and talking about our crushes. I was in love with Rob Drost, who had a lightweight blond mushroom cut and was often wearing a worn-out Offspring T-shirt. He would pass away when we were in our early twenties, but I still have the notes that Jen and Madi and I would write: *Zahra Drost* encased in a heart. I'd see Vinny, Eric, Ryan, Leonardo DiCaprio, Brad Pitt, Christian Bale, and all the other men I'd ever loved and had to let go of.

I'd have seen my cousin Rory and me as little kids, catching fireflies in a big glass jar and watching them twinkle in tandem with the stars overhead in the soupy July night air. I'd see myself crouched in a bush with my high school best friend Vanessa, hiding from the police after starting a wild party at a classmate's family's new home that they hadn't yet moved into.

I'd see the first cigarette that I smoked at age eight, and the first line of cocaine I did at sixteen, and all my other trysts with self-destruction. My dreadlocks and blue eye shadow in high school. The girls I shoved at parties, trying to act tough so no one would find out how weak I really was. The money I stole from my mother to buy pot and cheap, tacky clothing at Forever 21. I'd have seen real shame, the kind that makes you swallow your eyeballs. Shame of being fat, ugly, having sweat stains, being bad at kissing, being weird, having breasts before anyone took me to buy a bra. I'd see my mother helping me cut up all my clothing so I could look like Tank Girl, and getting sent home from school because of it. The kid with broke, lefty parents on a *we feel bad for you* scholarship, wearing knee-high baseball socks over purple fishnets and an old Army helmet to her blue-blood Republican private school, what could go wrong?

I'd see my dad dressed as Uncle Fester, and me as Wednesday Addams on Halloween in 1993, and as a leprechaun in 1998, and Pippi Longstocking before I knew how to read. The Humpty Dumpty costume my mother made me out of Hula-Hoops and a white bedsheet for the fourth-grade production of *Alice in Wonderland*. Learning to ride a bike. Breaking my clavicle. Seeing *Pulp Fiction* in the theater when I was ten. At Nassau Coliseum for my first concert, Dire Straits, and at Bowery Ballroom for the last Company Flow show. Having sex for the first time in my childhood bedroom in the tenth grade.

I'd see my mother making me chicken soup when I was sick, and us pretending to be crabs together at the beach, me clinging to her, loving her so honestly and purely, wanting to be as close to her as possible. I would see our fights that got so out of control when I was in high school that the cops would come, and her face when I spit in it and screamed *I hate you*, and then the morning after how I tried to pretend like we hadn't fucked it all up beyond repair. I'd see her teeth, crooked in the exact same way mine are, when she threw her head back to laugh.

And then I would see flames, and think to myself, *I don't want to feel myself explode. I don't want to watch myself catch on fire and burn to death. Not with these eyebrows.*

The problem with our lives flashing before us is that we

only see the bygone. I could not see that I would one day be a chef, and then a writer. I couldn't see that I would open my own restaurant at twenty-six, all by myself with no experience, or that it would be such a massive success and breath-grabbing gut punch all at once. That it would bankrupt me and also provide me with a stage to be charming, engaging, celebrated, hated and mean, inappropriate and electro charged. I couldn't see what all of that would come to mean to me, the shame I would feel or the ways in which I would try to change how I moved through the world because of it. I didn't know what professional success would feel like, that it was even an option in my lifetime, or what it felt like to be drenched in sewer water from falling in the grease trap, to skin a pig's face in one unbroken sheet to make porchetta di testa, to see my name in the paper. To realize that none of these things mattered nearly as much as becoming fluent in kindness and patience.

I couldn't see the searingly painful losses, some so bad that I would sob to my mother how I wish I had died in the bus accident. I couldn't see that loss can be the key to learning to love yourself. That, like eggs, we are meant to break in order to be truly functional. I couldn't see what it would be like to fall in love with someone who lived in Italy and never really get over it. I didn't know about pandemics or how much water could leak from my face after my dad died. I didn't know that I could really do anything at all, like cook or be loved, and though I still wrestle with these truths from time to time, I am accepting them more and more with the daily setting of the sun.

The knowledge that we can be loved, and that we deserve it, and that it matters to live and breathe with this recognition, is crucial to being alive. I often wonder, as I inch closer to being someone who believes I am capable and deserving, how much pain and destruction is caused by not understanding that we are born tender beings worthy of being cherished. I didn't know that I was born tender, or that one could get hurt this bad and live, and it's a shame, because if we are lucky, we do live, and wouldn't it be lovely and awful all at once to have *that* flash before our eyes? A little hope, a little perspective, a vision of true, honest, unbridled laughter? Sometimes a crisis is sadly the finale, but often it is the most pivotal scene. Scars are currency. *Please girl open your eyes and live to see how that can be true.* Like Nora Ephron's mother told her, *Everything is copy.* Like my mother sang to me, *Que será será. Whatever will be will be. The future's not ours to see.*

. . .

WHEN I CAME TO, I saw fire and smoke. I smelled gas. I felt the heat of dancing orange flames on my skin, like I was at the business end of a barbecue. I was staring at death and praying it would not come any closer. My brain ping-ponged between *this isn't happening* and *this is happening.* To fully embrace the latter was to give up every ounce of control that I had ever had. I had been so reckless with my life because I hadn't yet considered the value in it. But I wasn't ready to say goodbye, I'd only just arrived, my coat and scarf were still on. I heard the panic in other people's voices as they came to consciousness. Jeffrey grabbed my hand, which was essentially no longer functioning as such, just ripped skin and bones sticking out from a wrist attached to a scared child, and they pulled me up from the wreckage. The bus had miraculously landed with the door facing upward, making survival possible. Someone had managed to push the door open and we started to make our way out into the abyss of wherever we were.

Where we were was in a ravine about forty feet below street level in El Centro. The majority of the stretch of Route 8 between San Diego and El Centro is flat on both sides. The spot where our bus driver fell asleep at the wheel is one of the only places where such an incident could have even occurred.

El Centro is the largest city in the Imperial Valley of Southern California, and also the largest American city below sea level. El Centro is one hundred and thirteen miles from San Diego and roughly twenty miles from the US/Mexico border. El Centro has over three hundred and fifty days of sunshine and under three inches of rain annually. The 1940 El Centro Earthquake measured at a 6.9 on the Mercalli Intensity Scale. It was the strongest recorded earthquake to hit the Imperial Valley, and caused widespread damage to irrigation systems and killed nine people. Cher was born in El Centro in 1946.

I was not aware that we were in El Centro, nor was I aware that Cher had been born there, and as someone who has watched *Moonstruck* once a week for the past ten years, I cannot help but feel as though this was kismet. If Cher could make it out of El Centro, so could I.

I had not yet processed that the bus had crashed, or the severity of the injury to my hand, or that the fourth toe on my right foot had also been sliced nearly off, which would bother me for the rest of my life, the life that had not been ripped away from me, even though we had gone off basically the only cliff in El Centro. I did not realize that rattlesnakes were slithering beneath my feet as I jumped from the burning bus, or maybe they were not, but I picture thousands of them in the audience when I manage to picture it at all. Jeffrey grabbed me and helped me make it to the road where a group of us had assembled and were looking out at the burning heap of metal that we had just escaped from. I thought at that moment that we would fix the bus and continue the tour. I thought, *This must be some kind of mistake.* I thought, *Is anyone still in there?* I looked down at my hand and then at Jeffrey as he removed his sock and tied it tight around my wrist as a tourniquet.

Hold it above your head, he instructed. *You're okay.*

We were in El Centro and also nowhere. It was just after four in the morning, but time had stopped, and by now it could have been five past four or eight p.m. the next day, or Christmas or a dream. It didn't matter; we were dead or we weren't, no way to tell at that point. Catastrophe freezes time, and upon reflection I can see how silly and trivial everything I have ever spent time worrying about has been. Some days I walk around in stillness, remembering the silence between life and death and how the only thing that I could have ever wanted was to just keep being a person. Coat me in amber. Preserve the thoughts in my brain and the air in my lungs.

I wish that perspective, that recognition for the gift of simply existing, could always snap me from my sadness or agitations. I wish that I could report that each day since has felt like a gift, and that I used this precious second chance to right my wrongs, but the truth is there were times in the years that followed when I was cruel and careless. There were days, whole years even, when I forgot how lucky I was, and periods of deep selfishness and contempt for my good fortune. And there was, and is, and hopefully always will be, outrageous joy, laughter, and bouts of gratitude when I squeeze my hands together so tightly that my wrists could break from the pressure while thanking the cosmos for precious life.

If any of us had been in our bunks in the middle section of the bus at three forty-five a.m., we would have been trapped when we crashed. But instead, eleven of us had managed to make our way to the road and escape death or critical injury. Two of us were missing: the driver, who was still in the same seat he had been sitting in when he drove us off the edge of our previous lives, and the man who had ended up on top of me. I would later learn that he had broken his leg when jumping out of the bus and rolled underneath it.

Everyone I've ever talked to who has traveled the stretch of Route 8 between California and Arizona has noted how you could drive for miles and miles and never see another car. In the wee hours of the morning of December 3, 2006, there happened to be two semi tractor trailers driving by, both of which came to an abrupt halt, their drivers climbing into the ravine after we told them that our friend fell under the bus. Both our friend and the bus driver were rescued before the bus burned to a twisted metal shell. We all lived.

A woman driving by stopped to take me and a few others who seemed to be in the worst shape to the local hospital. I destroyed her car with my blood. I cannot tell you how much time I have spent trying to find out who she was so I could thank her and pay her for the damage I caused by spraying blood all over her car like an extra in *The Wild Bunch*.

When we arrived at the hospital, I walked through the door of the ER and up to reception covered from head to toe in blood, my right hand held high above my head as though I had a question, sticky red liquid rushing over the soaked sock and into my hair. The receptionist looked at me and said, *What seems to be the problem?*

The problem, Madam, is that my hand is coming off. The problem is that I am supposed to be traveling across the country on tour with my cool musician friend, being the absolute envy of everyone I know, finding myself, and coming home in two months to start my life as a famous painter and move in with some hot guy I met on the road, but my right hand is now steak tartare and I look like Carrie fucking White. I am drenched in my own blood, and other people's blood, and maybe I am also dying from internal injuries. This trip was meant to have been directed by Cameron Crowe, but it appears that he has been replaced by David Lynch. The problem is I can't tell what is real anymore. The problem is this was not part of my plan. The problem is plans in general, and how they so often refuse to be reliable. The problem is I am really just not done yet. I haven't sorted things out with my mother, and I want to, so badly, even though I would rather chew glass than admit it right now, but really I love her and I cannot die before we fix it. I have not figured out how to feel truly beautiful, and I want to. I haven't gotten to the part where everything not making sense actually makes sense. But really the problem is that I feel like I deserve to live, that I am supposed to, that the universe is watching out for me. The problem is that I thought I was a young woman with a long life ahead of her, and time to turn things around, but I have just been made aware that I am a tree branch, and all I want is to have roots. The problem is I hadn't died, and now I would have to justify my survival for the rest of my life to anyone who asks me my name. *I'm Zahra. I'm a chef because I got into an accident and got a settlement out of it. I know I don't deserve any of this, I'm just lucky.*

. . .

FIVE YEARS LATER I will look at my father seated at the bar of the restaurant I would open with the settlement money from this cataclysmic sojourn. I will watch him laugh and eat meatballs swimming in a pool of thick, tangy red sauce, and be his effortlessly charming self with the staff and patrons seated next to him. *That's my girl*, he will say to the couple to his right, pointing at me working garde manger. I will think of the Get Well card and the smashing of metal into boulders and the box-dyed hair and feel happy these flies were no longer in our collective ointment, and also unclear how we had ever managed to get them out. In another five years he will be dead from cancer. I will be angry at him for dying. But this moment at the bar has stillness to it, two ticks of pause, a breath out. His giant freckled hands gripping the copper bar as he enjoys the chuckle erupting from his belly and hissing through his nostrils.

If I one day do get the chance to scan through superlative moments of my life before I die, I hope I would see this one. And I hope I would see the bus barreling down that cliff, wheels popping off like hot corn, see myself careening toward a completely different story, a blessed second chance, a magical new existence and very complicated life, all right there in the palm of my chopped-up hand. *Not yet.*

EXTRA SAUCE

EXTRA SAUCE IS HOW I LIKE MY PIZZA AND ALSO HOW I FALL in love. If there is extra sauce, food will taste better and last longer. It will have more flavor, more texture, more squish, and more meaning. Extra sauce is messy, and messy is exciting, wild and free. Wild and free is how you evade death, for now, and how you manage to not feel it when it finally finds you. So by that math, extra sauce is survival.

Extra sauce is for sopping, dunking, and licking off your plate. Licking off your fingers. Licking in general. It is a tiny demand for freedom and hedonism. Abbondanza. Joie de vivre. Life has told you this is the amount of joy you get, and you say, *That is simply not enough*. Extra sauce is a craving and a need, an itch that is distracting until it is scratched. Extra sauce gets you into trouble sometimes. It can make you take chances that break your heart, but it can also mend the heart because it will go to the ends of the earth to find treatment. Extra sauce drips onto your white clothing and leaves a stain, and you should know by now not to wear white clothing, but you like white clothing, *and* extra sauce, and so the shirts continue to become soiled.

Extra sauce is a pleasure. It is asking for pleasure or making it for yourself. Sometimes pleasure is hard to ask for. Sometimes it is hard to give it to yourself, but extra sauce says, *God damn it you deserve pleasure*, so you take it even when you feel deflated or embarrassed. Extra sauce is a shot of tequila, or five. It is chain smoking. It is devouring a good book in a day and a half. It is the music turned up so loud that you know you are permanently damaging your eardrums, but you don't care because "Feels So Good #1" by Junior Kimbrough is meant to be played at an eleven. It's rubbing your eyes too hard and too long, three bowls of cereal, falling in love, and singing Cole Porter standards in the shower. It is a ten-page love letter written furiously on nice stationery and sealed with a kiss. It is how I would headline a personal ad in the newspaper if I was single and looking for love in 1987.

Extra sauce is a triathlon. A temper tantrum. A very large banquet with lobsters and ham and various petit fours. Pamela Anderson. Bootsy Collins. Bobby Short. Nicolas Cage and Anaïs Nin. Hard sex that leaves the sheets torn to shreds. Smeared makeup and claw marks. Heavy breathing and stars in your eyes. It is fucking instead of making love. Extra sauce is a meltdown that you didn't want to happen but couldn't stop. It is sucking giant shrimp heads dry, drinking wine from the bottle, and doing karaoke. A chip buffet. Anthony Bourdain. Liza. Divine. Jumping in the ocean at Robert Moses every New Year's Day. Extra sauce is taking big swings, and being swung at in return. It's revolution, vim and vigor, piss and vinegar, passion, zeal, rapture, and perhaps a concussion.

Extra sauce is how my mother orders everything, chicken francese arriving at the table at our favorite local hometown Italian restaurant floating in a lagoon of lemon butter sauce. She dunks turkey, coleslaw, and Swiss wraps into small buckets of Russian dressing they give her as a side at the Woodbury

Country Deli, and she hides a French fry in a Trojan horse of ketchup. When I am with my mother on Long Island, extra sauce is the expectation. It is our treaty, and if I decline to ask for more dressing or a side of marinara, I am abandoning her. When I ask for the spaghetti and meatballs at Sal D's, our local Italian American favorite, she tells me, *If you get it, I'd ask for extra sauce*. It's not a suggestion, it's an order, and I comply because I share her affliction, or gift, depending on the circumstance.

My entire existence has been extra sauce. Make it better, make it hurt less, make the bitterness indetectable beneath the thick coating of fervent delight. Become feral and tameless to eclipse the fear and shame. Extra sauce can mask even the driest, most bland chicken cutlet. *Don't be a bland chicken cutlet* was in the subtext of all my mother's suggestions to live with reckless abandon. Maybe I wanted to be a bland chicken cutlet, and maybe as a child I needed to be one, instead of going against every grain that suggested I just fit in. I was not a bland chicken cutlet when I kicked through the windshield of her car when I was seven, but had I been, maybe I would have been able to avoid dragging such painful and embarrassing memories around with me for decades like a sack of dirty laundry. I do want extra sauce on everything, all the time, always, but I have learned that what you want and what you need are often different entities. I want the moon, I need the earth. I want Kevin Costner in *Bull Durham*, I need Kevin Costner in *The Bodyguard*.

When I ask for extra sauce on my spaghetti and meatballs at Sal D's, I discover that Bobbie is right. Their sauce is delicious, and I am happy to have a surplus to sop up with bread. I ask for extra pecorino too, and I put a full foil-wrapped rectangle of butter on a chunk of seeded Italian bread, dunk it in the extra dressing that Bobbie asked for with our salad, and I am exactly where and who I want to be.

For most of my life I have eaten nothing but the sauce, and it has been delicious, and it has given me terrible agita too. A giant bowl of sauce is not a fully balanced meal. Nowadays I try not to use extra sauce when expressing displeasure with another human being. I try to order an argument undressed to avoid overstimulation and unnecessary calories when I can. I do not wish to bring a confrontation to a Sal D's level. I have learned that more tears and more struggle does not make love more real, it drowns the real thing, makes it forever out of reach.

As I age, I hope to become a better cook, and a better person. There is a benediction to restraint, and I have come to learn that sometimes less truly can be more. Simple, classic, chic, effortless. Clean lines. Very French. But I am not French, I am Italian, a quarter at least, but that quarter wants extra sauce, and that quarter leaves with it all over her white shirt, always. That quarter laughs loudly until she cries, and nothing in this world, not a million dollars or your name in the paper or a new car from Oprah, feels as good as laughing until you cry. That quarter has been known to drink five negronis like she was John Wayne's Italian cousin, and order one of everything. That quarter falls in love very fast and very hard and gets hurt very easily and very bad and very often. That quarter wears see-through clothing, and bright red lipstick, and eats with her hands.

I am scared of ordinary, but I am practicing becoming friendly with it, because ordinary can be stable. Hop in the canoe instead of the speedboat. I will learn to drink a cocktail in more than two sips, and take five seconds before I react to something unfavorable. And I will also try to eat slower, because it is ideal for digestion, but when I do, it will always be with extra sauce. Because it is okay to want more from our lives. To ask for it, yearn for it and pursue it, all of it. The key is to determine whether what we desire must be sought after or already exists within us.

My Favorite Marinara

I HAVE MADE OCEANS OF MARINARA SAUCE IN MY LIFE, AND I have loved all of them, even the ones I have accidentally burned because I totally forgot they were cooking and went on to doing something else. I have come around to thinking of this sauce as my favorite, both for its rich, bright flavor, and how wildly simple it is to prepare. No more sweating over the stovetop for you sweet folks, this sauce comes together in the oven, and is finished with uncooked crushed tomatoes. Not only does this reduce stress, but the addition of uncooked crushed tomatoes (try and use the best-quality ones you can get your hands on) adds a tangy freshness to this absolute delight of a sauce!

MAKES ABOUT 2 QUARTS SAUCE

½ cup extra-virgin olive oil
1 large onion, halved and thinly sliced (about 1½ cups)
6 to 8 whole garlic cloves
2 tablespoons kosher salt
1 (28-ounce) can whole peeled San Marzano tomatoes
1 tablespoon granulated sugar
½ teaspoon crushed red pepper
1 (28-ounce) can crushed tomatoes

Preheat the oven to 375°F.

In a medium to large skillet, combine the olive oil, onion, garlic, and 1 tablespoon of the salt and cook over medium heat for 5 to 7 minutes, until the onions become soft and translucent. Transfer the mixture to a medium baking dish (8 x 10 inches or similar). Add the can of whole peeled tomatoes, the sugar, crushed red pepper, and remaining 1 tablespoon salt. Make sure that you have at least 1 inch of space between the tomato-onion mixture and the top of the baking dish to avoid spillover in the oven. Bake for 30 minutes, or until the onions and garlic are super soft and the tomatoes are slightly charred on top.

With a hand mixer, or a fork if you don't have a hand mixer, pulse or smash the sauce. I like some big chunks in there, but if you prefer a smoother texture, you can blend it thoroughly.

Mix in the can of crushed tomatoes, season to taste with more salt, sugar, and red pepper, if desired, and bada bing, bada boom—you've got your new favorite marinara!

CHICKEN FRANCESE

MOST PEOPLE WHO KNOW ME THINK THAT I AM *VERY* ITALian. Like, *when you're here, you're family* Italian. Like *gabagool, mortadel, oh madone, Dante's Inferno* Italian. Like I just might know where Jimmy Hoffa is buried, or have a direct line to the ghost of Mother Cabrini Italian. While I do have a tattoo that reads *TAKE IT EASY*, I do not have a big family that gathers for Sunday dinner, or a dozen uncles who are not blood relations. Like America's sweetheart Robert De Niro, I am only one quarter Italian. While only twenty-five percent of my body is made of pasta fazool, it would be the quarter where my heart and my stomach are.

My grandfather John Tangorra Sr. was a first-generation Italian American whose parents hailed from Bari, Italy. He returned from the Korean War as a decorated fighter pilot. He was highly volatile and occasionally scary and abusive. If a family member wanted something to cry about, he would offer generously to give it to them. He was also a great storyteller, and a phenomenal and heartfelt cook. As a young father, he drove an oil truck back and forth from Long Island to the Bronx each day, and made spaghetti vongole with hand-dug clams and listened to Mario Lanza 45s by night. In his second act, he became a door-to-door Electrolux salesman. My uncle

Steven tells a story of how Grandpa John once took him on his sales route through a neighborhood a few towns over. He knocked on the door, and the two were welcomed in by the home's matriarch. My grandfather's sales pitch involved throwing a bag of dirt he had stashed in his pocket all over the prospective buyer's carpet, and then showing them how efficiently the Electrolux vacuum could suck it up. The woman begged him not to pour the dirt onto her carpet, but he had faith in the product, and so he dumped a huge bag of soil all over a stranger's shag carpet, only to learn after the fact that their power was out.

Aside from that hiccup, he was an excellent salesman, winning a cruise to the Bahamas for selling over two hundred vacuum cleaners in a year, and later, a 1978 Cadillac Coupe DeVille, which was his greatest pride and joy, aside from the brilliantly red, impossibly sweet and juicy *tomaterz* he grew in the backyard. *You can eat my tomaterz like an apple*, he'd proudly boast, his giant earlobes and turkey neck waving to and fro for emphasis. He was a devout but pharisaic Catholic, and a card-carrying member of the Knights of Columbus. He made the most delicious, rich, salty pizza rustica for Easter, and juicy meatballs that he would simmer in marinara sauce all day, as he kept watch from a tall stool next to the stove in his white undershirt, eating half of them out of the pot before dinnertime. He loved crusty, sesame-seeded bread, which left a trail of crumbs behind him wherever he walked. Thank heavens for the surplus of top-quality vacuum cleaners.

He was thrifty, and was known for regularly pulling mussels from the Cold Spring Harbor Bay, yanking dandelion greens from the cracks in the driveway to sauté with garlic and olive oil, and taking old seafood *off the hands* of local fishmongers, as though he was doing them a favor. My father told me on his deathbed that Grandpa John had killed my childhood pet rabbit, Habit, and made cacciatore with it. He was *very* Italian.

I chose to be Italian just like Bobby D. Growing up, I studied being Italian like a method actor, but also it was in my bones and my heart. I knew how to make it look realistic because despite it not being a core tenet of my parents' identities, it was a part of my bloodline. To me, being Italian also meant being someone special and exciting and different, and if I was a different person, maybe I could one day be a part of a loving family. To my mushy and growing little puddle of brain, this meant, in its truest distillation, safety.

I was inherently gutsy and sharp-tongued, and I could eat a dozen ravioli without breaking a sweat, and this meant I was Italian. When I was in private elementary school with a bunch of WASPy Gatsby descendants, I didn't want to be like the milk-drinking medigans, and so I was Italian. When I started in public school, I wanted to fit in, so I was Italian. When *The Sopranos* came on the air my freshman year of high school, and having a last name that ended in a vowel was cooler than having a Nokia flip phone, I was Mario fucking Puzo. When I wanted to open a restaurant at twenty-six, there was no question what type of food I'd cook, and from that point on I was Chef Boyardee.

My grandfather was certainly a factor in my journey to becoming a real Italian, but even more influential was an unassuming, divey spot on New York Avenue in Huntington Station called J & J Southside Restaurant. New York Avenue is a commercial road, otherwise known as Route 110, that stretches from the picturesque port of Huntington Bay on the North

Shore, to the equally lovely port of Amityville on the South Shore, about a half mile from the notorious haunted murder house. J & J's was planted in a working-class section of Huntington Station, between the firehouse and a store that sold medical supplies. My family had been regulars there for generations. As a teenager in the late 1960s, my dad used to hang out there with his friends and eat bar pies and smoke cigarettes and drink cold Budweiser. They went there between knife fights with rival bands of hooligans, and after they found out President Kennedy had been shot, and to pregame before the wedding where he would meet my mom.

The food at a restaurant doesn't have to be good for the restaurant to be good. I've had baked potatoes at Keens that have been in the food warmer since it opened in 1885, but it is still the greatest restaurant on the island of Manhattan. Good doesn't really exist, because for some people Per Se is good, and for others Taco Bell is good, and for me a diner tuna melt is better than Nobu. Good food is not ubiquitous, it is emotional and highly personal.

I remember the food at J & J's being delicious, but it was secondary, as all food should be in a restaurant. The true function of a great restaurant is to be an oasis. A great restaurant invites you to take a load off for a few hours. Cry in your beer. Celebrate your promotion. Have your last meal. This is not to say that lovingly prepared dishes are not welcomed or deeply appreciated, but the best thing a restaurant can provide is comfort and warmth, like the server at J & J's who always brought me extra sauce before I even had to ask for it, because she knew I liked extra sauce. And extra sauce was what I looked forward to as a kid going to J & J's.

J & J's was the place my family could escape to after my

parents went bankrupt and were forced to move back into my grandparents' house on Vidoni Place in Huntington Station. We would come here to be free from the low ceilings and brown carpeting, my grandfather's incessant badgering, and the feel of sadness and desperation. The restaurant was divided into two halves separated by a low wall made of frosted glass panels. One side was a bar filled with local drunks and working-class folks playing pool, shooting darts, and taking a break from life. Men with motor oil still on their thumbs and troubles they probably didn't know how to talk about. The other side was a restaurant lined with deep, red leather booths, tables covered with red-and-white-checkered cloths, and families sitting at tables heaped with plates of spaghetti and troubles they probably didn't know how to talk about. There were neon beer signs in the windows that cast a warm glow over the room like a state of perpetual sunset. The smell of red sauce from the restaurant side, commingling with cigarette smoke from the bar side, is branded on my brain as a talisman. I still am, and forever will be, an amalgamation of red sauce and cigarette smoke. There was a jukebox that made me an early Tom Petty fan, and a big window into the kitchen where you could see the steam billowing off the giant pots, and faintly hear the crackling of artichokes being dipped in the fryer over "American Girl." *God, it's so painful. Something that's so close, but still so far out of reach.*

At J & J's there wasn't fighting and sadness and separate bedrooms. There was jubilation in the form of penne alla vodka and roars of laughter, and cheers, and the occasional *Fuck, Jimmy, you wouldn't know a bull's-eye if you were a cattle farmer* coming from over near the dartboard. I remember being so excited just opening a menu and realizing that I could choose what I wanted to eat, and that the old ladies in the kitchen, with just the right amount of swinging arm fat, would make it for me. The waitresses were twins in their sixties, and they smoked cigarettes when they took your order, because this was a time before *supposed tos*. Sometimes my dad would even let me take a sip of his beer. I'd be given a pile of crayons, and between gulps of my Shirley Temple and nibbles of warm seeded Italian bread, I'd draw broccoli-shaped trees on the white paper placemat, "Born in the USA" playing for a third time.

I began to see restaurants, and more specifically food, as a vehicle for magic, the kind that can take the chill from the air and turn cold hearts to glowing red blobs filled with hope. No matter the location or context, food holds the potential for healing of big, ugly wounds. While that was not printed on the plastic-covered, red fabric–rimmed menus at J & J's, it hung heavy in the atmosphere, bound in the fascia where the aroma of toasting garlic met the clicks of billiard balls. There was, between the chicken scarpariello and the chicken marsala, an offer of admission to a life filled with warmth, happiness, and belonging, for $9.50 with a side of pasta. I'll have that, extra sauce on the spaghetti please.

At J & J's people seemed happy, or at least happier than they seemed at my grandparents' house, where my father lived in the unfinished basement and my mother upstairs in his childhood bedroom. The other families seemed like they knew things about each other, interesting things, soft and loving things. Chances are that many of them had equally or more dysfunctional lives than ours, that they glanced over at our table and saw what looked like a real Italian American family and yearned for it, not knowing that we were imposters too, not knowing that my parents had never really been in love, or barely had money to pay the check. *We're all bozos on this bus*, as my mother often quotes. But it didn't matter as long as we were there in the radiant glow of the Budweiser sign, dunking our bread in a big bowl of tomato sauce as we waited for our food.

. . .

THESE MOMENTS TOGETHER WERE fleeting, and vanished after my parents divorced when I was seven. After that I went to J & J's with them separately, but it was still a special treat to be there. When I went with my father, our standard order was a perfectly thin bar pie, followed by a dish called Chef's Special, which was stuffed shells, sausage, baked ziti, and gnocchi, all smothered in red sauce and melted, lava-hot mozzarella. It would arrive at the table steaming and perfectly arranged in the oval-shaped ceramic baking dish, and then with a few gusty cooling blows from my tiny mouth, it would be ready to eat. On the side, we'd order what I distinctly remember to be the world's largest and most delicious meatball. It was the size of a baseball and so tender that it seemed to break apart as soon as it saw your fork headed toward it.

When I went with my mother, we would always get the house salad (crunchy iceberg lettuce, salami, provolone, olives, pepperoncini, and a soaking of red wine vinegar), chicken francese with extra sauce and lemon, and a side of spaghetti marinara. Extra lemon, extra pecorino, extra sauce, always adding to make it better, to make it last longer, to be more enjoyable and decadent. Chicken francese is the sleeper hit of Italian American menus, the fluffy, egg-battered, incredibly tender thin-sliced chicken breasts generously slicked with a silky sauce of lemon, butter, and white wine. It is also one of the dishes that I would use if I were to sculpt my mother out of food. She never made it at home because to her, it was a dish that signified being out somewhere special, and I have rarely made it at home for the same reasons.

I wished we were a real family, one that enjoyed each other's company and loved doing things together. I wished my parents had loved themselves, because then maybe they could have loved each other, and could have better loved me too. My parents' disdain for each other, and for where their lives were, made me feel like a pair of handcuffs they had lost the key to. Thinking of myself this way made joy mostly feel embarrassing and out of reach. But here in the magical sauce palace I was not a burden, I was regular and wanted and happy. More than just happy—I was unafraid to be happy, encouraged even. This was an invitation rarely extended to me outside of J & J's at the time, and so I stored this information away: Food is love, better learn how to make that shit, and make it right.

I may only be slightly more Italian than James Caan, but the best parts of me are drenched in marinara and covered with melted mozzarella cheese. The fleshy, fiery parts. The saucy parts. The parts that wanted a real family, a big one that kissed each other on the cheek and made meatballs, and while that may have not been my reality at home, it was at J & J's. How I wish we could have set up a fort under our booth and lived there forever and ever. Italian food has a way of getting people to that safe haven where our problems get stashed by the door like wet umbrellas. I only have to hear the words *stuffed shells* and I am a million miles from anything that could harm me, besides a burn to the roof of my mouth. That is what good food does: it demands all of your attention. It wasn't just the shells, with their gooey, creamy filling and bright, tangy blanket of sauce; it was realizing that food had the power to make people happy, even my family, even when we were quite far away from it.

. . .

J & J'S CLOSED in 2007 without much warning. I never had the chance to stop in for one last bar pie and plate of chicken francese. It took me a long time to understand my true motivations for opening Brucie, which I did three years after that. I was so young that I barely had the self-awareness to know why I did anything at all. But upon reflection it is quite clear that opening an Italian American restaurant was a love letter not to my Italian American heritage, but to a life I wished I had lived, the one that I borrowed from time to time but never really owned. We often reenact the scenes we were never in. Appropriated sentimentality that somehow draws us closer to our true selves.

Being Italian was, and always has been, about exercising that small part of me that I wanted to be bigger and truer. We are all born with parts of us that grow and shrink as we grow and shrink. We experiment with defiance, conformity, passion, patience, and rebellion. We change our hair, we show off, we hide, we change the cut of our trousers or the sway in our gate, we dabble in the occult. We tug on different threads of the fabric we were born wrapped in and follow the ones that seem to dress us in the perfect outfit. For me the most compelling narratives will always be those of uproarious love and togetherness, and I have auditioned for them zealously, hoping to be convincing enough to be cast in the roles that portrayed a life I was not born into, but had very much wished to be.

Being Italian was a role I have always felt I was born to play, and so I fed that quarter of myself with meatballs, red wine, acrylic fingernails with French tips, and very dirty jokes. I embodied the part with my very own real feelings, my grandfather's accent and affection for fresh produce, and one day it began to take shape not only as fulfillment of a wish, but also my art.

Chicken Francese

BOBBIE REFERS TO US AS *THE LEMONHEADS*, BECAUSE WE HIStorically use more lemon on our food than sailors trying to ward off scurvy. *Excuse me, could I bother you for a little extra lemon?* Bobbie will ask the server as soon as a plate of what is sure to be not nearly acidic enough food is placed in front of her. Inevitably they will return with a few flimsy garnishing slivers of lemon, a valiant and kind effort to accommodate, but about as effective as throwing a hungry lion a piece of turkey jerky. *They call this lemon?* Bobbie says under her breath, smirking at me as she strains to squeeze at the slippery coins of citrus.

This is why I started making this chicken francese at Brucie and Zaza Lazagna, so I could take what I had grown up loving so much, and make it as lemony as the Lemonheads could possibly imagine! Chicken francese is often overshadowed by its more popular poultry comrades on an Italian American menu, and this is a shame because it is a true delight of a dish. The key to a perfect francese is in the light and fluffy egg batter. This preparation also works wonderfully with butterflied shrimp, flaky white fish like fluke and flounder, and tender scallopine of meats like veal and pork. Serve with a twirl-shaped pasta like spaghetti or linguine, in either the same sauce from the francese (in this case you'll want to double the quantity of sauce in the recipe) or with marinara, which I think makes a great pairing with the lemony, buttery sauce from the chicken. It also goes great with some garlicky sautéed spinach or escarole. This can easily be made ahead and reheated in the oven at 375°F for about 20 minutes.

SERVES 4

2 large chicken breasts, cut in half lengthwise and pounded out thinly, ¼ inch or so
1 cup all-purpose flour
3 teaspoons kosher salt, plus more to taste
4 eggs
1 cup extra-virgin olive oil for frying
5 tablespoons salted butter
1 cup dry white wine
1 cup chicken stock
Finely grated zest and juice of 2 lemons
1 tablespoon chicken-flavored Better Than Bouillon (optional)*
Chopped Italian parsley to garnish
Lemon wedges for serving (optional)

*I love a little Better Than Bouillon in the sauce for an extra kick of flavor and color! If you add it, you likely won't need any additional salt in the sauce. Go slow, it's strong stuff!

Assemble your chicken, flour, and eggs near the stovetop: Put the flour on a plate, mix in 1 teaspoon of the salt, and set aside. Crack the eggs into a bowl, add 1 teaspoon of the salt, and scramble with a fork.

Pour the olive oil into a large frying pan and heat over medium-high heat for about 2 minutes.

Once the oil is hot, dredge the cutlets in the seasoned flour, then fully coat in the egg batter, and drop them straight into the frying pan, in batches if your pan won't fit both chicken breasts together. Fry for 1 to 2 minutes on each side, until nicely golden brown. It's okay if they aren't totally cooked through, as they will continue to cook in the sauce. Remove from the oil and set aside on a plate.

Discard excess oil, but no need to clean the pan. Over medium-low heat, make a quick roux: Add 2 tablespoons of the butter and 1 tablespoon flour and stir together as the butter melts. Allow the flour and butter to come together for about a minute, then carefully add the wine, whisking as you do to avoid lumps in your sauce. Add the stock, lemon zest and juice, and remaining salt (or Better Than Bouillon, if using). Increase the heat to medium-high and simmer for 2 to 3 minutes, until the sauce starts to thicken and reduce. Lower the heat and whisk in the remaining 3 tablespoons butter. Add the chicken back into the pan and simmer for another 2 to 3 minutes.

Garnish with parsley and a few big wedges of lemon for fellow Lemonheads who like a little extra.

SPANAKOPITA

MY PARENTS HAD BOTH BEEN CHEFS IN THEIR TWENTIES and thirties, and began and ended their culinary careers before I could recite the alphabet. Bobbie and John were amazing cooks. They, like me, had no professional training, and little instruction from their parents. They only ever cooked professionally as a team, at businesses they owned and operated.

In 1973, they opened a specialty food shop and catering business called The Lovin Oven. This was the same year *The Exorcist* made people pass out in the theater. It was four years after the Manson family drove up to Cielo Drive that hot August night, and seven years before John Lennon walked through the archway of the Dakota for the last time that cold December evening. It was nine years before *The Silver Palate Cookbook* was made famous by its recipe for Chicken Marbella, and I think there is a *Sliding Doors* moment where The Lovin Oven could have become the household name in late-twentieth-century gourmet home cooking.

When I ask my mother about The Lovin Oven, she always begins by saying, *No one had even heard of quiche when we opened.* I am quite sure millions of people in France had, but I try to imagine a world before quiche, and all I see are muddy dirt roads covered in horseshoe prints, and people pushing wheelbarrows of cabbage and animal pelts, covered in dirt and slurping watery oatmeal from wooden bowls, and then here come my parents with their broccoli and cheese egg pies, and *voilà*—everyone on Long Island is wearing a beret.

Before they were chefs, though, they were nineteen- and twenty-three-year-olds who met at a wedding. My father stole my mother away from her date, and they got married at the Mariners Inn three months later. They were practically strangers, and from what I can tell, they were never really in love. Not the healthy kind, and not the *Casablanca* kind either. They were only a few miles away from being children. It was like they were stowing away on a train together, both desperate to escape from their former lives for very different reasons, and I think what they loved in each other was the possibility the other brought to that dream. At their wedding my father's salad was filled with chunks of broken glass, but my grandfather told him, *You better eat, salad doesn't grow on trees*, and although salad does basically grow on trees, my father ate the blue cheese dressing–soaked iceberg around the glass to avoid further conflict.

After the wedding and the glass salad, my parents did odd jobs like running an old inn on Shelter Island and managing a horse barn in Kent, Connecticut, which almost killed my father, as he was severely allergic to horses. They took what little savings they had and drove across the country and throughout Canada with their two dogs in the backseat. Or I should say my mother drove across the country and throughout Canada with my father in the passenger seat because he was too afraid of driving to learn how until he was forty. When they returned to Long Island, they began catering parties for friends of my mother's parents out of their tiny rented house in Huntington

Bay. Their events were highly theatrical, and sometimes included my mother and aunt Flo posing as mimes, or my father dressing as a tomato and putting his painted red face and puffy red and green hat through a hole in the buffet table so he looked like part of the crudité arrangement. They were in the business for the love of food, but equally for the need to burn off the creativity that filled their brains like kerosene, and this, along with my father's love of South African jazz and my mother's bottomless empathy, was passed along to me in my gestating days.

One day, they were driving past an old house turned bakery that had recently closed. A sign advertised *Kitchen Utensils For Sale*, so they went in. They walked out with a whisk and a newly signed lease on the property. They borrowed some money from their parents, and my father's uncle Sunny, who had been a master builder in the city, helped them do the renovations for free, and in four months' time they had a place to put their insatiable culinary creativity to use.

Their tagline at The Lovin Oven was *Try a Piece of the World's Cuisine*. Neither of them had ever left the country, with the exception of the road trip through Canada, but they became obsessed with the cooking of Morocco, Italy, Turkey, and my mother's Eastern Bloc heritage: sweet and sour soups and stews, dishes you could roll into phyllo dough or handmade puff pastry and sell in bite-sized servings by the dozen. My mother made their famous spanakopita, a dish that still to this day could better identify her than her dental records. Her spanakopita is perfect, buttery and flaky, with a crunchy outer shell and tender layers of phyllo laminated around soft, salty feta and spinach filling. She has always said that my first word was spanakopita, which is a classic Bobbie fib: always told lovingly, thinking that it would make me special and sophisticated, and yet signaling to *me* that just being myself was not enough. This is a lie with layers, much like the dish at its nexus. Nevertheless, The Lovin Oven's savory pastries were the crux of my parents' success and would one day be the cause of their undoing.

My parents were maximalists to the maximum. Every inch of the store was covered with a rare musical instrument, a tapestry, or a puppet. They collected African art, played world music, and decorated the shop with didgeridoos, Baule masks, and papier-mâché puppets my father would make on his day off. He had become obsessed with Persian dolls and bought a half dozen to sit atop one of the display fridges, just days before the Iranian hostage crisis in 1979. While making hundreds of Maida Heatter's sour cream praline loaves, Cornish pasties, pigeon pie, and samosas, he blasted the Wild Tchoupitoulas and got buzzed on homegrown weed and brandy and sodas. Years later, after their divorce, my mother told me that my father wore a dress to work. When I asked him about this, he got so mad that he punched a hole in the wall. *It was a god damn fucking dashiki!!* As memory serves, she was simply trying to tell me about what their lives were like and who they had been, but by that time, my father had covered up his past, and his work dress, in mud-colored suits and paisley ties in an effort, I believe, to hide from the loss of the only time in his life he was ever truly happy.

While his friends were off *Stayin' Alive* and out of the water (taking heed of *Jaws*), John was wrist-deep in dough for the latter half of the 1970s, spending eighteen hours a day in the kitchen making Swiss cheese bread, walnut torte, empanadas, and coconut cookies by the thousands. My mother handled most of the savory food and became a local celebrity for the spanakopita, as well as other delights like her eggplant rollatini, chicken pot pie, and vegetable curry. Their personal counterculture resistance took the shape of coq au vin en croûte and vegetable lasagna. They poured every ounce of creative energy they had into the culinary circus of The Lovin Oven. They were doing everything off the cuff and from the heart, and as bizarre as it may have been for Long Island in the 1970s, it also seemed to be working. The Lovin Oven was reviewed in *The New York Times* in 1979 by the one and only Florence Fabricant. The article hangs framed on the wall of my mother's kitchen.

> For the last few months, Bobbie and John Tangorra have been into Moroccan food. An exotic combination of minced chicken, raisins and subtle spices layered in pastry and dusted with cinnamon and confectioner's sugar is the latest addition to the ever-changing catalogue of savory ethnic pastries available at their immensely appealing takeout and catering shop.

Ms. Fabricant noted how they made everything from scratch with the help of a young assistant, and how although they were entirely self-taught, they were also extremely accomplished and creative cooks.

She loved the creamy cheese and scallions, the cinnamon-scented Greek lamb in phyllo, and the richly curried meat and vegetable samosa turnovers, and she raved about the ham-and-cheese-layered pizza rustica, though she found the spinach pie "overly dense."

Even so, my father was a fantastic baker right up until the

time he died, and the review made special mention of his decadent pastries, like his chocolate nut torte, whipped-cream-filled hazelnut dacquoise roll cake, and various mousses and pastry triangles.

The Lovin Oven also did a ton of large-scale catering for weddings and other festive events, and Florence noted my father being adamant about keeping prices low—$4 to $10 per person—in order to properly serve the community. While many of their customers and clients were definitely wealthy, there were plenty of folks in their community who were not, and as someone who was also not a part of the societal upper crust, my father wanted to make sure that The Lovin Oven was a place that everyone could afford.

The article ends with a quote from him: "We've sampled foods from takeout places in Manhattan and we feel we can compete. In fact, sometimes I long for a more appreciative audience."

It's so funny to hear them wax poetic about the exotic appeal of paella and savory pastries. These things are so commonplace today, but back then it was like, *Samosa? I hardly know her.*

Aside from the fact that you could have an entire wedding meal for less than the cost of a cappuccino today, the most surprising takeaway from this article is how well they must have worked together to create such magic. Thirty-two years later Flo Fab would write an article about my future restaurant's lasagna service. I couldn't wait to tell her about the full circle of the pieces, figuring we would both cry and she would include the parallel in her review of my restaurant, but when I mentioned it, she looked straight through me as though the wall behind me was saying something more interesting. I wanted to tell her how I learned how to make pizza rustica like my father, and his father, and a great many Tangorras before them. That the trick is in layering it right so the provolone sticks to both the prosciutto cotto and the dough. That you have to strain the ricotta and poke holes in the top so it doesn't become soggy. That it was one of the only things in this world that made me feel like I had a real family, somewhere, sometime, *before*.

The day after the *Times* review, The Lovin Oven was mobbed by new customers, stepping on one another to get their hands on the savory pies and chocolate nut tortes. Even Billy Joel was a customer, though he almost got into a fistfight with my father because he refused to accept that they did not sell Christmas cookie decorations. As their success continued, Bobbie and John decided to take their savory pastries to the national stage. They sold The Lovin Oven in 1984 and moved down to Boca Raton to follow an opportunity to wholesale their savory pastries en masse, and be closer to my mother's parents, who had migrated there along with all the other sixty-year-old Jews from Long Island in the mid 1970s. They had gotten huge contracts selling hors d'oeuvres to a few hotels in South Florida, all of whom took ages to pay them, or refused to pay at all. My mother blames this on the mafia, but no matter the reason, it put an incredible financial strain on their new endeavor.

Over the next two years, they worked toward opening a space in a food hall in Boca, which they called Zaza's Hot Hors D'oeuvres, named after me, little Zaza, two years old at the time. They had sunk all the money they had from selling The Lovin Oven, plus a loan from Bobbie's parents and a loan from a local bank, into the new project. The food hall went bankrupt shortly before opening day, and my parents lost everything. They weren't even allowed to go in and collect their equipment, so my father broke into the boarded-up space and stole back their dough sheeter, which they sold to be able to afford to drive back up north to stay with his parents while they figured out how and if they could recover.

Completely dejected, they strapped all of our belongings on top of their old Toyota and we headed back to stay at the house my father grew up in. We stopped along the way in North Carolina to sleep at a motel, and in the morning, all of our worldly possessions, which had been stashed atop the maroon Corolla, were gone. We arrived in Long Island with only the clothes on our backs and their broken hearts. This was the same year as the Chernobyl disaster, and the vibe at my grandparents' house at Vidoni Place was a similar one.

My parents' broken hearts, coupled with my grandfather's fierce protection over his tiny kitchen, kept them away from the cooking, and they became totally disinterested in food. My father would only eat fast food, TV dinners, and something he called *chow chow,* which was sautéed ground beef that he smothered with cottage cheese and ketchup. After emerging to eat, he'd retreat back behind the dusty velvet curtain in the basement like a vampire, where he slept on a single mattress on the floor and made toys and masks and other oddities out of papier-mâché. Then Bobbie would tiptoe out from my father's childhood bedroom upstairs, where she always kept the door closed and the lights off, to make herself a meal of brown rice and tofu or Rice Dream vegan ice cream bars. Meanwhile, I would have fish sticks and pizza, or sneak raw hot dogs from the fridge and dip them straight into a bottle of KC Masterpiece Barbeque Sauce. It was a very lonely and isolated time for us all, and while I would eventually come to value the ability it gave me to enjoy and embrace solitude, that feeling was ill-fitting and baggy at the time.

When I tell people that I am a chef, and that my parents were both chefs as well, the assumption is that my early life looked something like a Nancy Meyers film about a culinary family. There must have been trays of freshly baked croissants and legs of lamb everywhere. Platters of ratatouille and terrines and bubbling pans of lasagna with homemade noodles. Lavish weekend breakfasts where my mother and father and I all sat around a table covered in fresh-cut flowers and mile-high stacks of blueberry pancakes. They'd send me off to school with a wholesome sack lunch: cold roast chicken and potato salad, apple slices and a small square of Swiss milk chocolate for dessert. On holidays we would all gather in the open kitchen, and I'd help peel vegetables and pick herbs while my parents seared off veal shanks for osso buco and carefully stirred risotto Milanese, the smell of saffron mixing with the sound of *Miles & Monk* coming from the record player. We would vacation in a small East Coast village and crack open steamed Maine lobsters, my mother eating the guts from all of our shells, with cold white wine in paper cups to go alongside. Even I was allowed a sip, my parents were chefs after all. But alas, my father hated lobster. My life might have looked more like this had they kept The Lovin Oven going for just a little longer, or had they loved each other with stronger conviction, or more realistically just been two entirely different people altogether.

Hearing their stories about The Lovin Oven, like the time that one of their employees stepped on a wedding cake and destroyed it hours before it was to be served, or when my father stopped short while driving hundreds of individual cups of pineapple mousse to a wedding and they all flew into the front seat, blanketing my parents in an impossibly creamy tropical foam, I feel a pang of heartache because I wish I could have known these people. It feels like hearing how someone you love was the life of the party, but all you got to see was the epic hangover the following day. My parents' hangover lasted decades, and in some ways never fully subsided. Their love of cooking was stolen along with their clothing at that motel in North Carolina, and thus, the Nancy Meyers film about the family of chefs would never go to production. I did not grow up getting to know them as happy people, or bear witness to their passion and talents, or see them as fixtures of the community.

I would have given anything to be a part of the before. Before they hated each other so much that they refused to be in the same room together. Before my father did everything he could to make my mother's life a living hell. Before, when they reimagined provincial Slavic cooking for the hippies, yuppies, and housewives of the North Shore of Long Island. When they spoke the same language, casting spells with butter and flour as a culinary folie à deux. In the aftermath, they again became strangers to one another, and I wonder what they missed more, each other or what they were able to do as a pair. For as mismatched as they may have been as lovers, they were the only two people who could have ever created what they did as a team: the chicken paprikash, crab strudel, red plum clafoutis—and me.

This is a problem with how we are taught to digest love; we are told that to be true, it must be sweet, like an apple turnover or a jelly doughnut. But pastries are not only sweet, sometimes they are filled with curried lamb, and Bobbie and John knew that better than most. Their love was the savory sort, the kind that is offbeat but still delicious. Their love was about their ability to learn, grow, and expand their minds beyond the confines of their parents' homes. To rock each other's worlds with creativity, to find the most obscure thing in *The Store Cookbook* and convince North Shore WASPs to serve it to their dinner guests. But every pastry has a last bite, and I think they were both too afraid to take it, so they let it rot.

I never saw my parents kiss, or make a meal together, and because I knew they once had, I came to blame myself for the way it all dissolved. The more I learned about my parents' mythic past, the more I believed that I must have been the broken spoke in the wheel of their great adventure. I lugged this inaccurate assumption around for far too long, mostly because neither of them had the sense to tell me it wasn't so. They had been alive before, back when *Black and Blue* came out. When Stevie Wonder scored their early mornings, as dozens of Russian black breads baked in the ovens, my father twirling my mother around in the kitchen, flour on their cheeks and noses.

I believe when I fall in love with you it will be forever.

. . .

THE BUILDING AT 8 West Shore Road has been a dozen things since they sold it in 1985. It's currently a yoga studio. When we drive past, my mother always says, *The Lovin Oven,* in a deeply nostalgic tone, an even mix of longing and gratitude for auld lang syne. I feel the same strings in my heart being tugged when I pass 234 Court Street, where Brucie once was, which I do at least once a day because I still live close by. Some places are like stars: their power and light are brilliant, but they were never made to burn in perpetuity. Places where you lost your mind in all the right and wrong ways, where everything you touched was your canvas, and your spirit the paint. *Lovin* and *Oven* may rhyme, but they are also two words linked by the idea that food and love existed together as perfect, inseparable teammates. This was the most important thing my parents ever passed down to me, despite their efforts to hide it.

Maybe we only get one true masterpiece, one magnum opus, a slice of history where we lived as our true selves. I wish I had been there, but The Lovin Oven bound me to my family even after we crumbled. I started attempting to make my mother's spanakopita in my mid-twenties, after we stopped being mortal enemies but before I opened Brucie; after Michael Jackson died but before Prince did. I struggled at first with managing the phyllo, somehow sticky and dry at the same time. I soon came to realize, though, that even if the phyllo breaks, you can fix it by slathering it with more melted butter and wrapping another sheet over the cracked one. When I finally managed to get it right, no one would have ever guessed how messy it had all been on the first attempt. It was the same with my father's pizza rustica. It looked so sloppy and disorganized going into the oven because it turned out that I was not a natural at crimping the edges of the dough together, but when it comes out of the oven it's like seeing the ceiling of the freaking Sistine Chapel. And I realized that even with these dishes that were their specialties, my parents were, like me, making it up as they went along. The best things they made were encased in dough that hid the broken parts well, that may have been lumpy or irregular, but were filled with rich, perfectly seasoned fillings.

A few years ago, my mother and I decided to exchange free

presents for Christmas, as an attempt to make gifting more meaningful. We sat on the couch on Christmas Eve, before our annual dinner at Bamonte's, and she handed me a long lumpy object covered in an old page of *Newsday*. I unwrapped a very old whisk, blackened from oxidation. *This was what we bought from the equipment sale the day we walked into Lovin Oven. Your father made a lot of carrot cakes with that thing*, she told me.

My father's carrot cake was one of my favorite things he made. He had riffed on a recipe from his personal queen, Maida Heatter. Warm, cozy spices, freshly crushed pineapple, and plump sweet raisins, baked into an impossibly moist cake and covered in an almost equally thick smear of fluffy, slightly salty cream cheese frosting. It's one of the only things besides pizza rustica and pea soup that he never really stopped making after my parents lost their love of cooking. For all the good times that I missed out on with my family, there are foods like my mother's spanakopita and my father's carrot cake that are as much a part of me as my fingers and toes.

I was born with my father's nose, long and bumpy and a bit hooked at the end, and my mother's wry smile, and their combined penchants for the overly dramatic. I inherited their interpretation of what enough salt meant, and how to measure a cup of sugar in shakes, despite never being given a lesson in this, or much of anything else. I did not need a book of recipes or Saturday morning pancake tutorials, although I would have liked them, and wished for them on a soul level, but that information came caught up in the web of neurons along with the freckles and slightly mournful eyes that all the Tangorras seem to have. What was not baked in was the truth that this all fell apart well before I became a human being, and there was nothing I could have ever done to save it; it was ash in its inception, but it was fun while it lasted. I would spend the next four decades trying to fix everything, and break everything, and fix what I broke and also the things I did not. I would misinterpret all these impossible-to-read recipes, going through much of my life interacting with love and romance that was incorrectly proportioned at best, and all too often completely inedible. It would not be until much later, when all those freckles had faded and the man I got them from had died, that I would realize the life I had wished for was never mine to lose, and I was not to blame for its failure to thrive. Despite all our effort and creativity, some dishes simply do not turn out the way we wish them to, and others become treasured despite them not having a recipe.

Spanakopita

MY MOTHER ROLLS HER FAMOUS SPANAKOPITA WHEN SOMEONE has a baby, a birthday, or a bad day. She brings them to cocktail parties, bakes them for holidays, and keeps them in the freezer for when guests come over. When I was eight, we had a bake sale at school, and I brought my mother's spanakopita to sell, which was the one and only time in the history of the world they were not appreciated, as most children prefer pink frosting to Greek savory pastries. They are soft and salty, just like she is, and when I die, I wish to be buried in a casket made of phyllo, packed with spinach and feta cheese.

After Bobbie taught me how to make her spanakopita, like any child would, I have put my own riff on something that needs no improvement. My spanakopita is my mother's spanakopita, with a few small adjustments to solidify myself as an individual. My additions are listed as optional at the bottom.

MAKES 20 TO 25 HORS D'OEUVRES PORTIONS

3 sticks salted butter (¾ pound), divided
1 large sweet onion, finely chopped
1 cup coarsely chopped scallions, green and white parts
1 10-ounce package frozen chopped spinach, defrosted
1 pint full-fat cottage cheese

1 pound feta cheese, crumbled by hand, with some larger chunks
½ cup finely grated Pecorino Romano cheese
1 egg plus 2 egg yolks
¾ cup fine unseasoned breadcrumbs
½ teaspoon grated nutmeg
1 teaspoon freshly ground black pepper
½ cup chopped fresh dill (optional)
½ cup chopped fresh cilantro (optional)
½ cup chopped fresh mint (optional)
½ cup frozen peas (optional)
1 1-pound package phyllo pastry sheets (defrosted in the refrigerator)

Melt 1 stick (¼ pound) of the butter in a large sauté pan, then add chopped onion and scallion and cook until golden brown, about 5 minutes.

While the onion cooks, squeeze out all the liquid from the defrosted frozen spinach and put it in a large bowl.

Once cooked, remove the onions from the pan and let them cool, then add them to the bowl with the spinach, along with the cottage cheese, feta cheese, and Pecorino Romano cheese. Stir to combine, then add the egg and egg yolks, breadcrumbs, nutmeg, and pepper, and the dill, cilantro, mint, and peas, if using. (Either way it's going to be mind-blowingly delicious!) Refrigerate for at least 2 hours or overnight.

Preheat the oven to 375°F.

Melt the remaining 2 sticks (½ pound) butter in a small pot and remove from the heat.

Okay, phyllo time! This part can get dicey, but I believe in you. Phyllo can get crumbly, but remember that some cracks and crumbles might happen, in cooking and in life.

Take the phyllo sheets out of the fridge and place a dry kitchen towel on top of them to keep the dough from drying out. Assemble your melted butter, a large cutting board, and your bowl of spinach filling next to the phyllo dough.

Place two sheets of phyllo on the cutting board, oriented horizontally, and using a pastry brush, brush them liberally with butter. Repeat this process two more times so you have a stack of six sheets total.

Fold up the bottom edge of the buttered sheets of phyllo to create a 1-inch border. Then, using a tablespoon, spoon the spinach filling along the folded border from one end to the other, smoothing it out slightly to make one even row of filling.

Placing your fingers under the dough, fold the phyllo border over the filling and continue to gently roll up the spanakopita.

Using a serrated knife, cut the roll into 2-inch pieces, and place them on a cookie sheet lined with parchment paper. They can be placed close together, but not too tight. Give them a pencil's width of space between.

Brush the spanakopita pieces with the remaining butter, then bake for 20 to 30 minutes, until golden brown.

The spanakopita can be served hot or at room temperature. You can refrigerate or freeze them, and then reheat them in the oven for 20 minutes at 375°F.

My Father's Carrot Cake

MY FATHER WAS A GIFTED BAKER. HIS CHOCOLATE CHIP COOKIES were legendary, his walnut torte was divine, and his coffee cake could bring you to your knees, but my favorite dessert he ever made was this perfect carrot cake. John had bright orange hair right up until the day he died—the chemo never managed to take it from him. This cake is orange, sweet, and complex, just like him, and that is why I love it.

SERVES 12

CAKE:

2 cups all-purpose flour
2 teaspoons baking powder
½ teaspoon baking soda
1 tablespoon kosher salt (I use Diamond Crystal)
1 tablespoon ground cinnamon
½ teaspoon ground nutmeg
4 large eggs
1¼ cups extra-virgin olive oil, or sunflower or avocado oil
1 tablespoon vanilla extract
2 tablespoons blackstrap molasses (optional)
Finely grated zest of 1 orange
1 cup granulated sugar
1 cup packed dark brown sugar
2 cups coarsely grated carrots
½ cup golden raisins

½ cup chopped pitted prunes
1 cup crushed pineapple, fresh or canned
1 cup finely crushed walnut pieces, plus a few walnut halves for garnish (optional)
1 tablespoon grated fresh ginger

CREAM CHEESE FROSTING:

2 sticks (½ pound) unsalted butter (if using salted, only use 1 teaspoon salt), softened at room temperature
5 cups powdered sugar, sifted, divided
1 tablespoon vanilla extract
2 teaspoons kosher salt
8 ounces cream cheese (straight from the fridge to keep the frosting from becoming too soft)

Preheat the oven to 350°F.

Butter two 9-inch cake pans and line them with parchment paper. Springform is easiest!

Make the cake: In a large mixing bowl, sift together the flour, baking powder, baking soda, salt, cinnamon, and nutmeg.

In a separate large bowl, whisk together the eggs, then whisk in the oil, vanilla, molasses (if using), orange zest, and sugars. Once thoroughly combined, add the carrots, raisins, prunes, pineapple, and walnuts.

Add the dry ingredients to the carrot mixture one-third at a time, stirring until combined. Be careful not to overmix.

Divide the batter evenly between the two prepared pans. Bake for 25 to 30 minutes, until a cake tester inserted in the middle comes out clean. Allow the cakes to cool for 10 minutes in the pans and then transfer to a wire rack to cool thoroughly. I find it easier to frost the cakes when they are cold, so I stick them in the fridge or freezer for a few hours after they have cooled on the counter before frosting them.

When the cakes are cooled, make the frosting: In a large mixing bowl or the bowl of a standing mixer fitted with the whisk, combine the butter and 3 cups of the sifted powdered sugar and beat on high speed for 1 minute (start on low and work your way up to high once the sugar is combined to not have powdered sugar fly everywhere). Add the vanilla, salt, and the remaining powdered sugar and beat on high for another 30 seconds. Add the cream cheese in two halves, beating for 30 seconds in between. Once all the ingredients are combined, beat on high until fluffy, about 1 minute more. You are looking for a soft, smooth, fluffy frosting with no lumps.

To frost, place one cooled layer of cake on a plate and spread half of the icing evenly on top. Place the top layer over the frosting and slather with the remaining frosting. Garnish with a few walnuts if you're feeling wacky, and refrigerate for at least one hour. Serve chilled or at room temp depending on your preference, though serving chilled does make it easier to cut.

A JOE'S SLICE

I LOVED NEW YORK CITY BEFORE THE 2003 BLACKOUT AND before Hurricane Sandy. I loved it before I watched it become covered in a thick white blanket of toxic ash on the TV in the commons of my Long Island high school on September 11, 2001. And I loved it more so after witnessing its resilience. I fell in love with New York when the subway only took tokens and Griffin Dunne had to run around all night trying to find the money to afford one. I loved it when Penn was still filthy and reeked of Auntie Anne's pretzels, and Sammy's Roumanian was still on Chrystie Street. I wish I had been there for the good old days when the Beatles played Shea, and everyone in Corona Park was there to twist and shout. When Meg Ryan came while eating a sandwich at Katz's, back when Nora Ephron presided as mayor from her headquarters at the Apthorp. When Marsha and Sylvia started hurling bricks at the enemy down at 53 Christopher, and SEEN was keeping the trains lit up. I loved it before I knew it would be the place I hope to live in until I pass away, and I love it still, and will forevermore.

I recently got into a tiff with a strange man on the street in Gramercy, and he asked me if this was my *first time in New York,* and I had never been so offended in all my life. I almost cried, and as I felt the tears prickling underneath my bottom lids, my friend Mary, who was walking with me, laughed and said, *Ooof, he got you good, Z*. In my time on this earth as a New Yorker, the city has become as much a part of my identity as it has a place where I sleep and wake, because it saved me from another life that held no promise. I don't remember my first time entering the city limits, but it lives deep under my skin, as deep as my pancreas, and it helps me to digest the world much the same.

There is a Tangorra family legend about my great-grandfather Francesco, who was a stonemason, and worked for the Piccirilli brothers after coming over from Bari, Italy, in 1901. In March of 1929, they were working on a big, beautiful building right near the George Washington Bridge, when Francesco was struck by a steel beam attached to a crane. The beam was apparently set to strike his coworker, but Francesco pushed him out of the way, saving his friend by giving his own life. This is not an *only in New York story,* but it is a *New York story,* an *immigrant story,* and in many ways, a *love story*. A true New York love story is not about a meet-cute while hailing the same taxi cab, or getting engaged on a rowboat in the murky green pond in Central Park. A true New York love story is about deliverance.

My great-grandparents had come over from Bari at the turn of the century in an effort to *take-a their-a piece of-a da pizza pie*. To make what they thought would be a better life for themselves and their seven children, one of whom was my grandfather John Senior. They made it from the heel of the boot to the south of the Bronx to free themselves from economic, religious, and political oppression and instability, and for a chance at a better life. It is ironic how much space there can be in a thirteen-mile islet, but more is more when it comes to a variety of cultures, cuisines, and ideas, and the cornucopia of traditions and imagination in this small slice of the planet has always made the city an epicenter of inhalation, even when the air gets thick. True love is not meant to make things perfect, it is meant to make them possible. They lived in a modest brick house and made friends with their neighbors. Francesco helped to carve the lions that guard the New York Public Library. His wife, Giuseppa, made ravioli, which she dried on the bedsheets in the afternoon sunlight, pizza rustica on Easter, and Sunday sauce each week for a family that continued to grow and grow. And then, the steel beam. But the steel beam doesn't end the love story, it's in the DNA, it is intergenerational and intergalactic.

Another New York love story: My grandmother Violet arrived on a boat from the former Yugoslavia to Ellis Island in 1941, where she had to live in quarantine for six months on account of her four-year-old son, my uncle Joe, having a case of the chicken pox. She had two small children, and was pregnant with a third, and married to a man twice her age. Violet's life was riddled with trauma. Her father and older sister had died in a concentration camp, while her brothers had joined the French Resistance. There was a bridge that connected Senta, where she grew up, to the neighboring towns, but until she was forced to flee, she didn't realize that there was a world on the other side. Upon finding herself far from a home that was now mostly rubble and bones, she took refuge in her new surroundings. She lived in a tenement in South Williamsburg and commuted to Manhattan to work day shifts cutting diamonds for Madison Avenue hausfraus to wear to dinner at the 21 Club and night shifts as a caterer. She left the old, mean man she was forced to marry, and made the painful decision to put her children in an orphanage, visiting them as often as possible. She hustled her way from diamond cutter/cater waiter, to print model, until one night at the Griswold Hotel she made the acquaintance of a soldier just home from war, who became my grandfather Bill. She could finally get her children back and tried to provide them with the life they deserved.

My mother would be born in New York, but she knew Violet's story from the foods her mother would make to bring her past into her present. She would wrap steamed cabbage leaves around beef and rice and braise them in tomato sauce sweetened with gingersnaps and dried fruits. My grandmother's famous stuffed cabbage had made its way from Senta to Brooklyn, baking in an oven she knew how lucky she was to have.

I loved New York City before anyone in New York City had ever ordered, or even heard of, a matcha latte. Before matcha was even discovered in the twelfth century. Back when everyone drank muddy coffee, and the only milk to put in it was animal. I loved it when you had to press your ear to a greasy pay phone and figure out who to call when your train came in, like Holden Caulfield. Back when Capote still worked in the mailroom at the *New Yorker* and Keith Hernandez was a Metropolitan, smoking cigarettes in the dugout between innings. When Scorsese ran up and down Mulberry Street in short pants with a Super 8. When Spike questioned what it meant to do the right thing, and George Gershwin worked as a song plugger on Tin Pan Alley. I love it all the way down in my roots, like I have been a plant in this small corner of the earth since the world began to spin. I have a borrowed nostalgia for every raindrop that has ever fallen upon 40.7128 N 74.0060 W.

Sometimes people ask me if I will ever move away from the city, and my reply is always, *You can't live without your heart.*

...

I GREW UP IN a little harbor town on the North Shore of Long Island, called Northport, which is about fifty minutes from midtown Manhattan without traffic. You could drive there and back in about the time it takes to watch *When Harry Met Sally,* and yet, I had dozens of friends and classmates growing up who had never once put a pinky toe across the western border of Nassau County. I was lucky enough to have parents who loved the city, and would take me in often for special trips. This was back in the 1990s, when working-class families like mine could go to see the Knickerbockers play, hot dogs and a foam finger included, for less than the cost of a first-class plane ticket to Tokyo.

Next stop and last stop is Penn Station, the conductor would say in his Massapequa drawl, and then the train doors of the LIRR would open and we were in another world that smelled like burnt sugar and urine, where everyone was in a hurry and holding a newspaper. People didn't hurry in Northport, and so I assumed people here were doing more important things.

Almost everyone in my hometown looked the same: white, suburban, amalgamations of ordinariness personified. There were variations on the theme, but my day-to-day experience of the people around me felt largely synthetic. To my small self, who did not yet understand the cruelty and injustice of poverty or the perils of capitalism, New York City was a carnival, where you couldn't tell the audience from the performers, and everyone lived off hot dogs and candied peanuts. My parents may have been born and bred in Long Island, but they didn't fit into the same mold of many of the other folks in our town. Sure, they liked a chrome diner and a deli san', and said *cawfee,* but they also owned tagines and hung Keith Haring prints on their walls, and I knew as soon as I stepped off the train at Penn that many others in that sea of people did too. We belonged here in the pandemonium, where we could flow with the current. Where my mother's pink hair and nose ring would be almost boring by comparison. Neither of my parents ever lived in the city, and I have always wondered how their lives might have played out had they settled in a place, so close yet worlds away, that was more tailored to their eccentricities. They chose to live thirty-five miles short of their creative potential, but being with them in the city always felt like a journey through the proverbial looking glass.

In my elementary and middle school years, Bobbie and I used to go into the city all the time before she met my stepfather, Rob. Back when Dinkins lived up at Gracie and the only naked cowboys in Times Square were at Show World Center. She would take me down to the Village, and we would spend the afternoon popping in and out of weird head shops that sold aggressive silver jewelry and vinyl clothing and then grab a slice from Joe's. What makes a plain slice at Joe's so special is how ordinary it is. They don't use the highest-quality cheese or mill their own flour. The guys making the pies are not Eleven Madison Park alums, the floor is dirty, and there is cheap garlic powder and parm to shake on top, and yet I have never had a slice so perfect. A Joe's slice has a thin and simultaneously crisp and tender crust, a generous layer of tangy sauce, and just enough cheese to make it gooey, but still light enough that a single slice feels like a snack. But none of that is really what makes it so good. A Joe's slice is among the most well-balanced in the city, but it is beloved for the same reason all old-school slice shops are: It is an egalitarian space where every kind of person in this city is there for the same thing, a simple delicious triangle of happiness that is only *this* good in *this* city. Everything you need to know about New York City can be explained from hanging out at a local pizza shop, and Joe's happens to do it a bit better than most, and in a great location.

Slices secured, we would then head down to SoHo to check out the Patricia Field store, Hotel Venus, that was below a wacky furniture shop called DOM. We would look at rare animal skeletons at the Evolution Store, thumb through records at the flea market on Prince Street, and get big steaming bowls of tortilla soup for dinner at Great Jones Cafe. My mother was cool, cooler than any other mom that ever lived, and I would return home from these excursions feeling like I had been somewhere secret and adult.

My other outings to the city, with my father and new stepmother and stepsister, felt like they were on the polar opposite end of the spectrum: extravagant and plush. After my parents split up, my father put himself through graduate school as an art history major by working as a bartender at a local country club for rich WASPs. He never did anything with this degree, but he did wrap several members of our extended family in layers of papier-mâché and force them to lay still for eight hours at a time while it hardened. He eventually pushed his artistic pursuits aside altogether and worked his way up the ladder, getting promoted from bartender to server captain, and by the mid-nineties he was promoted to general manager at the Huntington Crescent Club. While he hadn't become rich by societal standards at the time, the climb up to big boss man afforded us access to perks that made it feel like he was a real hot shot.

A guy who owed my dad a favor from the club would get

us a stretch limousine, and we would pile in, then drive into the city to see the Rockettes make Christmas look sexy at Radio City. My stepsister, who was the same age as me, would glide around the rink at Rockefeller Center under the twinkling shadow of the impossibly big tree, while I clung to the wall like I was an eighty-five-year-old woman afraid to break her hip. We visited Santa at his vacation home on the seventh floor of Macy's in Herald Square, and devoured giant soft pretzels covered in the kind of salt used to melt snow, smeared with globs of tangy yellow mustard. We ate dinner at Planet Hollywood, and while this may have been rather vanilla compared to the adventures I had with my mother, I loved it all the same. Even now, having lived in New York for longer than I have not, I still hold the shiny and the grimy parts of this city in equally high esteem.

As early-onset adulthood hit me around age fifteen, I rarely if ever went into the city anymore with either of my parents. Instead, my friends and I would skip school every few weeks, scraping money from our classmates to ride the train to Penn, grab a slice at Joe's, of course, and a look at some sex shops on Sixth Avenue, then catch the LIRR back home for dinner. *I know a spot in the Village that has the best pizza,* I would brag. New York was beginning to take shape as a refuge, one where I could imagine myself melting into the crowd effortlessly, like low-moisture mozzarella cheese on my favorite pizza.

The rickety foundation of my childhood had given way to a collapse by the time I was a teenager, and upon entering the ninth grade, I had little support or stability to hold on to. My father occasionally gave me brief and confusing pep talks, the subject of which was most often Chet Baker or some other drug-addicted jazz musician, as an example of why not to throw your life away with the baby and the bathwater. *Listen to this and then tell me there is no such thing as a waste of talent. You don't want to end up like this cat, kiddo, trust me,* he'd lecture, handing over the four-song CD of the Ennio Morricone–produced *Chet Is Back!* I never did try heroin, and it was because of Chet, and also because I saw what it did to Leo and Marky Mark in *The Basketball Diaries*. By the time I was fourteen, things had become painfully awkward at my father's house, and we both thought it best for me not to spend too much time there. I craved the taste of belonging, just to be somewhere I could fit like a puzzle piece, even if just an edge. Somewhere that felt exotic yet inclusive, where I could observe rather than be stuck under the glare of a magnifying glass. A foreign place where I understood the dialect. That same year, Rob had moved in with my mother during the summer while I had been shipped off to a sleepaway camp, and I only learned of this when I returned home to find he had taken over the spare room, which my mother had gifted me the year prior for my thirteenth birthday. Gone were the bean bag chairs and lava lamps and posters of Leonardo DiCaprio. Instead, there was a bent wood dresser filled with Rob's socks and underwear, topped with photos of family members I didn't know. There was no communication or patience surrounding the massive shifts taking place in our home and life, but had there been, perhaps this new arrangement could have allowed us to become a family rather than pitting us against each other as competitors. The unfortunate lack of explanation and sensitivity sent me to that familiar, wicked place where I assumed I was not good enough, and it truly broke my spirit. My mother and I barely spoke outside of screaming at one another, while Rob and I became adversaries, each pretending the other did not exist, unless to exchange insults, until I was nineteen. Rob had no children of his own, and although I have over time come to love and adore him as a real father, back then he didn't understand children or how to interact with them, and it made for a truly miserable and emotionally detrimental half a decade.

One's teenage years are at best a test, and at worst a trap. I may have looked kind of like an adult, but in fact I was only separated from building forts and believing in the powers of a benevolent billionaire fairy who pays for old teeth by a few dozen months. My adolescence felt untethered from adults I could trust, or people who really loved me. I had plenty of friends and a very active social life, but with such chaos and loneliness at home, I still often found myself dissociating, like someone had hit the mute button in the middle of a wild party. There were times when the clouds parted and the vibe was kinetic and the laughs were genuine, but there was always this impending dread of going home to a place where I was disliked and unwelcome that kept true joy at bay.

I was alone, in the worst sort of way, and because I felt so powerless and weak, I became fastidious in self-sabotage as a means to control something. I know that there are some people from troubled homes who double down on productivity as a means of escape, but I was the other kind of person, the kind who was determined to self-destruct to show everyone how much I was hurting, placing bad bets and breaking my own knees for missed payments. When you have been hurt and disappointed before, your brain tricks you into hurting yourself before anyone else does, like chemo making you sick because it kills the healthy, viable cells as well as the cancerous ones. I flunked classes, cut my own hair, quit sports teams, all so that my parents, especially my mother, got to see me fail. I reveled in these moments like my peers would by showing off their A in chemistry or three goals in soccer. If there was an opportunity to make myself sadder, I would take it, and there was no one to stop me. I got into fights. I smoked as much weed as I could scrap from my friends or get with my five dollars of lunch money. I drank shots of warm Georgi vodka at lunch. I threw my homework in the garbage as soon as I walked out of class. I would rip up precious family photos and throw priceless childhood gifts in the trash, and then get as high and drunk as possible because this was the only way to convince myself that I wasn't breaking my own heart.

No one wins in this scenario. The parents I was attempting to punish either did not or could not care, because if they did or could, I would not have been in the position of needing to self-immolate to get their attention. But as a kid, I didn't know this, or much of anything really, and I set myself ablaze, not for a righteous cause, but because I lacked the language to say, *I am hurting, please help me.* I so desperately wanted to be heard, but I was speaking in tongues to a nonexistent audience. Finally, when I kept burning and burning and no one came to put the fire out, I just stopped going to school altogether.

In the morning, when I was meant to go off to the eleventh grade to learn chemistry and French and dissect the works of Ray Bradbury, I lay in my bed, in a room covered in cloud wallpaper that had been installed when I was eight and my mother and I still liked each other. My mother protested at first. She screamed and yelled and stonewalled and slammed kitchen cabinets, and ultimately gave up after a few weeks, and in my bed, under the clouds from another lifetime, I remained for the next three months. I was eventually expelled, only to be allowed to come back after attending a monthlong program for troubled teens.

I don't remember what ultimately forced me to go to this program—threats of unimaginable punishment, or my one last shred of self-determination, a tiny voice saying *don't fucking die yet*—but I went. This was a place I didn't feel I belonged, and honestly without judgment for the other children that were there, I think that instinct was correct, but just barely. The class consisted of ten teenagers ranging in age from thirteen to eighteen, all of whom had very serious drug addictions and mental health issues. Even though I dabbled in these subjects, I was not an expert, but I was there, so perhaps it is possible I belonged more than I wished to have believed. I made it through the thirty days, scared and sick to my stomach as fights broke out and threats of suicide were hurled at the teachers on a daily basis, and reenrolled in the eleventh grade about a month after being kicked out.

I returned to school very sad, but trying desperately to hide it between humor and intimidation, and low-rise jeans with the waistband cut off to reveal the fluorescent thong that I had matched to the eighty-seven layers of eye shadow caked on my Long Island eyelids. I had no real hopes or aspirations, but not in a normal way, in an intentional and avoidable way. Get through the day, try to be loved, fail at being loved, blame self, hate body, hate parents, hate life, get blitzed, eat food that made me feel sick, cry self to sleep, repeat.

The only bright spot was Mrs. Minardi. Like many dysfunctional teenagers in both movies and real life, I had one great teacher in high school who I felt truly got me. She was a short, blonde, beautiful woman who had a twin sister, and had told us she once dated Stanley Tucci. She looked a lot like Edie

Falco, who had also dated Stanley Tucci and gone to my high school. I looked forward to the breathing room I had in Mrs. Minardi's class, an unpolluted air that was nearly impossible to come across anywhere else during this tumultuous time in my life. She saw how badly I was struggling and grabbed my hand before I could sink to the slimy floor of the Long Island Sound. I think she saw the same drowning person that my parents did, but was perhaps better trained as a lifeguard. Or maybe she was just brave enough to look out at the surf to try to find the person struggling to swim. It didn't take great depth of character to realize that I was having a hard time, despite my best efforts to cover it up with makeup I stole from the drugstore, but it did require genuine care to not just dismiss me as a lost cause, and that is a very loving act that I did not have the emotional intelligence or wherewithal to thank her for at the time. But I hope I can now; I hope that she reads this and knows that if not for her, there would probably be no memoir.

I was seventeen, and had not yet considered the possibility that I might attend college. College was for kids who went to class, who had parents who believed in them, and who believed in themselves. I had no real ambition, no vision of a future or a version of myself that could survive, let alone thrive. No one ever proposed the idea that I could be something when I grew up, and as things became increasingly tense at home, the only thing I thought that I could ever be was a disappointment, or at the very best a party girl like my hero Parker Posey, before she became a librarian. I was creative and had a great appreciation for the arts, but I was so consumed with just getting through the day without wanting to disappear that I really did not have the space to dream of a happy life, or figure out how to put my talents to use. Mrs. Minardi must have seen me, even though I made every attempt to hide any hope I had in my heart, as hope is vulnerability, and vulnerability made me an open target. I did everything I possibly could to avoid exposing the bull's-eye, and yet, she saw a round red orb glowing through the armor.

Mrs. Minardi asked me to stay after class one day so we could talk. I assumed it was to tell me that I was in trouble for coming to class high, or in danger of failing for cutting too many times. The bell rang and I told my friends I would catch up with them in the commons so we could go take bong hits at the beach and get bacon, egg, cheese, and hash brown sandwiches for lunch at the Northport Deli. I prepared myself for the one adult that I liked to tell me that she did not like me back, but instead she proved that she had been thinking about my future more than I ever had.

Have you considered the Fashion Institute of Technology? They have a pretty great fine arts program there. Maybe I could help you get your portfolio together, Mrs. Minardi offered in a very matter-of-fact tone, which was the only possible way of getting through to me. She made FIT seem just okay, and realistic to get into, and I allowed my brain to take me there, back to the big city where everyone was too busy to notice me, and away from the small harbor town where I had come to feel like Leatherface. It was close to home, which comforted me, and even though home was such an uncomfortable place to be, it was still the devil I knew.

And I felt comfortable in the city. When I would ride the train into Penn Station with my friends, I would look out the window as we headed west and see the world open up, like how the bay becomes the ocean, becomes the sea. Maybe I could live in the sea, the sea of Manhattan where I could just be a wave, moving along with the other waves from Riverside to Battery parks, until the tide pulled me home to my apartment for rest. Maybe I could be an artist, or a good neighbor, or a wife. Maybe I could have a future. Maybe I deserved one just as much as anyone else. Maybe I wasn't as bad as I thought, and maybe with a little perspective and a little space I could reach a vantage point where I was able to really see that. Maybe I could grow upward, toward the sky, like the buildings all trying to do the very same thing. Maybe I could be a New Yorker. My grandparents had all lived there; I knew how to hail a cab and buy a MetroCard, and where to get the best slice of pizza. I was basically Fran Lebowitz.

With Mrs. Minardi's help, I got into FIT as a fine arts major—I would be a New Yorker after all. This was to be more than a day trip, more than a dream or a Chloë Sevigny movie I watched a hundred times. This was going to be the beginning of a real life, one that I never thought I deserved or would have maybe even lived to have seen. A life that had the potential to be bigger than the one my parents had. A life that might prove that I was more than a mistake. I had no way of knowing then that this was just the first time I would be lucky enough to survive the odds, but looking back, it feels like the city saved me from a very near brush with death. Maybe not the same kind of death that happens when you fly off a cliff, but missing the opportunity to have gotten out of the vicious cycle that I was stuck in in my high school years would have been the death of my spirit and perhaps my body too. I don't know how much longer I could have kept the flame of myself going. It needed air—smelly, smoky, noisy, wild New York air that filled my lungs with a surge like I had been given CPR.

I would walk around my new neighborhood, passing by

the Chelsea Hotel every day, wondering if the sidewalk had felt the same beneath Patti Smith's Converse when she walked these same streets when she was my age, hand in hand with Robert Mapplethorpe. I wondered if I would ever be a part of the city's tessellation the way she was. If it would fuck me or ask me to slow dance. Either way, I had made it far enough to find out for myself. I had made it through the fights with my mother where the cops would come. Through the emotional hurricanes at my father's house and the levee breaks at my mom's. I made it through dabbling in cutting, and the multiple infections from trying to pierce my own belly button. I made it through dozens of joy rides with drunk drivers, and through swimming in frozen water while on mushrooms and skiing through mountains of cocaine. I made it through the vicious diet culture of the 1990s that gave me bulimia. Out of the depths of sadness, alone in my cloud-covered bedroom. From the precipice of giving up. From the edge of throwing it all away, like Chet.

I have fallen in love dozens of times in my twenty-plus years in New York. I have fallen in love with boys in terrible bands, boys in pretty good bands, bartenders, drunks, liars, chefs, and nice guys that I wasn't really ready for. I have fallen in love with people who have hurt me, and who I have hurt. I have fallen in love with the chaos. With strange nooks in Prospect Park, Fat Beats, Kim's Video, the Strand, and the latkes at Barney Greengrass. With watching pickup games at the courts on West 4th Street, an Italian Combo at Faicco's, and a late afternoon screening of *A Woman Under the Influence* at Film Forum. With sitting at the Temple of Dendur for fifteen minutes to clear my head, and a martini at Bemelmans to make it cloudy again. With the lions guarding the library that Francesco helped build, and steaming bowls of ginger scallion congee at Noodle Village in Chinatown. I have fallen in love with the way everyone seems to know the same dance to different songs.

I love New York because it saved my life by giving me the space to blend in. It saved me by demanding I use my creativity for good. It saved me by introducing me to so many interesting and special people who taught me far more than I could have learned in school, even if I had gone to class. Somewhere in my subconscious was the awareness that there was a place that I could escape to for a fresh start, like my grandparents had. That saying, the last part, on the green lady who watches over us—*yearning to breathe free*—I felt that all my life growing up, that aching for the kind of air my lungs could process. It felt like falling in love, the thrill of passion, of belonging. It saved me the way falling in love does. It's not the object of our love that gives us salvation, rather it's the mirror reflecting back our own magic, and the promise we hold within, to be loved, and to give it back whenever possible.

BOUILLABAISSE

I'M MOVING TO FRANCE, I TELL MY MOTHER. SHE IS SHOCKED, but quickly realizes that by moving I mean visiting for three months.

I was visiting France because I was twenty-four, and I had a great sum of money from surviving the bus crash in the desert two years before, and I wanted to use it to find out what a real croissant tasted like. I wanted to hear people speak fluently in another language and walk around with a baguette sticking out of my bag, eating tears of it as I smelled the lavender blowing through the purple hills of Provence. I would become sophisticated and cultured, and return with stories about my time abroad, and this would make people forget that I used to cut the waistband off my Mudd jeans and match my thongs to my eye shadow. I had survived a freak accident, and I felt like the proper thing to do in celebration of my existence was to see more of the world that I was still lucky enough to be a part of. Even in the darkest moments of my parents' lives, they had always been, and continued to be, top-tier celebrators, and this insistence on festivity was passed down to me along with my facial features and sarcastic sense of humor. I had lived, and there was much to see through the fresh eyes that I had been gifted after the accident. *I am moving to France. I am celebrating.*

I am not embarrassing and crass anymore. Bonjour world, here I come.

Moving to New York had awakened my lust for life and given me a literal canvas for my creative inclinations, but I still had not really considered how I might use these tools to build a future, and now I felt intent that I should make something out of my second chance. It all seemed very big at the time, like not dying meant that I had to live better than I would have had it never happened. I set out on an adventure to France with money that I would have never had if not for almost losing my life, in an effort to make it count. I know now that life counts no matter what, but I thought growing up that mine didn't really, and now it could. This twenty-four-year-old logic seems awfully silly now, but no matter how crudely that map may have been drawn, it led me down an unimaginably meaningful path.

It was late summer 2008, and my then-boyfriend Matt and I embarked on our collective first venture outside of George W. Bush's post–9/11 America. I had been uneasy about the long flight, so a friend had given me what she thought to be a Xanax to soothe my anxiety. It is funny how easy it is to grab an ecstasy pill instead of a Xanax when you're casually reaching your hand into a glass jar containing dozens of tablets and capsules. I began rolling as the plane took off. It was the Fourth of July, and fireworks burst in neon webs over the Atlantic Ocean, and I imagined whales huddled up with their families watching from below and grilling ten-foot-long hot dogs underwater while horseshoe crabs set off Roman candles on the shoreline. To make things even more complicated, one of the passengers died and was moved to the row behind us and covered with a blanket for the duration of the eight-and-a-half-hour flight.

Matt and I had swapped our dingy South Williamsburg studio with Marie, a young French architect who had a gorgeous flat in a community just outside the Marseille city limits, called Le Jardin d'Eden. The outer left window of our Brooklyn apartment was boarded up and covered by wire mesh, and a rat had gotten stuck there, then passed away and became petrified. It had been there for months because both of us were too afraid to touch it, but with our new French houseguest arriving the next day, Matt was tasked with breaking the dried rat in half, prying both dusty pieces from the wire that had killed it, and chucking them into the trash. This is all to say that we got the better end of the swap, but Marie had the time of her life being in New York, and we very much enjoyed waking up to peacocks strolling outside on our terraced garden every morning.

We were playing grown-up, and it was exciting. I had never pictured myself as someone with a bank account and a passport, but alas, here I was with both of these things, saying *oui* and eating *pain aux raisins*. Looking back, I was more mature than I am now. When I was twenty-four, I wanted to come across as forty, and now in my forties, I wish to come across as six. But it was healing to feel grown up for the first time in my life, to be in a place where I could detangle adventure from disaster. I knew then in France that I could potentially grow into a person whom I felt good about being, and while it would be a slow climb to get there, the privilege to be able to look at my past from such a remarkably special place felt like a call to take everything more seriously. I was not accustomed to gifts of this magnitude, and I did not wish to waste them. So we drove all around the countryside of Provence eating savory galettes and giant oysters and roasted chickens, drinking

Châteauneuf-du-Pape right out of the bottle, and this was a growing up of the most decadent and elegant sort.

Despite my rocky teenage years, I had never believed that I would become a delinquent and dysfunctional adult, never leaving my hometown and eventually ending up in rehab or worse, but I had also not been honest with myself about how close I had come to that reality. It's ironic that I ended up going over a cliff, because I had been teetering on the edge of one for some time preceding that descent. I had spent a lot of the foregoing years looking over the edge of my life, tossing rocks over and watching them smash, wondering if I should jump or walk home and have dinner. Somehow being physically thrown off helped me become more grounded, and it is worthwhile remembering that when I am tempted nowadays to look over the sides of bottomless canyons.

I had flirted with disaster on many occasions but never went to bed with it, unless you count the accident, but that was really more of a surprise blind date. For all the ways in which my parents made me feel untethered from them, there were still memories and moments of true love, whimsy, and revelry. There was a rope of connection to peace and emotional prosperity that was often stretched to the limits of snapping, but was never fully atomized. Real hope that got just enough air to never become totally extinguished. I am, and always have been, a very sincere laugher, and even in the most terrifying and lonesome moments of my life, seismic tremors of jubilation have cracked apart the cynic in me. If there is laughter, there is hope.

It came to me on that trip, as clear as the pure blue skies above the red hills of Roussillon, just how lucky I was to have been in France instead of jail or a cemetery or living in my parents' basement. Not lucky in the regular way, lucky in a George Bailey way, finding Zuzu's petals after a frenzied fever dream: *I am still here, thank heavens.* Cue the tears and the townspeople.

During my time in France I learned to drive down winding cliffside roads without being afraid of flying off them. I learned that you serve from the left and clear from the right, and that it is rude to remove someone's plate before everyone is finished eating. Less is more, unless we are discussing butter, in which case more is a finish line that turns out to be a mirage. I learned that when you buy a whole chicken in France, it comes with the feet still attached. Because we did not have a well-sharpened knife or pair of kitchen shears at our flat, I learned how to remove them by breaking and twisting them loose from the body with my hands, and then hacking through the rubbery skin with a dull blade. When my mother came to spend a week with us, I re-met the person who I had had adventures with as a little girl. She was a playful and engaged lover of life and a very dear friend, and I had the opportunity to see the bottomless wells of her magnificent enthusiasm for the world. She would fill like a helium balloon with childlike delight while walking through the markets and meandering through the cobblestoned streets of medieval towns, and it was a mending of a great big wound to see her as a real person through my own rapidly maturing eyes.

Matt and I drove to Italy and I learned how to make Bolognese the traditional way, in Bologna, from a real-life nonna. You use ground pork, ground beef, pancetta, chicken livers, mirepoix, chicken stock, just a touch of crushed tomatoes, salt, pepper, nutmeg, and white wine, then simmer until it's almost dry. I love seeing people do their own takes on classic dishes, but there is a part of me that winces anytime I see a liquidy Bolognese. I learned that Matt was sweet and patient and would have stayed with me through anything until the end of time, and that I was not yet ready for that, or maybe even built that way in the first place. I learned what it felt like to fall in love, and also not to know how to nurture that love. It wasn't until a decade or so later that I learned that this is okay, you're not supposed to know. It's okay to not be born knowing everything, including how to love properly, or that Bolognese is meant to be dry. I learned that there was a lot that I did not know and more that I had not even ever thought of. Had I been given the choice, I don't think that I would have willingly made the trade of being in a traumatic accident for a three-month trip to France, but we seldom, if ever, have a say in such matters. I was deeply aware of my privilege, though, and not just for the delicious food or beautiful scenery, but the privilege of realizing how small I was in relation to the world in such an exquisite way.

. . .

THE HEARTBREAK THAT WAS starting to heal in France was an old one, over a decade old in fact. When my mother and my stepfather, Rob, first started dating, I was ten. We would have him over and cook him elaborate meals to coax him into being a part of our family. I'm not sure that Rob knew what to make of these over-the-top dinners, or of my mother's relationship with me, which at the time was as if Nichols and May had been doing their act live from Grey Gardens. It had been a long time since my mother had made a meal for me, partially because she was a single mom with a full-time job, and also had a residual aversion to cooking left over from the dissolution of her business with and marriage to my father. While it was exciting and new to see my mother cooking again, it also sparked a building resentment. When it had been just the two of us, she never put this effort into preparing food for me, and to be fair, of course she didn't; I was a picky eater and she was just doing her best to get by, but my extra-sensitive child-brain told me that meant she preferred him to me.

One weekend when they were first dating, my mother decided she wanted to make Rob bouillabaisse, the Provençal seafood stew of mussels, clams, shrimp, and cod in a pungent saffron-laced tomato broth. She pulled Julia Child's *Mastering the Art of French Cooking* down from the shelf for inspiration and we got to work simmering shrimp shells for a stock and making rouille, thick saffron aioli, to spread atop crusty bread that would soften in the rich, fishy broth. This is one of the only meals I remember making and eating as a trio of happy people at this time, and I can still taste it if I close my eyes.

Those first few years, Rob really tried the best he knew how, and he was at somewhat of a disadvantage without children of his own to educate him on the complexities of being a parent. He was and is kind and accommodating, and he truly adored my mother; he had a genuine sparkle in his eye for her that has not gone out till this very day. Things between us became incredibly strained in the years to come due to my mother's inexperience with dating, and the extra care required in doing it while having a young child freshly bruised from her parents' divorce. But there were nice moments between the missteps, and cooking with her were among the brightest. For all the pain and trauma that was to follow, I am grateful for the times we spent together in the kitchen, and for those moments when I first got to realize how lovely Rob really was. It is a shame and a sadness that we would hurt each other so much in the years that followed, but also one of the greatest and most meaningful joys in my whole life is that we found our way back and built a beautiful relationship as adults. Like Papa Hemingway said, *The world breaks everyone and afterward many are strong at the broken places*. Our broken places have become little gardens from which grows our gratitude for each other, and we pluck the bounties from it to make all the special meals we didn't have the recipes for all those years ago.

When my mother, Rob, and I became sworn enemies over the course of my teenage years, I would think about this bouillabaisse she'd made to prove her culinary prowess to him, as well as her consistent choices to prioritize him over me. She was a caring and smart and passionate person, but she was not a good parent at that time; as a mother, she was disinterested and avoidant, and it broke my heart. My father didn't help matters, and once, in a cruel maneuver to pit me against her, he claimed she was planning to move across the country with Rob and leave me behind. And while she never did disappear without a trace, the very thought of it was like skywriting that followed me everywhere that read *YOU DON'T MATTER*.

In the depths of that pain, I had no bandwidth to dream about what I wanted to be when I grew up, or that France even existed. Never in my wildest dreams could I imagine that one day I would be able to get on a plane and be transported to a place filled with fields of fresh lavender, and markets lined with stalls selling every kind of olive and dried fruit by the kilo to the soundtrack of clanging church bells and calls of *bonjour madame*. Or that I would rip a dead chicken's feet from its cold, featherless body with my bare hands, and realize that I just might have a passion and a purpose after all. Maybe I could return home and keep ripping off chicken feet and make some sort of life out of it. Maybe I could find a way to put myself into the magic of The Lovin Oven all these years later. This was not a clear thought or goal, but more like a strong current pulling me closer to shore. At the time all I could really think was, *How did I end up here, driving above the Gorges du Verdon, instead of haunting a rocky ditch off Route 8 in El Centro, California?*

I had, and still do have, a hard time reconciling why I was this lucky. I'd sink my teeth into a real croissant, and as its shiny brown shell shattered like autumn leaves wrapped around a cirrus cloud, I'd think, *Why me?* Someone once told me that there are only three ways one can make sense of life: karma, randomness, or God. I have always been one to mix condiments, and so I chose to believe that life is more like a Russian dressing, with ketchup as the karma, randomness as the relish, and of course mayonnaise standing in for God. With regard to my salvation, I believe going on the tour was the ketchup, the bus driver falling asleep was the relish, and ending up on a balmy August evening in the Vieux Port in Marseille watching seagulls snatch oysters from the harbor and smash them on the rocks below, instead of being a twenty-two-year-old skeleton, was one hundred percent mayo. I will never know why I was so lucky, and why others are not. Maybe everything is simply chaos, and if so, I will whip and twirl around in it with gratitude as long as I am allowed. Gratitude that I had scars, because scars are for the living, and I was never more aware in my life until that point what a privilege it was to wear them. I had not only survived, but my brush with death had rewarded me with a fresh start and a trip to Europe.

In a tiny restaurant on the harbor, as I sat by the crystalline water of the Mediterranean Sea looking up at the Calanques, sharp jutting fjords that guard the shoreline like knights on horseback, the server brought me bouillabaisse. The broth was rich and zesty, the garlicky rouille aromatic on top of the perfectly golden crostini. I had chosen to come here because Marie lived in Marseille, but I had also learned that Marseille's most famous dish was bouillabaisse. There was promise and healing in the way the word rolled off the tongue. Perhaps this stew really was magic. Though my mom, Rob, and I had started to reconcile before the accident, it was the bouillabaisse that really felt like the symbol of the love we all needed from each other. Perhaps it could bring us all back around that table and allow us to make different choices, and be different people to each other. Back in my teenage years I was *à bout de souffle*, or out of breath, but here in France I was like the film's more hopeful English translation—breathless.

. . .

AT THE END OF the trip, my best friends Alexis and Kyle came for a visit, and one lazy afternoon we found ourselves at a small yet cavernous-feeling restaurant that clung to the edge of the terraced hilltop town of Gordes. It was run by a sweet couple in their sixties, one of whom was the chef and the other the waiter. There were no more than twenty seats, and the two men lived in an apartment behind the kitchen, separated from the dining room by a thin white lace curtain. The waiter presented us with a small chalkboard, upon which he'd scribbled the day's menu in that ubiquitous French handwriting, curly and whimsical with "1"s that look like small pine trees. There were a dozen or so *plats du jour* to choose from, all made fresh to order by the waiter's lovely other half, smiling out at the eager diners from the tiny open kitchen. When I say made fresh, I mean that he rolled out sheets of yolk-rich yellow pasta and filled them with creamy chèvre to order, sautéed the ravioli in butter that tasted of grass, and finished them with a drizzle of pungent green pistou just out of the mortar.

It was one of those meals that was so special that all you can talk about is how you can't believe where you are and what you're eating. The four of us sat there, young and hungry for the braised lamb shanks with prunes and cognac that we could smell being prepared just for us, but also for new ideas for how to live, ideas that were flowing through us like the geranium-rich breeze coming through the open windows of the tiny bistro. I watched the two men as they tripped the light fantastic together, complementing each other's movements gracefully, swaying through their service with casual expertise. You could tell this from every detail—the fresh flowers bookending the pass, the mismatched plates and glasses they probably collected at weekend markets from sellers who knew them by their first names—that they loved it. I thought of my parents, and how they must have known similar steps at their shop, and it all felt like a dance that I somehow knew too.

Our eyes rolled back as we let artichoke hearts cooked silky-soft in lavender and chicken stock melt in our mouths. We sopped the juices with chewy, crusty baguette, and washed it down with wine that was so minerally it was almost crunchy. The four of us had eaten hundreds of ravioli over the years, but never ones like these, that felt like satin-covered pillows bursting with creamy cheese so tart it made our eyes water. There was duck confit with skin that cracked like crème brûlée, topped with bittersweet orange marmalade. The meal finished with liquor-poached nectarines topped with a quenelle of goat's milk ice cream sweetened with local honey. The food was gorgeous and lovingly prepared, but also simple. The space was casual and warm. It felt like being in someone's home, because it was. This was their life, making beautiful food for people to remember, because it pleased them to please us.

I knew by the time we left the table three hours later that this was what I wanted to do. To learn these routines, and attempt to give an experience even one hundredth as special as this to others. I have never been as elegant as these two, especially not at twenty-four, but I did have an awful lot of heart and felt desperate for somewhere to put it. I also had an unexpected windfall of money and wanted to do something meaningful with it. I did love to cook, I had it stretching in my bones, begging to let me grow.

I knew on the plane home that I was changed. I was not high on ecstasy this time, but rather on the realization that I had come to see I had a passion, finally, and I was ravenous for the chance to get to work. The picture was revealing itself to me as such: being good at something makes people love you. I was good at cooking. I had money that I never thought I would ever have, so I should use it to make people like me, and also to make *me* like me. If I played my cards right, if I soaked up everything about France and cooking and having good taste, I could ensure that no one would ever try to move across the country from me in the middle of the night again. This was my karma. This all happened so that I could rewrite my future to erase the past, and I would do it by making the most complex broth that anyone has ever had. I would fill it with the bounties of the sea, and overhead, high above the shoreline but below the clouds, the sky would be written with something less aching.

FRIED BUCATINI

When I was growing up, Harrison Ford was president. Kevin Costner was a baseball player, Bruce Willis was a cop, and Arnold Schwarzenegger was pregnant. There were twenty-five movie stars, and a quarter of them banded together in the mid-nineties to open a chain of restaurants, and in my very qualified ten-year-old opinion, they were the peak of gastronomy. I loved Planet Hollywood, the Rainforest Cafe, and Mars 2112, even though I was deathly afraid of outer space. Beyond the heaps of Asian-inspired chicken salads and sizzling fajitas, I was left with an even more important imprint lesson: anyone could open a restaurant, even a Bengal tiger or Sylvester Stallone. Maybe this is why I too thought that I could open a restaurant with no experience. Or maybe it was because my parents had done it that way, or because my brush with death a few years back had convinced me that I was now invincible.

Sometime after Planet Hollywood, and before I went bankrupt, I lived on a dingy block in South Williamsburg just around the corner from Andrew Tarlow's sister establishments Marlow & Sons and Diner, and I became a regular at both. As someone who had believed that the only restaurant cooler than a monster-themed establishment in Midtown called the Jekyll & Hyde Club, where mummies took your order and

Dracula made virgin piña coladas, was a clubby Thai place in Williamsburg called Sea that had a pond in the middle, this was an illuminating experience for me. Tarlow's restaurants featured local, house-made everything; young, cool staff; and a daily changing menu of wacky ingredients written in ballpoint pen on your white paper tablecloth by a server who moonlit in your favorite band. Grass-fed burgers. White burgundy. And what the fuck was pozole? I wanted to create something similar of my own, a social club for people who listened to MF DOOM and were horny for ramps. As I matured I would come to realize the value of community and how a local small business can be an integral part of one, but at the time I was fueled by a hunger to be admired more than anything else for what I believed to be my interesting taste. That's not a crime, but it is also not the best frame of mind to have when making a commitment of this sort.

There weren't many good restaurants in Brooklyn back in the early aughts, back when Williamsburg was all farmland. Back when people wore smelly black tapered jeans and sniffed cocaine out in the open air, in addition to Diner and Marlow, there was DuMont, Moto, Sweetwater, and Bonita. Roberta's was still a twinkle in her mother's eye, and Saul and The Grocery were far away in Cobble Hill and for adults. If you were in the city, you could go to Barrio Chino to drink grapefruit margaritas and eat tongue tacos with pineapple salsa before casually trying to make out with one of the Strokes at Max Fish, or trying not to get roofied at Welcome to the Johnsons. The Odeon was for pretending to be a grown-up and learning how to like martinis. There was Keens or Bamonte's if it was your birthday and your parents were paying, and Mesa Grill if you wanted to go home with a Patrick Bateman–type, overdose on blue corn, and have a funny/scary story to tell your friends. Those were the only restaurants in all of New York City.

I loved going to Marlow for breakfast and devouring massive biscuit, egg, and cheese sandwiches and sucking down lattes, which I had just discovered was a classier alternative to a caramel Frappuccino. I had thought that scones were strictly for old English detectives until I tasted theirs, studded with gobs of tangy peaches and coated in crunchy demerara sugar. Marlow and Diner were really the first spots in New York to do market-driven casual fine dining in this way, a beautiful synthesis of exotic and approachable, drunk on naturally fermented Gamay and scored by James Murphy. My friends and I would sit at the bar at night and pretend we knew the difference between Wellfleet and Conway Cup oysters, slurp Hemingway daiquiris and endless glasses of Muscadet, and smear pounds of butter onto homemade sourdough bread, then use it to soak up the juices left over from the chicken that had been roasted under a brick. There was a heavenly chocolate caramel tart with sea salt on top and reclaimed vintage sinks in the bathroom. This may seem commonplace now, dated even, or silly, but to twenty-three-year-old me, who had previously thought the Steven Seagal burger was haute cuisine, this was a rapturous experience.

There were amazing people working at Diner and Marlow in those days too: Merica with her long curly red mermaid hair and perfectly fitting vintage Levi's; AD, who had an effortlessly cool and mysterious vibe; and Guy, cuing up playlists peppered with Suicide tracks, reminding all the lucky diners to *dream baby dream*. The graduates of these places have gone on to open some of the best spots in the city, like the wonderful Cervo's, Leo, and the Meat Hook, spreading the gospel of simple, thoughtful food served in a warm environment by interesting and sweet people.

When I moved out of my studio in South Williamsburg, and away from Marlow and Diner, I took what I had learned with me so I could replicate it in my new digs over in Fort Greene. It was 2008, two years before I opened Brucie, and I was twenty-four. My friends Alexis and Kyle would come for Sunday dinners at my apartment, and I would make things like homemade ravioli filled with sweet corn and goat's milk ricotta sautéed with fresh apricots and browned butter, or pork shoulder braised in lambrusco served over taleggio-laden polenta. Never a classic dish or simple recipe, always multiple courses with too many ingredients, but all made from scratch with local seasonal ingredients from the Fort Greene market, which was set up directly across from my apartment every Saturday.

This was an exciting and experimental time, but more so it felt like salvation because I had finally found something to be good at. Cooking became an obsession fueled equally by passion and a primal urge to outrun my past self, whom I had deemed defective and unlovable. Cooking was my liberation, and the ecstasy in this newly found freedom coupled with the naivety of being in my early twenties was what drove me to open Brucie. I had a very real, inherited passion for food and cooking, and a lifelong quest for companionship, love, and family, and so Brucie was born out of both my history and my desperation to outrun it. I had essentially won the lottery by way of a near-death experience, and rather than invest it in a house, or in an IRA (whatever the hell that was), I decided to use the money I'd gained in the settlement with the bus company to buy myself a new life and career.

It's not necessarily a terrible idea to use some unexpected

funds to finance a dream. It was also not, on paper, the most irresponsible thing that I could have done, and had I had any experience working in a restaurant, or a partner that could look after the financials, this could have even been, dare I say, a sound investment. I did not open Brucie in a conscious effort to get people to like me, and while it has been established after much therapy and personal reflection that this was indeed a massive motivating factor, I honestly did think I was making an "adult" choice. I believed that the careless choice would have been to spend it all on lavish vacations and Fendi bags, and that opening a business was a mature decision. I wish I had focused on the pendulum in its resting position. I wish I had had the patience and soundness of mind to realize that opening a business could absolutely be a good way to use this money, *and* that I should spend some real time making sure I knew how to run that business in a healthy way before pouring every last dime I had into it. But alas, at least I didn't piss it all away on a Lamborghini or whatever the fuck.

My early concept for Brucie was a New York–style pasta shop that used all locally sourced meats, dairy, and produce. I'd been inspired by Mr. Sausage in Huntington, and the classic Italian American pork stores and Italian specialty shops of that ilk that are such an important fixture in Long Island food culture. Everything would be made in-house: butter, fresh cheeses, filled and extruded pastas, and sauces: marinara, vodka, and pesto, but not just pesto Genovese—purple carrot pesto with Marcona almonds, and broccoli and mint pesto, and fermented yellow pepper pesto to bring home and toss with golden, saffron-laced tagliatelle! We would butcher whole pigs and make sausages that glowed neon pink from the addition of beets, and cure our own pancetta from the pork bellies.

Every time I saw a new heirloom variety of vegetable, or came across a dish I'd never heard of in *The Silver Palate Cookbook,* I pictured how to put my own special spin on it. I wanted to reinvent the wheel, and I wanted to make it out of 00 flour and stinging nettles. My young mind blazed magma-hot because I was naive and unfazed by the arbitrary nature of conformity. I look back at this young woman who set about to create a rococo red sauce renaissance, and I admire her gumption, but if I could have given her one piece of advice, or one thousand, the first would have been to learn to make a perfect carbonara before you run.

When I was a college student at FIT, I had interviewed famed rapper Aesop Rock, aka Ian Bavitz, for an essay I was writing about a *New York person, place, or thing*. Aesop had gone to my high school, and had been a personal hero of mine for years. As a nineteen-year-old fine arts major, I felt that I had no use for life drawing or intro to photography. I was an artist, and I was just there to make art the way I thought art was meant to be made. I had no interest in learning the basics, and I told Ian this much during our phone chat, which I took while spending the weekend at my mother's house, in my childhood bedroom, on a clear wall phone, the kind where you can see all of the wires inside.

If I can tell you one thing, it's how important it is to learn and respect the basics, he said in his briny low vibrato.

I was shocked, offended almost. I felt betrayed. Here was one of my heroes, someone so strange and unique in his own medium, he might as well have arrived on earth in a wide circle in a cornfield—why was he telling me that respecting and honoring tradition was paramount in one's quest to be a creative person?!

My contempt for his opinion was actually embarrassment at the arrogance that made me think I knew better than time-honored tradition, better than Frida or Georgia. I thought because Basquiat was so esoteric, that meant that all conventional ways of thinking were for the birds, never considering what he may or may not have studied before, or the fact that he never lived to be old enough to be elected president. I'd never been raised with boundaries—my mother would say, *In this house we only have two rules, no saying bad things about other people, and no blue food,* which haunted me like Giovanni Bragolin's *The Crying Boy*. But obviously Aesop was right, and the fact that I was not willing to take this advice tells you all you need to know about the level of misguided, albeit well-intentioned, self-assuredness I was committed to as a young person. Today, I am often pummeled by waves of sadness over how it all ended at Brucie, but the truth is that I needed to get tossed in the surf in order to learn to tread water. I wish it had not taken such force to free me from my misconceptions about how the world spins and my place in it, but I am glad it did because that humility is priceless.

Brucie morphed from being a psychedelic pasta shop into a full-service restaurant in phases, fully embracing the latter not long after opening our doors. During our first days in business, we were still struggling to find our identity as a restaurant, and I was personally caught in the same struggle as I tried to figure out what it meant to be a chef. Is a chef anyone who steps into a kitchen and declares themselves so? Or is it a title bestowed to you after a certain amount of time spent sweating out your will to live at the sauté station or learning to make a French omelette with one hand behind your back? I had thought we could be the exception in making a market/restaurant work, but it became clear shortly after opening that Brucie was going to be a full-on restaurant, and so we ditched the open fridges filled with Italian sundries and fresh veggies, and started fine-tuning our service.

People loved Brucie straightaway, and after a few months of doing embarrassing things like making people come order at the register, having servers pin their handwritten tickets to an old rope functioning as a ticket rail with fucking clothespins, and refusing to serve coffee, we got our act together and ran a tight ship with delicious and exciting food for six wonderful and insane years. But if I could have done it all over again, I would have taught myself the importance of restraint, in cooking and in being. I would have mastered carbonara, pesto Genovese, and zabaglione, and learned how to cost out dishes, budget, manage my temper, and handle stress. Life drawing is important, because you should really know how to draw a hand, even if you prefer a foot. The reason students are made to learn to draw hands first in art school is that hands are the hardest thing to do. It makes everything you create better if you first understand the fundamentals, in drawing, painting, music, cooking, and being a part of a team.

. . .

I FOUND THE SPACE at 234 Court Street in Cobble Hill in the spring of 2009, and within a few weeks had signed a lease with my very Italian American landlord. He had four dozen or so brothers who helped us with the construction *for a price.* We got to work ripping and building and installing mason jar light fixtures and a custom-built copper bar top lined with stools meant to resemble tractor seats, which were not only terribly uncomfortable to sit on, but also had a propensity for falling off their posts at random. In the front dining room, the walls were papered with a baby-blue-on-white pattern that you might find in a grandmother's kitchen, if she lived on a sprawling cattle farm in Kansas in the 1950s, and in the back dining room, with thick navy and white stripes that made you dizzy to look at. Beyond the tractor-seat bar stools, which were just a few inches short of the proper length from the bar, making them impractical as well as painful, each seating option was more unfortunate than the next, ranging from small backless stools that looked as though they had been lifted from a preschool classroom, to an assortment of rickety wooden vintage chairs, constantly threatening to collapse, to the benches at the *picnic tables* I thought looked amazing crammed in the private dining room in the back.

Within the first year, we changed much of the seating and decor, some for the better, like replacing the nausea-inducing striped wallpaper in the back room with a mural of the constellations that my friend Mary had hand-painted in a whimsical homage to Ludwig Bemelmans, and the terrible bar stools with classic bent wood ones. We changed the 1950s Kansas grandma style of the front dining room to Ralph Lauren children's collection wallpaper that featured a repeating image of a map of the world on a tan background, and when Brucie would close for good, we would tear off pieces and sell them to regulars for $5 a pop.

I think of Brucie now, and the twenty-five-year-old version of me who designed it, and I cringe a little, but then I laugh, and feel gratitude for being someone, for at least a portion of my life, who was so confident in her bad taste that it made something good. We need a certain amount of feral gaucheness at points in our lives to find our way to grace, and in those early days, putting this fanciful project together, it was equal parts passion and precipitousness that brought it to life. Blessed be the sweet mistakes that form the stars in our own constellations.

I needed this arrogance, foolish optimism, and total disregard for logic to have the gall to do something as outrageous as to open a restaurant at age twenty-six, on my own, with no professional training or experience. I often ask myself if I would do it again. On many days the answer would be no. I would have taken the three hundred thousand dollars that I pumped into and lost with Brucie and bought a home. I would have trained in other restaurants and understood the basics, how to draw hands and make a perfect omelet. Instead I watched YouTube videos on how to break down a pig, and threw myself off another palisade.

But on the odd days of the week, I can't imagine it ever being any other way. When I spend a day with my friend Becky, going to the movies and almost choking on pizza crusts because we are laughing so hard, or when I blow out the candles on my Fudgie the Whale cake that Dan got me for my birthday, or go to Robert Moses beach with Mary to float in the sea and eat deli sandwiches crammed with potato chips under our umbrellas, or when one of them is there to hold my sadness when my arms tire, or better yet, when I'm cuddled in a pile on the couch with all three after drinking too much wine, I realize that all my foolishness, all my throwing of paint at the wall and calling it art, was worth it. If I hadn't done it that way, I wouldn't have ever met my best friends, and getting to be a part of their lives and have them in mine has been the luckiest thing that has ever happened to me. Not knowing them is not a life that I want to imagine living, and so all the mess and years peeled off my life by the stress and the chain smoking was worth the trade. I wish that I could have had it all: the patience and appreciation for honing a craft, and the unbridled creativity and drive, and an IRA (I'm still unsure what this stands for), and a house, and the perfect carbonara, but alas, like my mother always says, our greatest weaknesses are also our greatest strengths. I eventually learned how to make perfect carbonara, and I am glad for that, because the adult me adores simplicity. But I also made carbonara at Brucie by smoking house-made bucatini and tossing it with parmigiano and cream and crispy lardons of bacon, frying it like a doughnut, and then topping it with a raw egg yolk, and it was pretty darn amazing. There is room to grow in life, and sometimes we do it in reverse, when we are ready.

I have a tendency when looking back at Brucie to chastise myself because there are so many ways in which I feel like I came up short. I feel embarrassed for how terrible I was with handling the finances, and ashamed of all the times I willingly lost my temper. I sometimes feel like I have to preface every recollection of this really huge effort with an apology or some kind of self-deprecating joke about how young and dumb I was. And I was young and dumb, and I do feel badly for how I treated people and myself at times, but I also look back and feel proud. Our brains are so hard-wired to define things in a binary way, but life and memory has taught me there is value in the fluctuation, the in-between. Not having any experience at all made cooking thousands of different dishes for thousands of people very challenging at times, and caused the restaurant and me to burn out quicker than we probably had to, but there was a luminescence to it all that could only have shone so bright without one inch of caution to shade it.

RICOTTA ICE CREAM

Z, THE FREEZER DOESN'T SEEM TO BE RUNNING. ALL THE ICE cream is melting.

I look down at the sous chef, Steven, and see lavender ricotta ice cream melting all over his hand. It is dripping from an adorable little vintage bowl that I got at one of the local thrift stores in Long Island near my mother's house. I wish I could call my mother at this moment to come pick me up, take me home, and put me to bed. I wish she had told me not to open a restaurant, because I feel so far in over my head that I can feel the bends settling in. I thought it would be cute to serve ice cream in these bowls the moment I laid eyes on them. I thought, at twenty-five cents apiece, *What a bargain.* I thought this would all have been much simpler: the restaurant, being a chef, being in charge. It is not simple, and this is why I call my mother at least two times per day.

Do you think we can send this one out? Steven asks me this in his British accent, which annoys me in crisis times. His cadence implies that he should have a solution, direct orders from M or something. Or maybe it was me that should have had the fix, but I was burnt from everything always being on fire. He is melting too, sweating through his shirt. We all are.

Certainly fucking not, I say in my Long Island accent. *You look like you were taking tickets at a bukkake festival.*

He dumps the contents of the ceramic bowl into the trash, places it in the dishline, and moves toward the sink to wipe his hands.

It is a Saturday night in June 2013, and the restaurant is on a two-hour wait. Some people are on first dates eating tagliatelle with tomato butter and house-made stracciatella, others are talking about their dead parents, some are breaking up, some are falling in love, others are irritated by the volume of the music, some think the green tomatoes with bagna cauda are too salty, and others sop up every last bit of that melted anchovy butter with our homemade sourdough. Many of them are sitting on the small backless stools at a communal table, and they clearly hate this. I thought small wooden stools around a large communal farm table was a great idea because I thought of it in the year 2010, and in the year 2010 this made sense. In 2010 bacon found its way into any and everything consumable, teeny tiny cabbages called Brussels sprouts were sweeping the nation, and people still thought it aspirational to work for David Chang. It was the time of whiskey and Edison bulbs and lots of silly little mustaches, and thus I selected small wooden stools and spray-painted the words *Eat* and *Drink* on them. We will keep these stools until the restaurant closes six years later, even though by then I will think they are so lame, and they are, and to me that is funny. I will store two of them in my mother's garage, and sometimes when I go to visit her, I will sneak in there and sit on one and have a good cry among the cobwebs and old rusted beach chairs. The people sitting on these ridiculous stools on this particularly busy Saturday evening in June are feeling the consequence of my poor seating selection in their lower backs, and they are envious of the people sitting at tables that have chairs with proper support. They are jealous of the four top that got the last whole roast chicken with strawberry agrodolce and charred scallions violently protruding from the neckhole.

The sound of Frank Ocean's voice braids with the sounds of forks dropping and people having a good laugh. People saying *yum* and *wow* and *What is bottarga?* Everyone is in the weeds. The ticket machine is spitting up so unrelentingly that I start to grab its regurgitations and stuff them into my bra.

George, who is working the line at the hot station, shouts over from the fryer, *We lost one, Z!* He gestures to an egg yolk–stuffed arancini whose guts have seeped out through a crack in its coating and oozed into the fryer, making it unusable.

Then throw it away and start over, Jesus fucking Christ, I say. I have convinced myself it is acceptable to be rude to my friends and employees when I feel stressed, an inherited aggressiveness that I picked up from reading *Kitchen Confidential* one too many times and totally misinterpreting it to align with my personality flaws and insecurities. It is okay for chefs to be aggressive and intimidating, because after all we are doing the lord's work here, saving a life with each order of Caesar salad we heap onto a plate. Most other times I am extremely friendly. Most other times I am everyone's favorite. But oftentimes I am rude, and I hate this about myself, but not as much as other people hate this about me. I have heard my father was like this in the kitchen, and many other times too, I know, speaking to people as though the volume is down.

Is that rice ball coming by carrier pigeon? I think that if my tirade, now aimed at George, is funny then it makes it less abusive. Perhaps this is true, but it doesn't make the arancini fry any quicker. It also doesn't make George feel valuable. It doesn't help me sleep better. But at the time, these are self-doubts that I shove down to make it through dinner service.

Cameron the GM walks into the kitchen to ask, on behalf of one of the servers, where table twenty-three's food is, and predictably I shout at him to *ask fucking George.*

They share a look, and it is a comradery that makes me feel ashamed, so I shout for my old friend Michael, the bartender, and order a round of shots for me and the kitchen and one for him and Cam too. This gives me the false sense of redemption that I need to keep pumping out tagliatelle after tagliatelle without the wheels coming off.

When I opened Brucie three years before, on September 25, 2010, I had no real restaurant experience, but I had worked at various different pizza places in my hometown of Northport throughout high school. First, San Carlo's, run by an Irish guy in his mid-forties. He was so thrifty that he would mince up any unsold pizza slices at the end of the night, roll them into uncooked dough with a little sprinkling of cheese, slice them into rounds, and sell them the next day as *pizza rolls,* which we all referred to as *stuffed yesterdays.* The next was run by an Italian man who could have been thirty-five or seventy given the lighting. He was heavily into drugs, leaving lines of cocaine on the back of the toilet tank for his high school–aged employees and handing out Vicodin at the mere whisper of a headache. I was a pizza delivery girl, which was a more dangerous job than I gave it credit for at the time. *Come in for a second while I grab my wallet,* said a middle-aged man, home alone for the night, then groped my exposed hip bone as I fumbled to get him his change. I cringed so hard I pulled a muscle and ran out the door without a tip. *Do you party?* asked a strung-out twentysomething after taking a pepperoni Sicilian from my hands. He passed me a small clear baggie filled with beige powder, that I only knew not to snort from watching *Basketball Diaries* seventy-nine times between 1998 and 2001. I tossed the heroin in the bushes and ate a garlic knot that I had snuck from his order on the way there, then continued on to the VA hospital, where I got trapped in an abandoned building and had to escape by jumping out a second-story window and running across a frozen field to my 1987 Volvo.

This is all to say that my experience in the food business was minimal and highly specific.

As Brucie's ticket machine continues to churn, we take the shots and the tequila goes to work loosening the knots in my stomach and brain. My friend Becky, one of our servers, walks into the doorway of the kitchen and asks if her table's entrées are coming soon, and I smile at her instead of scowling, because the tequila has helped me to step back from the edge. I survey the tickets and let her know that her table is mere moments away from a hot date with their double-cut pork chop and mile-high stack of sourdough sitting atop a thick swoosh of our house-made cardamom-pistachio butter.

We are getting back on track. I apologize to George and we hug, and I settle into the delicious certainty that this will turn out to be a good night. In a few hours the customers will have left, and we can blast the music to an even more unreasonable level as we wipe the gaskets of the lowboys and sweep the dried pasta strands and charred Brussels sprout leaves from the ground. Cameron will count the money and give the servers their cash tips. We will all change into our human clothes and gather around the bar to get drunk and talk about the craziness of the evening. I will say funny things and everyone will like me again, or pretend to at least. Then we will go down to Henry Public, and Marty will give us free shots, and we will eat French fries, and the chaos of the evening's service will be like a bad dream you can barely remember upon waking.

But this world is hours away, and in a busy restaurant on a Saturday night in June, many things can occur between now and French fries and free shots. This is always when disasters happen. Floods, fires, injuries. The health department coming in on Valentine's Day, or the heat breaking on a nine-degree day when there is a rehearsal dinner buyout, or a Beastie Boys song randomly coming on while Mike D is eating brunch at the bar. Maybe it is Murphy and his rude law, or Newton's third, but no matter the reason, in a restaurant, the worst possible things happen at the worst possible times.

Broken freezers do not unbreak with a shot of tequila like bad moods do. They remain broken until properly fixed, like bones and childhood traumas. The freezer was leaking freon, and I didn't want to spend the money to have it fixed straightaway. The freon leak caused the freezer to warm. The freezer warming caused the ice cream to melt. The melted ice cream caused Steven to present me with a hand that looked to be covered in semen, and this in turn now propels me down the narrow stairs to the basement to stick my metal-handled, stainless steel knife into the back of the freezer in an attempt to turn the temperature down.

I have never been one to stop and think things through before catapulting myself into action, and tequila might warm the brain, but it cools one's rationale, much like freon. I have seen Jacob the refrigerator repairman dial down the thermostat a thousand times. In my phone he is *Jacob the Fridge,* and this makes me chuckle to myself every time I see it, which is often, as the freezer is always on the fritz. But Jacob the Fridge used a plastic screwdriver to turn down the thermostat. And now the stainless steel knife making contact with the electrified thermostat on the back of the walk-in freezer causes me to be violently electrocuted, blown several feet backward from the rear of the freezer into the concrete wall behind me. I disconnect from time, just as I had when the bus divorced from the road in El Centro, California, all those years back. The lost moments of the walking dead.

The melted ice cream seemed so important, like life or death. It was important enough to convince myself I could be nasty to my beloved coworker. It was important enough that I risked my life to stop it from melting without a second thought. But it was just whipped-up ricotta cheese, cream, sugar, eggs, and lavender. If the table who wished to order it was told that it was no longer available, they could just choose something else or get a pint of Ben & Jerry's to eat in bed while watching *Breaking Bad*. But this is not the freon that I run on. My freon tells me that if the ice cream is unavailable, or the rice balls take too long, or a server waits to clear the dirty plates from the table, I am a joke. That the accident was for nothing. That my whole plan to convince my friends, family, and community that I am worthy and lovable would erode and I would be washed away back to the lonely island from which I came. There is simply no reasoning with someone operating from this state of mind. Sticking my knife in the freezer was desperate and careless, much like the person attached to the handle. It is a good thing to care about your work, and to be brave and bold and take deep pride in what you do. But there is a difference between dedication and desperation.

Cameron rushes over to help me up. *Are you dead?*

Maybe? I genuinely do not have a definitive answer. My hair is frazzled like a cartoon, and my right hand, my bad hand, is covered in black soot. I slowly shuffle back to the rear of the walk-in to grab my knife. The force of the electricity cut a quarter-inch groove into the tip of the blade. After I see that, I look back up at Cam and struggle to push out a more steady *maybe*. We both laugh with tears welling in our eyes.

Well, you look like the fucking Blair Witch, fix yourself up before you go back up there, he says, helping me smooth my hair, wiping the mascara stains from underneath my eyes. Cameron and I were born three days apart, and we are very similar. He often says something mean to let me know he loves me, and the *Blair Witch* dig gives me the laugh I need to keep going, it reminds me that I am alive for real. That there are people in my life who love me enough to tease me in the worst of times, and I them, and this is what it is actually all about, not ricotta ice cream.

I wish that I had done a better job of trying to keep the people around me in working order as much as I had the kitchen equipment. A few years later, Cameron and I will have a bad falling-out. He would leave to go work at a very famous Brooklyn restaurant, and I would be devastated and heartbroken, but instead of saying that, or admitting the role I played in our fractured relationship, I would decide that he was awful and a traitor, and we would never speak again. It hurts me to think about this, because he wiped the mascara from beneath my eyes dozens of times, and teased me like the brother I had prayed for as a child, and I don't think I ever got a chance to tell him how much that meant to me. One time, when I was commiserating about an embarrassing mistake I had made, he told me, *In the moment we all think what we are doing is right. That we are smart and mature and have it all figured out. And then you look back at that person, the one from months or years ago—the brilliant genius that knew everything—and you realize that person was an idiot, but that's okay, because that is how we grow, and everyone feels this way. It is what it is to be a person.*

Now, Cam tells me that he thinks I am, in fact, alive. He hugs me and says, *Go get 'em tiger,* and I turn and run back up the narrow basement stairs, taking them two at a time, and straight into the bustling kitchen ahead.

86 ICE CREAM!

COFFEE BUTTER

When I was around five or so, and my parents and I were still living with my grandparents at the house on Vidoni Place, I created my first original recipe. The kitchen was small and featured appliances from the 1950s that I would die to have now. One afternoon I snuck into the kitchen, took the reacher that my four-foot-eleven grandmother used to grab things from the cabinets, and retrieved the peanut butter and grape fruit roll-ups. I turned on the oven, probably to five hundred degrees, and waited for it to warm as I spread peanut butter that I dug out of the jar with my fists atop the leathery fruit snack. On a sheet tray and into the oven it went, and when my mother smelled smoke, she came into the kitchen to find me sucking peanut butter off my fingers, the same fingers that I had used to turn on the oven. She snatched the bubbling mess, and once it cooled, she tried it.

There were many times at Brucie that we came up with dishes on our daily changing menu that sounded about as appealing as broiled fruit roll-ups with peanut butter, but much like my mother, our guests took a chance on them. While the combinations were whimsical and often completely wild, they really worked. The recipes were not tested, because there were no recipes, just instinct on the part of myself and my chef de cuisine Jennie that strawberries, anchovies, and peanuts when tossed with cilantro, scallions, sherry vinegar, and peppery olive oil would make something exciting but also familiar happen in one's mouth. We did not make wild things to shock people or to go viral on Instagram, because this was back in the 1700s when Instagram was just for taking blurry pictures of your dog, or a lake you visited, and editing them to be super high contrast with a caption that read *What is time?* We made mischief out of mozzarella for the sheer joy it brought to us and our guests. And we knew the swings we took would connect. Classics like spaghetti and meatballs and eggplant parmigiana would share the stage with fried purple sweet potatoes with coffee aioli, hazelnut brittle, and a drizzle of smoky, peaty Laphroaig for balance. As strange and esoteric and *American Psycho*–esque as a dish like swordfish and fava bean lasagna may sound, the flavors and presentation were as approachable as chicken parm.

Getting to be creative each day in an uninhibited, almost childlike way was the most fulfilling and grounding part of my life thus far. I felt like I was doing something that mattered professionally for the first time—a starring role in the play, a reason to get up in the morning. At that time, I was still very much living under the misconception that being the center of attention is the best seat in the house, when really it's like sitting in first class: Sure, you get to stretch out, but you pay a hell of a lot for it, and in the end if the whole thing crashes, you're the first to die. But I did not know any of this yet, I was still in the puppy love stage of a bad romance. The thing that's so addictive about professional cooking is how quickly the hit of validation reaches the brain. You work hard making something that is a representation of your talent and within hours you will receive feedback, hopefully in the form of praise, and that's that; the mouth feel of your fresh fettuccini with sweetbreads and figs has cemented your role as the second coming of Christ.

But there was also a purity to the pride I felt in opening Brucie. I felt inspirationally annexed to my parents in ways we hadn't been able to tangibly connect face to face. There was a telepathy of sorts that I plugged into in the restaurant kitchen, a trust fund of congenital culinary adroitness that I had finally reached the proper age to access. I hope with all my heart that our guests enjoyed eating the fruits of our fever dreams as much as we enjoyed preparing them. All that I do know for sure, though, and what I will cherish for the rest of my days, is that for a slice of my life I had the great privilege of true creative freedom. It came with a hefty price, and I was too young and arrogant to protect it, but god damn am I lucky to have been able to touch something so ethereal.

. . .

BRUCIE BECAME KNOWN FOR our whole roasted chickens, which were prepared differently according to the season and our mood. In the winter, they might be served Caesar style, with a tangy, salty, heavily dressed salad of charred cabbage and raw bitter greens, a thick slice of our homemade sourdough, and a snowy mountain of grated parmigiano. In the summer, we'd take inspiration from caprese salad, and there would be juicy heirloom tomatoes, a mound of house-made stracciatella, and pillows of pistachio pesto atop the birds. These whole chickens were served, well, whole. We refused to cut them into manageable pieces, and tables that dared to ask were basically told to fend for themselves with a dinky steak knife. What can I say, it looked so dramatic on that big oval-shaped ceramic platter, it would have been an insult to the chicken to chop it up merely to make it easy for the guests who had just paid fifty American dollars to enjoy it.

We dreamed up an endless rotation of small plates: fried mozzarella with carrot romesco and tahini; fresh shelled English peas with tuna conserva, pickled raisins, and a sharp sesame dressing; kale sprout caponata; egg yolk–stuffed arancini in smoked bone broth. Early spring menus had us dramatically plating mushroom parmigiana; butchering heritage breed pigs for bone-in double-cut pork chops that we'd serve with pickled rhubarb, tzatziki, and a pile of fried artichokes; and stuffing whole cauliflowers with lamb sausage we'd made in-house, studded with almonds and prunes, then drenching the whole thing in preserved Meyer lemon and caper berry vinaigrette. In summer, we'd make Korean-style rice flour pancakes with burrata and radish kimchi; cucumber, blueberry, and sweet corn salad with diced pickles, red onion, and Cabot clothbound cheddar, tossed with a tangy, lemony yogurt dressing and freshly popped popcorn for a surprising crunch; and pan con tomate, kicked up with warm anchovy butter and bomba calabrese. We would layer lasagnas with shrimp Bolognese, squash blossoms, and paper-thin ribbons of pickled zucchini, and top it all off with crunchy, fine breadcrumbs made from Caputo's famous lard bread. Fall menus featured entrées like thick, tender steaks of butternut squash alla Milanese, atop a generous swoosh of saffron aioli and crowned with a sky-high pile of lemony arugula salad, an aggressive amount of raw red onion, and a blanket of grated parm.

We reveled in all the unique produce we could get our hands on. I was a chronic over-orderer from Lancaster Farm

Fresh, awestruck by the heirloom varieties they had to offer each week: soft, buttery graffiti eggplant, candy-sweet sungold tomatoes, crunchy little watermelon cucumbers, aji dulce peppers, juicy berries, currants, watermelon, stone fruit, red kuri squash, fresh baby corn, noodle beans, purple Brussels sprouts, flowering broccoli rabe. You can find Jimmy Nardello peppers all around the city nowadays, but in 2014 there were only a few dozen restaurants working with ingredients like these, and we fawned over them, like a bunch of teens seeing a Playboy centerfold for the first time: *So that's what it looks like.* We would take the Nardellos and stuff them with rabbit sausage and braise them with fresh shelled borlotti beans, sherry, and chicken stock, and finish them with a glug of olive oil made by Arianna Occhipinti herself.

You might think that changing a restaurant menu every single day would mean that a decent percentage of dishes would miss the mark. I am not saying that everything that came out of the kitchen was a perfect ten, or could not have been made better with testing, but I will say with conviction that I was proud to serve every single plate that came off the pass.

In Brucie's six years, there was only one disaster dish. During one of our morning brainstorms, Jennie and I came up with a small plate of calamari tubes stuffed with an unctuous and creamy pâté of house-made ricotta whipped together with pistachio-laced mortadella. The calamari were tied shut with a long chive, then broiled and garnished with a pungent fried rosemary salsa verde. In theory this was meant to dazzle and amaze, and it did, just not in the way we had hoped.

As the first tables were sat, and diners ordered the appetizer that was sure to change the way they thought about calamari forevermore—which the sweet servers described as *a guy from Bologna moves to Amalfi*—we lined our pork-stuffed cephalopods on sizzle trays, drizzled them with olive oil and a sprinkle of kosher salt, and slid them under the broiler. When they came out, Jennie dressed everything with a healthy sploosh of salsa verde and a glug of fancy olive oil, and off they went to win us a James Beard Award. We waited patiently in the semi-open kitchen to hear the *oohhs* and *aahhs*, but instead came cries of *ouch* and *why god why!?!*

What we had not accounted for was the pork fat from the mortadella and the whey from the ricotta melting together with the juice from the cooked calamari, essentially creating a balloon of molten mixed animal juice. When the customers cut into them, seemingly all at once, the blazing lava-hot liquid shot out at warp speed, blasting them in their faces. It was like the opening scene in *Saving Private Ryan,* but with squid. People on first dates clutching each other for safety. Grown men telling servers to *get this note to their mothers*. Friends ducking under tables to hide from the enemy. Limbs being torn off by violent, fishy magma.

Cameron walked into the kitchen with two plates covered in oily shrapnel, horrified by the carnage he had seen. *What were you guys thinking, this is a disaster,* he scolded, forlorn and traumatized. In the dining room, servers were running to the tables who had not yet activated their calamari landmines, grabbing their plates away and rushing them back to the kitchen.

A panic set in. How could Jennie or I not have tried the dish? Though we didn't formally test our recipes, we always tried things before service. But between the cleaning of the squid, piping in the filling, and then tying the slippery little bastards with a god damn CHIVE, which had given our prep guy Eduardo so much grief that he nearly quit over the whole thing, this particular dish was regarded as too precious to taste. I had reasoned that I knew they'd be good, and they would have been good, great even, if I had added some breadcrumbs to the filling to soak up the juices and tighten it all up, but I did not, and so we experienced the one true failure to come out of the Brucie kitchen.

Like any good slapstick disaster, once the panic and shame subsided, then came the laughter. All of us in the small kitchen, cooks and servers, were hysterically, out of control, crying laughing at the destruction that lay mere feet from us in the dining room. We triaged as we always did when the wheels came off, with generous pours of free prosecco and gifts from the kitchen, then prayed for the lost, took big shots of warm tequila chased with cold beer, and carried on. *One small change to the menu this evening,* the servers repeated for the rest of the night, *we are unfortunately out of the calamari.*

In addition to a sense of humor about kitchen nightmares, our team was monumentally creative, and the wacky food combinations were honest and pure reflections of their unimpeded artistry, deep personal cravings, and desire and excitement. Some of the dishes at Brucie were a challenge for the customer to understand on paper, but at its core, our cuisine was very simple and un-tortured. It was not tweezer food, it was genuine and unpretentious and extremely laid-back.

For a stint, George was our sous chef. He was a tall, lanky metalhead from Connecticut, with a sense of humor and performative hamminess that could have made him the Jim Carrey of his generation had he taken his act to the screen. He came to Brucie early on, in 2011, with little professional experience, and started as a line cook. The first time I asked him to slice prosciutto, he started by cutting off all the fat and throwing it in the garbage. But George was all in for Brucie, and we became fast and close friends.

George and I would work the dreaded Friday shift from ten a.m. till midnight, go out and get drunk at Boat Bar, then return to work at eight the next morning to work a brunch double, followed by Saturday dinner service, which would finish at one in the morning. Saturday mornings would start with us both comatose, floating in a state of half hallucination while mixing pancake batter and warming meatballs. We'd chug our coffees, which would give us just enough energy for a joke or two before the caffeine peaked, leave us teetering on the edge of a nervous breakdown for a bit, and then eventually level out at around eleven with a shorty Bloody Mary. We had a bit where we would punch the eggs open into the pan instead of cracking them, and we would often pass the entire brunch service by talking like Andrew Dice Clay. After the seemingly never-ending shift was over, we would sit in the backyard drinking beer, chain smoking, and doing our best John Wayne impressions until four in the morning, much to the chagrin of our upstairs neighbors.

In the early days of George's tenure at Brucie, when he was still a line cook, the sous chef was Max, who was highly volatile and abusive. It didn't take much to send Max into a tyrannical fit, and one very busy Saturday night, complete with a two-hour wait and an overflowing ticket rail, he threw two full pans of spaghetti at me, dousing me and everything in the garde manger station—all of the prepped ingredients for salads and pastas, and the finishing touches like picked herbs and grated pecorino cheese—in tomato sauce, scalding my chest and rendering the mise unusable, then walked out the door, leaving George and me to fend for ourselves. George rushed over and wiped away the sauce and tears. We stood there for a brief moment, unsure how to forge ahead with service, and then George grabbed my hand and said, *Come on Z, we can fix this.*

We flew down the stairs to the walk-in, furiously grabbing ingredients to refresh the demolished salad station, almost dropping the cambros of herbs and shredded cheeses all over the floor because we were laughing so hard. *You look like someone just gave birth to you,* said George in his comforting baritone voice. We barreled back up the stairs and had the entire station flipped in under five minutes, and cruised through the rest of service like we were god damn Butch Cassidy and the mother fucking Sundance Kid. Georgie was my right-hand man, my true ride or die. He did not come to Brucie with a passion for food, but he left with one, and I left with the pleasure of spending thousands of hours with one of the finest humans I have ever met.

But my truest, deepest love at Brucie was my chef de cuisine Jennie. Jennie Lupo walked into Brucie in 2011, responding to an ad for a line cook that I posted on craigslist. Lupo means wolf in Italian, and in ancient Roman mythology it is said that a she-wolf saved the city's founders Remus and Romulus when they were thrown into the Tiber by the king as infants, and nursed them back to health, making it possible for the great city to flourish. Jennie has piercing, almond-shaped hazel eyes and a mysterious nature, much like her namesake. She moves carefully and quickly with intention and has a restrained, quiet coolness to her, but she could kill you in a split second if it ever came down to it. She is whip-smart, hilarious, and a classic beauty, truly timeless and unparalleled in her class and grace.

When Jennie came in that first day, I felt an instant kinship. She was from New Jersey, which is basically like being from Long Island, and had an air about her that suggested she had struggled in life, but knew how to laugh about it and roll it into pasta the same way I did. I knew she was a good cook before I ever tasted her food—I could tell by how little she needed to prove herself. She was humble and tactful and said *cawfee* and *tawk,* and so I hired her on the spot.

Jennie turned out to be the most talented cook I have ever met. Her food is sharp and punchy, like her sense of humor, and you can taste the history in it. Unlike me, she had cut her teeth in various New York City restaurants that underestimated her talent, merely using her as a set of hands to chop and fry. When she first started on the line at Brucie, she did so with the same humbleness that she brings to everything she does, despite the fact that she is often the most gifted person in the room in just about every way possible. She could do anything I could do better, but never made a point of proving it, rather throwing herself in wholeheartedly whenever needed, never expecting special recognition. But it was clear how good she was, and before long she became the sous chef, and shortly after that the chef de cuisine.

Jennie and I matched each other's creativity in the kitchen. We had a shared nostalgia for classic tri-state-area red sauce cooking, punctuated by childhood trauma. We are perhaps the only two people who appreciated the intersection of chain restaurants and Fellini, and had a propensity toward the whimsical and fantastic, which gave us a distinctive shorthand while creating the daily changing menu each and every morning. We would serve tuna noodle casserole—house-smoked tuna folded into sheets of homemade fazzoletti pasta and baked together with Cabot clothbound cheddar and peas—alongside wild boar osso buco over risotto Milanese topped with bitter salad in a garlicky anchovy vinaigrette. We would get whole pigs' heads once a week and run them as large-format specials. *Let's do this week's Irish coffee–style,* Jennie would say, and then she would go about braising the head in whiskey, espresso, and cream with a hearty dose of balsamic to cut through the fat, then plate it atop a bed of buttered cabbage and bring it to the table with a shot of Jameson for each diner. We stewed short ribs negroni-style in Campari, gin, vermouth, and tangerines, and filled polenta pancakes with roasted butternut squash and chèvre, then topped them with miso butter and amaro-spiked maple syrup.

Jennie was just as psychedelic when it came to menu planning as I was, but more pragmatic, so she was forced to be the voice of reason hundreds of times while making the day's menu, like a mother telling her toddler that she could not have four scoops of ice cream with homemade waffles and an entire birthday cake for breakfast. It wasn't that she didn't think house-made seafood sausage in lobster broth with crispy guanciale sounded fabulous, it was just outrageously expensive and laborious beyond the point of reason. She was right, and I am sure at times it felt as exhausting as managing a toddler to talk me off the edge of bankruptcy every morning. We would sit there day after day at the copper-topped bar, over coffee and big bowls of cut-up grapefruit, and finagle our way out of the previous day's culinary hallucination into a fresh one, rearranging pasta shapes, vegetables, and sauces into new and radical inventions. We would scribble, scrawl, and rub our eyes, and pull at our hair until we had solved the puzzle and found new ways to surprise and impress each other.

There was a succinct rhythm to the way we created the menu, like good jazz. But there were also many times when we hit walls, not fully understanding each other's ideas, which felt almost like a betrayal of the trust we had for each other's talents. The unfair part, the one that I know built a resentment in her, was that I ultimately had the last word, even if that was never the tone of the conversation. I looked at us as equals in the process, and we were, but even if I rarely vetoed her suggestions, I think the fact that I had the *power* to do so left a feeling of disease between us both. I didn't want to have the authority to make the final call, or be the one to take all the public credit for the work we both put in, but because we had not built this business as partners, because I signed the paychecks and paid the rent, that tension hung in the air no matter how fluid the concepts that bounced between our brains were.

Jennie and I loved and still do love each other like sisters, but neither of us ever had an actual sister to be a reference for how complicated the depth of this type of love can be. At the time, I didn't always feel deserving of recognition for my culinary skills because I felt I hadn't earned them. I had not been handed a check by my rich parents and told to go have fun playing restaurant, but the power dynamic between Jennie and me at times made me feel like I had. She had taken out the student loans to put herself through culinary school and sweated over the grill having her ass pinched by her coworkers in hot kitchens all over the city, and here I was, a rube with a stack of cash who bought myself a career. She was the one who deserved to have her name in the paper, not me. I know she cared for me, it was evident in every move she made, but I know to some extent she felt that way too. Even though I told countless journalists who wrote about the restaurant exactly how things were done, and how important Jennie was to the creative process, it didn't matter because the myth of how Brucie was built—the chef parents, the near-death accident—was in place before Jennie walked through the door.

And I leaned into that storyline all the way too. No matter how inclusive I tried to be, I was also a showoff and a scene stealer. It is in my nature to be loud and outrageous and command attention, and that made it difficult, if not impossible, for Jennie to shine. Despite the balance we brought to even our most fantastical dishes, we struggled at times to find it in our relationship. I would have given Jennie half the restaurant in a heartbeat, but in the years it took for us to evolve into a more comfortable partnership, there wasn't much to give except a huge sales tax debt and a business that I was actively thinking about how to sell. No matter how deeply we cared for each other, that imbalance was a stain on our relationship that was very tricky to wash off, much like the beet juice we used to dye heavy cream to make into neon pink stracciatella.

When Jennie got married in 2015, I wore a bright red dress to her wedding and refused to just blend in for once and let something not be about me. But I also helped her make all of the food, and gave a speech that began with a Rodney Dangerfield joke. *I think I might be an alcoholic. I went to the doctor today to give a urine sample and there was an olive in it.* It went on like most wedding speeches, praising the couple for the outrageously high bar they set with the love they shared, how no other two people complemented each other so well, and how Jennie was the most beautiful person I had ever known, but it wasn't just schlocky hyperbole, every word was as true as fire burns. I ended it simply, with a sincere wish: *I hope you have the best time*. I believe when you truly love someone that is the most genuine desire you have for them, that they have a beautiful life, that at the core, beyond all the ways in which we miss one another, you wish that every bite they take will be more delicious than the last.

I wish I could have better organized our relationship like I did our mise en place, putting the herbs in a row, making sure all of the drippy and flaky things don't make a mess of the other ingredients. In relationships, the messy things usually make their way into everything sooner or later, just like grated pecorino cheese. I love Jennie, and her contributions are immeasurable, just like the food she made; food that could never be replicated because there was no recipe—but even with one, no one could have ever made food that tasted the way hers did.

There were times in Jennie's and my relationship marked by pain and disappointment, where I know that I came up short and took her for granted. Our bond was at times arcane, similar to how the dishes read on the menus we created together, but ultimately made for a truly perfect bite, unexpectedly complementary and filled with pure delight. Brucie would have never been the magical place it was without her profound contributions, and I would never have been able to stretch my own creative muscles to their maximum potential without her as my teammate. Jennie and I transcended friendship. When she had her bachelorette party at Hunk-O-Mania and wore a white dress and no underwear, not realizing she was going to get pulled up onstage and flipped upside down, I pulled her into the bathroom and gave her mine. I know that sounds gross, but love is often gross and that's what makes it so fantastic. No matter how we have broken each other's hearts, we live within them, and have stayed committed to the relationship, scars and all. We were both born to live a life without real sisters, but we came as close to it without sharing a bloodline.

The greatest loves are the ones that call on you to stretch further than your tendons might allow for, to expand your imagination, compassion, and threshold for emotional proliferation, and this can be agony at times—the kind of growth that only such authentic care can conjure. What a gift it has been to have a friend like Jennie, who never let go of my hand, even when it was very hard to hold. She is the magnificent she-wolf whose love made it possible for Brucie to flourish.

. . .

WE ALL AT BRUCIE may have fawned over weird peppers and tomato varieties with human first names, but we were not a very *chef-y* bunch. No one had pig part tattoos or brought their special knives to work. We used the shitty but well-sharpened ones that clung to the knife rack hanging threateningly by the sink right above head height. Many of us, myself included, had never worked in a professional kitchen, and certainly not one as ambitious as Brucie.

Haji, who made all our fresh pasta, cheese, and bread in the second half of Brucie's run, was an old friend of mine who had once had a career in the music business, and Amelia who preceded him in that role had never worked in a restaurant before either. I had met her at a mutual friend's house on the Fourth of July 2011, skinny dipping at midnight, and when she said she wanted to work in a restaurant, I replied, *See you Tuesday then.* She started baking what would come to be our highly acclaimed sourdough boules that we would serve with a seasonally rotating list of homespun butters, in flavors from anything from coffee to peach and bacon. Folks went wild for the coffee butter, and so it made its way from adorning Amelia's tangy, chewy sourdough, to topping polenta pancakes, to being tossed with Haji's hand-rolled cavatelli.

Simple yet creative things like the coffee butter became a throughline over the years—food that reflected the vibrant spirit of our team. We didn't draw sketches of dishes we dreamt about, or plan to stage at Michelin-starred restaurants, or reference Escoffier, or even know who Escoffier was. We didn't brunoise vegetables, we often chopped them unevenly and roasted them without peeling them or setting a timer. And we certainly did not call each other *chef*. We just loved food and got a rush out of preparing and plating and eating it. We got into and out of the weeds almost every night, and we equally loved and hated the brutal grind of working the line. We smoked cigarettes and drank American beers on ice out of plastic quart containers, took shots, and stayed out late at dive bars near work. We superglued our cuts and always had slug-shaped burns on our forearms, and we all became stitched into the lining of each other's hearts. We also despised each other for at least thirty minutes per day at a minimum, and laughed until we cried at least double that. The most chef-y thing we said was *corner* and *behind you* because we did not wish to have hot oil splashed in our faces or be accidentally stabbed in the gut by a coworker.

(Here is the thing about saying *behind you:* it has become chef and food service worker satire, but each and every one of us around the globe, from all walks of life, should be saying *behind you*. If animals could speak, they should say it too, as their sneaky presence is equally if not more threatening. Unannounced, we are all essentially living booby traps. I say *behind you* each and every time that I am, you guessed it, behind someone. I get sideways looks and eye rolls, since people unfamiliar with restaurant work sometimes take this as an offense, as if I am rolling up on them, being pushy and aggressive. *Au contraire, mon frère,* I am simply trying to avoid you swinging around and splashing your hot coffee down my shirt, or unknowingly slicing me in two with that live chainsaw you are holding, and because I fancy a clean shirt and how my top and bottom halves look attached, I politely announce myself: *right behind*. Do not take offense, this is best for us both.)

While our cuisine and candor may have been unhinged and unconventional, we were professionals where it counted. In addition to being absolutely amazing at saying *behind you,* the kitchen was sparklingly clean, the walk-ins and dry storage were labeled and audited meticulously, and we set up, cooked, and broke down with precision. Saying *corner* can prepare you for avoiding potential disasters, but not for a wall socket catching fire during service, or a drunk celebrity ripping a bookshelf off the wall while waiting for the bathroom. We took the important parts seriously, and made the rest our own peculiar, enigmatic brand.

The pace moved very quickly, all of us working in the kitchen scrambling to make a new restaurant each day in the six hours we had between walking through the door and firing the first orders for dinner. There was an incredible amount of pressure on both the front and the back of the house staff to learn a new menu every day, and I often had unrealistic and unfair expectations for the staff to understand the daily offerings as they existed in my head, without ever having sampled them or practiced their preparation. I would get agitated and salty with servers, many of whom were my best friends, or snap at them if they forgot a detail about a dish and came into the kitchen mid-service to ask about it. It would have been ten times easier to just answer their question with a smile—*the herb in the pesto is shiso*—than it was to shame them and assume that they didn't remember because they didn't care. They did care a lot, and they proved it every shift with their hard work, attention to detail, and the warmth they shone upon each other and the guests.

There were dozens of times when one of the talented cooks missed something on a pickup at the sauté station, forgot to set a timer on the bread, or left something out of the fridge overnight by accident, and instead of taking a beat and realizing how demanding their jobs were, and that it is more than human to make mistakes, I blew my top. I could blame it on the fetishization of the stereotype of the angry chef, or that I was not taught the importance of controlling my emotions as a child, and while those things are true, it is truer still that being kind and patient are the absolute most important parts of being the captain, and failing at that is my deepest regret of anything that ever happened at Brucie. I believed that kitchens were a place where misfits went to fit in. One where people with unresolved traumas came to exorcise their demons in a hot, sometimes highly aggressive environment, like a hardcore show, or a boxing ring, and maybe this was it for some folks. But while restaurants may attract people who are looking for drama and a little bit of violence, they need to be a place where everyone feels comfortable, happy, and safe. That is eight million times more important than validating anyone's need for sadomasochism; that is what doms are for.

Brucie was not run in a militaristic manner, nor was it a

place where the vibe was overwhelmingly abusive, but I know that at the time I believed losing my temper was okay because it ultimately helped people learn, and this is wrong. If I could change one thing that happened at Brucie, it wouldn't be the exploding calamari or the hideous, uncomfortable stools; it would be that. Do not, under any circumstances, be mean to your team, ever. It is not as cool as your television makes it out to be, it's not cool at all. My advice for any young cook or business owner of any sort is: do not sign a lease until you are certain that you know how to be a lighthouse to your staff, a dependable and guiding light, no matter the weather.

Brucie was a piquant love affair with food, saturated with red sauce and tequila. It had a Cassavetes-like quality to it, all intuition, imagination, and heart—plus Peter Falk worked Saturday nights behind the bar! It was set to an ear-piercingly loud soundtrack of 1990s top 40 rap, acid jazz, dirty jokes, uproarious laughter, and occasional screaming fits. There were love affairs, table dances, pig heads, broken bones, and grotesque burns, but it was more than that, much more than what you would see in the trailer. The blood that pumped through the heart of the restaurant was the people who gave their time, effort, and love to make it so special. Even though we always announced it, we always knew in our bones that we were right behind each other.

Desserts: brown butter ice cream sandwich: rosemary caramel
chocolate cookie:
chocolate tart: shortbread crust, vanilla ice cream, salted caramel
Pana Cotta: candied mint, whipped cream, bourbon caramel
Apple crostata: greek yogurt moose, pecans ~~hazelnut~~
Fig → mini personal pie

Bfast 4 Diner: $18
Savory "Croque Monsieur" French toast:
Marscopone slick
Mortadella
Caccio cavallo
Parm baked in
fried egg

brucie

April 9, 2014

ONE

CHICKPEA brussels, egg, harissa - 10 (Pureé roasted soft / Raw fried chickpea / w/ bread)

BEETS lentils, capers, pistachio, sesame - 11 (Roasted / lime vin (tangy touch of sweetness from honey))

LEEKS anchovy, house ricotta, breadcrumb - 12 (cooked in white wine butter, lemon / parsley - black pepper)

KALE SPROUT CAPONATA - 12 (Sweet/Sour Raisin/olives/tomatoes / Sugar / vin. olive oil)

PARSNIPS mortadella, apricot, smoked yogurt, honey - 14 (thin slices of roasted / cubes / fresh mint. / Ricotta salata)

RADICCHIO mushroom, meyer lemon, sage pesto - 13 (Shaved / shaved raw / chips / walnut)

TWO

RISOTTO wheatberry, chicken sausage, olive, lentil - 18 (green / butter/lemon/pork-rabbit stock / (Parm. scallion. oil))

PAPPARDELLE carrot, leek, brussels - 18 (HM / roasted / long cooked / Pernod cream / black pepper and pecorino)

TOFE short rib, orange, cauliflower - 18 (Negroni braised / mint/olive oil / breadcrumb)

SPAGHETTI & MEATBALLS - 18

THREE

CAULIFLOWER SPEZZATINO - ~~$~~18 (ricotta salata / Stew / over creamy Polenta. / Sicilian flavors: fennel/caper/anchovy/saffron/olives/tomato)

PORK MILANESE kale sprouts, fried egg, grilled lemon, parmigiano - 24 (Pecorino/lemon / 1/2)

POLPETTE ricotta gnocchi, chickpea, brodo, salsa verde - 25 (2 beef: cheddar - dill - garlic - red wine - bacon fat - dill / (4) / regular / Pork broth / → jalapeno/arugula)

CHICKEN FOR TWO ALL'AMATRICIANA - 45
-tomato/bacon/onion/pork belly/white wine/thyme
• black rice • arugula

CHEESE

KUNIK cow & goat, new york - 9

Pecorino Jenepro: Softer Pecorino that's rubbed in juniper

SIDES

BREAD & BUTTER - 3 coffee

MARINATED OLIVES - 6

SAVORY PASTRY - 6 Meat grab bag tom/raisin

KALE - 7

2lb Ribeye: $120
• Winter veg braised in red wine
• Anchovy butter • herb salad
• garlic aioli

no substitutions please. xoxo.

Coffee Butter

WE CREATED THIS FABULOUS WHIPPED BUTTER AROUND 2012. We wanted to serve Amelia's delicious sourdough boules with something that had a Brucie twist. I don't remember how the coffee got into the butter, but once they met, they were truly inseparable. Coffee butter is so simple to make, and pairs well with anything from fresh bread and pastries, to steak and pork chops, to pasta and risotto. It just dawned on me, this could change the way we eat popcorn forever!

MAKES 1 CUP

2 sticks (½ pound) salted or unsalted butter (I am not fussy about salted butter. If you use salted, be gentle with any additional salt.)
2 tablespoons finely ground coffee (any roast you like)
1 tablespoon granulated sugar
½ teaspoon ground cinnamon
Salt to taste

Put all the ingredients into a food processor and process for about 1 minute, until thoroughly combined. Store in an airtight container for up to two weeks. (Yes, that is it!)

TAGLIATELLE

A GOOD LIE IS ONE WITH NO REAL VICTIM AND LOW-STAKES subject matter. The last Christmas we had together, my father bought me the ugliest necklace imaginable, and I told him at least once a month for the following year how much I loved it, and how it matched everything I wore. I never once put it around my neck to step outside my house, but it was probably the best lie I ever told because of how happy it made him. *The train is delayed* is the greatest and most beloved of all New York City lies, even though everyone knows it is code for: I couldn't decide what to wear. *I loved* Breakfast of Champions: lie, I hadn't read it yet, I just wanted to impress my date. *I'm coming!:* I'm not, I just want the date with Kurt Vonnegut guy to be over.

Running a restaurant also makes you into a great liar. My father had been very skilled at dealing with upset customers on the spot by making up little white lies to neutralize his blunders. Most notably, he had told me about a time at The Lovin Oven where a customer brought in a hazelnut dacquoise cake she had purchased earlier that day, in which she had found a quarter.

Oh my god, Bobbie, get out here. We have a winner! my father said, calling for my bewildered mother to come to the register and witness his wild ride from shame to benefaction. *Ma'am, you won our grand prize! You found the quarter in the cake! You see, in French provincial folklore, where this cake hails from, they hide loose change in the cake this time of year to celebrate the coming of spring, and whoever gets the piece with the money in it is said to have great prosperity in the coming year. So we have a contest going here where the customer who finds the quarter gets a free cake! And you have won!!*

The woman went from outraged to overjoyed, and all it cost my parents was a cake, hopefully this time free of pocket change.

I had taken pages from this book from time to time at Brucie. I had once made a whole chocolate olive oil cake for a private party in our back room, and forgot to grease the enamel baking dish that I baked it in. When the top broke apart from the bottom as I was about to plate and decorate it, I did not succumb to the meltdown hovering behind me like an old wet Victorian ghost. Instead, I smushed the crumbled cake back into the pan, covered it with fresh whipped cream, edible flowers, and some stray thyme sprigs, and I proudly paraded that thing into the baby shower, asking in my most Martha voice, *Who wants spoon cake?!?*

One woman said to her friend, *I've never had spoon cake!* to which her friend replied, *Oh, it is so good, it's very trendy right now.*

I felt invincible. No matter the gaffe, there was a made-up tradition or recipe that could save us.

I didn't have much of a leg to stand on when I opened Brucie. I was suffering from intense imposter syndrome, a diagnosis that continues to give me tension headaches and itchy skin until this day. I felt like I was lying to everyone by merely showing up and saying, *I'm a chef.* I hadn't done much more than make dinner for my twentysomething friends who thought homemade pesto was a revelation. I was opening an Italian American restaurant, in Brooklyn, with a measly twenty-five percent Italian American genetic makeup. I had chef parents who had taught me next to nothing about cooking, who had historically taken me to chain restaurants and made me boxed and microwaved food growing up instead of home-cooked meals. But I did love food, and preparing it was the one thing in life I felt truly confident about. Despite the lack of gabagool twisted in my double helix, my command of the cuisine of Italy was deep enough to make me at least the groundskeeper of the Olive Garden.

. . .

THE FOUR TOP SITTING at the middle of the big table are getting really pissy about their food taking so long. They cursed at me, and they are just being awful, do we have an ETA on their mains? Paulina, one of our beloved servers, asked exasperatedly.

It was a Saturday night, somewhere in the fourth quarter of Brucie's run, and we were in a classic bottleneck that inevitably happened at some point on every busy night. The restaurant sat around seventy-five people, and the kitchen was two hundred square feet, and no matter how strategically we tried to seat people, or how mindfully the servers tried to stagger putting their orders in, there was always one point in the night, usually around nine or so, that it all became static despite how furiously we were all moving and twisting and frying and tossing. When tables were waiting longer than usual for their food, we would always send a gift from the kitchen—some homemade sourdough or a bowl of something fried tossed with pecorino and chili flakes, or at the very least a round of prosecco—and this was almost always enough to dissolve any edginess about the wait.

This group, however, was an anomaly, and was giving Paulina a very hard time about it, verging on cruel, and totally entitled. I had a zero-tolerance policy for customers being rude or abusive to our staff, and the staff knew that if there was an issue they could come and tell me, and no matter how deep in the weeds I was, I would drop everything and take care of it. My go-to move was approaching the offending guests, asking them how everything was, and then informing them that their meal was finished, and on the house, and that we would look forward to never seeing them again.

On the evening in question, I made a beeline for the center of the communal table to give them the old manager's special. *Gentlemen, what seems to be the problem?* I asked with a syrup-sweet smile, twisting the sword behind my back and readying myself to split them through the center at any second, to make a scene and prove a point, and let my Robin Hood complex bask in the glow of their shared humiliations.

We have been waiting, like really long, for our entrées, and I mean this is just honestly bullshit, their spokesperson shrieked.

I wound up for the swing, and in that moment, something stopped me, something innate and familiar, but slightly odd fitting, like walking in your mother's heels for the first time. *Well, I am very sorry you are so upset, folks, but unfortunately one of our servers died earlier today, and we are all just trying to get through the night the best we can.*

I was just as shocked by the story that came out of my mouth as they were. Where had this come from? Earlier that night, one of our staff members had been dealing with a serious mental health crisis that kept them from being able to come into work. But that wasn't why the veal parm was taking forever, you could blame that on seventy-two people ordering at once, or George hearing *fire veal* instead of *fire two veal,* or me for not actually saying to fire two, but insisting I did. (Wow, I am starting to sound like a real Pinocchio here, but really I've never been much of a liar, not any more than the next guy. We all tell little lies sometimes, especially people who are trying to make their restaurant popular.)

But this lie erupted from somewhere deep within me. I think in this moment I wanted to teach these people a life lesson, one that made them look like the assholes, rather than the other way around, which was what always happened when I grabbed some jerk's plate of pappardelle mid-bite and told him to take a hike in front of his date. I wanted a supersonic moral bitch slap that reminded them that they had no idea what happened to make their food take so long, or what Paulina had been through that day, what any of us had, and if their food had taken another two hundred years to be ready, it still didn't give them the right to be rude to a total stranger. And the irony here is not lost on me, because they too could have been coping with the imaginary or real death of a loved one, and I had had dozens of irrational outbursts myself hurled against my staff, but alas.

These guys were mortified, and that is to put it lightly: dust bunny, feather boa, puff of smoke lightly. *Oh my god, I am . . . we are . . . oh my god . . . we are so sorry. I cannot believe what a jerk I was being. Please accept our deepest condolences,* said the man who had just seconds ago been ready to threaten me with a bad Yelp review or maybe even a lawsuit.

It's fine, how could you have known? Really. But just to keep in mind for next time you're at a restaurant and your food is taking too long, or it comes out imperfect in some way, someone could have died. I gave them a sympathetic smile, and actually felt tears welling up in my eyes, and darted back toward the kitchen.

What happened out there? Paulina said as I returned to the kitchen.

I replied, *Well, I was going to ask them to leave, but instead I told them one of the servers died earlier today, and we are all in mourning, so just go with that.*

What? Why? she asked in an elated state of disbelief.

Well, I guess I just wanted to give them a little perspective, I answered, then hugged her and then whipped around the corner into the kitchen. *Okay, where were we? George, that's two veal all day, baby, how we looking?*

Some lies create unexpected good; this group of gentlemen became some of our most devoted and loyal regulars. They were at our closing party, toasting the beloved restaurant that had surprisingly charmed them out of their frustration with the untimely and tragic death of an imaginary person. Others are engineered to make something good even better, like the Legend of John Tangorra Sr.'s Meatballs.

The meatballs at Brucie were the only thing that stayed on the menu, unchanged from the day we opened until the day we closed. They were tender and fluffy, packed with milk-soaked sesame-crusted Italian bread, loads of chopped parsley, sweet garlic and onions, grass-fed organic beef and pasture-raised pork, and an almost equal amount of pecorino. One surprise ingredient made them bright and punchy, something you don't usually find in a meatball: lemon zest. I love lemon zest, and I find it to be a sneaky way to give a little burst of pizzazz to things that can otherwise fall a little flat. It's a way of adding an imagined acidic or herbal flavor without actually adding acid or herbs. Lemon zest is how the French say, *What the fuck is in this thing?*

Not long after we opened, reporters started trickling in, wanting to write about the restaurant and our unconventional approach to cooking Italian food. I was flattered, terrified, and honestly shocked. When asked about what were fast becoming our famous meatballs, I created a legend, which was in fact a tiny lie, that these were my grandfather's meatballs. It came from a nostalgia for a childhood that I had not lived, but always wanted, and one that I could tell the journalists wanted too. This wasn't *A Million Little Pieces of Lemon Zest,* just an innocent fib that would make people less sad than the truth, which was that my family never once ate dinner together in my whole life, and though my grandfather made delicious meatballs, he was also an outrageous bully who not only never taught me his amazing meatball recipe, but would have cracked me on the head with a wooden spoon for suggesting something as tony as putting the zest of a fucking lemon in them. *Lemon zest is for shrimp scampi, now get the hell out of my kitchen, you hippy bastard* is what he probably would have said, had he lived long enough for me to give him recipe suggestions. What we both put into our meatballs was time, care, and intuition, and what we got out of them was adoration for a job well done. I would have loved to be a part of a family, especially one with such collective culinary acumen, that celebrated treasured recipes together, but what I got was one that, for better or worse, allowed me to write my own.

But there are some mistakes so horrifying that not even Tom Ripley could talk his way out of. In 2014, because of Jennie's incredible leadership in the kitchen, I no longer had to be on the line six nights a week. I still worked in the kitchen most of the time, but I had time to be on the floor and interact with the guests more, which I loved. This particular evening was a busy Friday in the early summer, and I was helping to run food through the crowded dining room. Brucie was a tight space, and there was an art to carrying plates through it, an art that our skilled and seasoned servers had mastered, and I had not. What I had mastered was the art of being a complete and total ham and showoff. I was wearing something sexy, the music was way too loud as it always was, and everyone was having a great time. It was an especially magical evening, which I remember because of how palpably hard I brought the vibe down.

Table 43, seat one spaghetti, seat two tagliatelle, Jennie instructed as I took the pastas from her at the pass. I sashayed away, plates in hand, hips swaying side to side, grin ear to ear, channeling my inner Diane Chambers, headed to a two top near the front window. As I made my way through the narrow pathway between the bar and the communal table, I held the plates above my head. I was going to show these servers how to do the job with style. I sauntered past the edge of the communal table, so thrilled with myself at how good I was at doing every job in the restaurant, when the plate in my right hand tilted to the side, spilling a hot, wet, red tangle of spaghetti and not-my-grandfather's meatballs on the head of an unsuspecting woman who was simply trying to enjoy a nice meal at a restaurant she heard was supposed to be cool.

This was the first of two times that I literally ran away from something that scared me, the second being when I saw my father's dead body, and in all honesty this memory makes me squirm harder. At Brucie I always stepped up to handle anything that came flying at us, but there was something about spilling spaghetti all over this woman that triggered a deep flight response. I was so ashamed I didn't even have the wherewithal to reach for a classic Tangorra family fib to make it all better: *Oh my god, whoever gets magma-hot pasta dropped all over their face gets the keys to the restaurant and all the money in my wallet. Congratulations! Goodbye forever!* And then I would have left the restaurant and my old life behind and headed west until I hit the desert, met a handsome man who fixed cars, changed my name to Dee and got a job bartending at the local dive, and old spaghetti-head could have figured out how to make caramel corn work on a wedge salad. But I froze, then made a brisk but heartfelt apology, then ran into the kitchen and hid in a corner and cried until she left, and service ended, when I laughed about it until I almost peed in my pants.

. . .

I ALWAYS SAY THAT I decided to close Brucie because I was tired, and I was. I was completely exhausted mentally and physically. But this was a lie, one I had to tell myself and everyone else to avoid the truth, which was that I was defeated.

I defer to the lie because it is less complicated and embarrassing than the truth, which is that on top of being tired, I was broke, afraid, lonely, and desperate to get out of what had clearly become an abusive relationship. As someone who had been in an abusive relationship before, I knew that they are not as easy to detach from as we would like, and despite being subject to harm at any moment without warning, we often stay because the memories of when things were sweet and alive have a boa constrictor–type grip around our hearts. Toxic relationships are reenactments of early trauma. We think if we can act out a similar pattern and create a different outcome, then perhaps the serpents in our pasts will transmute as saints, allowing us to find salvation and freedom from all future pain. Fairy tales are enchanting, but real growth comes from finding the strength to sever the ouroboros.

My relationship with Brucie had become toxic because I was pumping all my time and energy into something that was fundamentally broken and unfixable, in the hopes that if I could just work harder or do better, it would thrive and all the shame and regret from my past would melt away like soiled snow patches on the first warm day of spring. It was toxic because in my quest for this release I gave in to all my worst instincts. In my efforts to find myself I was losing my handle on the plot.

Owning a restaurant is a very hard thing to do on your own. I was lucky enough to be surrounded by talented and loving people who made it possible to open the doors every day, but ultimately the burden of operations fell on my shoulders. It was always too heavy to carry, but by late December of 2015, when we had been open for almost six years, I simply couldn't hold it anymore. Over the last year, I had been thinking of closing, or restructuring and starting over in some way, and then one night, when I was alone in my apartment, I decided to call it quits for real and close Brucie after Valentine's Day. I owed over one hundred thousand dollars in sales tax, and more than half that to vendors, and that was what had been keeping me going: I had to just find a way to make up the money so I could walk away clean. But I was so burnt to a crisp by that freezing cold night in December that I really didn't care what would happen to me.

Maybe I would go to debtor's prison, but as long as the staff got paid and we had a good celebration on the way out, the rest would just happen, and I would get through it. I couldn't be this person anymore, a perpetually exasperated young woman who at times would resort to yelling and cried herself to sleep. I didn't want to participate in the capitalist structure of restaurant ownership, where I was the boss and other people were my employees; it was all in conflict with my values, with the kind of person I could actually feel proud of being. I couldn't afford to pay people as much as they deserved, which even back then would have been at least fifty dollars an hour to be able to afford the cost of living in New York City. I just wanted to be one of the gang. I wanted to love myself more than I wanted anyone else to love me. And even though I wouldn't begin to really know how to do that for another eight or so years, I would have never even moved one centimeter in that direction if I had kept Brucie open.

When I was young, after losing The Lovin Oven, my mother worked in a hospice, then went back to social work school and has been a psychotherapist specializing in bereavement and grief ever since. For as long as I can remember, the walls of her therapy practice have been adorned with dozens of quotes meant to inspire her clients while they waited for their sessions. When I entered adolescence and grew to detest my mother, so did I detest her wall of quotes. Only in hindsight, and with the healing that has transpired between us, have I been able to realize how special it is to have a full wall of the musings from the greatest thinkers in world history to stop and take a look at every day. Through the years the quotes have made their way onto kitchen corkboards and picture frames in the living room. I don't remember when I first saw *Leap and the net will appear—John Burroughs* pinned between

Rumi and James Baldwin, but I do remember that it was what I heard over and over again in my head the night when I decided to close.

For better or worse, I have never had a plan. I have always been a leaper. I was born with a fear-filled brain, and have found that the only way to conquer the neuroses that aim to keep me stuck and paralyzed is to leap. Not to run, or hide, but to leap. Leaping is different from running. Running is using all of your energy and aliveness to stay a few steps ahead of that which chases you. Most of my time at Brucie, no matter how wonderful and precious it was, was spent running, sprinting as hard as I could to just make it a few more yards. But leaping is choosing to surrender to the unknown rather than your prospective captor, like Harrison Ford in *The Fugitive,* when he jumps off the dam, free-falling into either death or freedom. I knew at that moment that I would rather endure a proverbial death than let Tommy Lee Jones in his sweater vest and jeans keep chasing me through the sewer. *Leap and the net will appear* does not specify the net. The net could be made of snakes or shards of glass, or feather pillows. The net doesn't matter, it is all about the leap.

To psych myself up for the leap, I had to believe that the net was made of marshmallows. If I had known at the time it was barbed wire, I would never have had the courage to step off the dam. The net was made from filing for bankruptcy and losing my apartment and living out of the trunk of my car and showering at the gym. It was made from unfulfilled attempts at new projects, lost friendships, a flatlined sense of identity, total humiliation. It was made of taking shitty personal chef meal prep jobs, making chicken fingers for rich people's kids, being depressed and drinking a little too much sometimes. But I was free. There was a lot of loss attached to that, but I hadn't died when I jumped.

That night, I wrote a corny breakup letter from Brucie to New York City and sent it to *Eater:*

Dear New York,

How do I explain how deeply I love you? Your vivaciousness, your energy, your people, the smell of your hair. . . . . .

It has been my greatest honor to be in this relationship with you these past 5½ years. Every day that we spent together was a new adventure. I felt privileged to have lasted in a love affair with such a fickle and fiery partner, knowing that the tenure of our union was in fact a testament to my character as well. When you bestowed gifts upon me, when your inhabitants filled my room, when your critics sang my praise, the world stopped. I never imagined that I could have lasted so long with someone like you, and the fact that you showed me love for so long and love so great has made my life feel like it meant something.

But, as you might be sensing from the melodramatic tone of this letter, I need to say goodbye. I need to move on and find my peace, my real purpose, my grown-up identity. Every second was a gift and a pleasure and while you will probably soon forget me, please know I will never forget you or what you have done for me, it has meant everything, and I will love you the most for the rest of my life.

Goodbye New York, I will be closing my doors February 15th. I don't know where I am going, but I know where I have been, and it was in the arms of the greatest city in the whole wide world. My staff and I look forward to all the new adventures and opportunities you have to share. While this part of our relationship is over, I really think and hope we can stay friends. Thank you. I love you. Take care.

Oh, you left your toothbrush here, I'm just going to throw it out. . . . . .

Love,
Brucie

Like many breakups, it was both for the best and a potent dose of grief. I had convinced myself that Brucie would fix me, but like in any relationship, we cannot be fixed by things or people outside of ourselves. Great loves can change and nurture us, or create chaos from which we can mature and grow, but true transformation and healing happens within the parameters of our own skin. When I think about the effort I put in, the relationships that blossomed there, and even the missteps and disasters, Brucie was the most formative time in my life, but I would come to realize that it was the loss that would have the most significant impact on me. Loss is blindingly illuminating. I wish this wasn't true, but it is also comforting to know that there is unmatched healing power in such deep pain. If I had known this at the time I probably would have tried to avoid swallowing such a bitter pill, but it was one I had to take to be ready for subsequent losses that were to follow, and to really learn how to live the life I wanted, one where I was awake.

When I walked into work the next day, I cried as I talked through the plans to close Brucie with the staff, many of them who had been there for the entire life of the restaurant. We had seen each other through deaths, heartbreaks, and marriages. The thing about restaurant work is that it feels urgent at times, and maybe that seems ridiculous, because it is, after all, just making fucking spaghetti. But making that spaghetti, and doing it well, and seeing how for fifteen minutes fucking spaghetti can tamp down the aggressions of the world that are beating down on the person who is enjoying it, is actually important. At its best, fucking spaghetti is a kindness, and it is unfortunate that the stress and pressure of getting it out of the kitchen often causes unkindness toward the people who work hard to get it from a pile of flour and eggs to the customer's mouth. The act of preparing and serving food as a team has so much sweetness in it.

We had bonded over this sweetness at Brucie. We had bonded over our dead parents and troubled childhoods. We taught each other about music and '70s B horror movies and how to cook. We got drunk and crammed into photo booths late at night, kissing each other and feeling all of the insanity it took to pull off another night of service wash away like pollen crusted on cars after a heavy rainstorm. I know that I had made a mess of things a thousand times over, but the tears from my friends and colleagues that day and in the weeks that followed were real, and I felt incredibly blessed that these people still loved me despite my failings.

My coworkers at Brucie had educated me on something that I had never really known before: how to be a part of a family. And there were many times when I took this incredibly precious lesson for granted like a spoiled child, but it was the greatest gift I had ever been given. I didn't know that you could be terribly imperfect and loved at once because I was used to being punished. And here I was disbanding that specialness because I was too *tired* to keep it alive. I hadn't taken the warning signs seriously. I hadn't done anything to address the burnout or the financial instability, and it meant that the best thing that had ever happened to me had to die.

I will run toward love so fast that I trip and smash my face every time, because I still believe that this is the necessary speed. Sustaining real love requires taking risks, but it also requires a slow pace at times. Looking where your feet land, and taking heed of roots and slick patches of grass so you don't fall and break your teeth. I never looked with Brucie, I just ran, and in the end, I bought the farm. I tried so hard to keep it going because I dreaded being perceived as a failure. But attempting to outsmart the truth that I was not happy, and the restaurant was not financially viable, did not make me a failure, and I was not willing or able to keep hurting myself to prove that to the world, who mostly couldn't have cared less anyway. My business might have not prospered financially, but that does not mean I needed to wear the scarlet F of failure. Failure is not a word we should ever reach for to describe ourselves. Replace it with adventurer, or prospector of meaning. Risk taker. Lover. Romantic. Rhapsodically inclined.

. . .

A FEW WEEKS INTO opening, we came up with what would come to be Brucie's signature dish. It lasted almost as long as the spaghetti and meatballs, but it was so popular that it actually started to annoy me, and so I took it off the menu for a few months to spite . . . myself? It had started to feel a bit like how an actor might when they score a hit role, and everyone refers to them as their character for the rest of their lives.

Hey, Spock, over here!

The name's Leonard, okay?

The famous Brucie pasta was tagliatelle, sautéed with a

luxurious tomato butter, and topped with fried Brussels sprouts, stracciatella cheese, and scallions. (The original version also had sweet corn in it, but we ditched that when corn went out of season and it never made a comeback.) In 2010, the fervor surrounding fried Brussels sprouts felt comical, so one of the cooks challenged me to work them into a pasta as a dare, and thus the Brucie tag was born from a joke. As much as I came to resent its popularity at times because it caused people to ignore all of the other interesting things on the menu, it really was a special dish. The contrast of textures, temperatures, and flavors was so satisfying and strange, and yet it also felt like something you grew up eating as a child. It had been conceived on a whim and ended up being one of the most memorable things about Brucie.

One night when I was running food, I had to bring four plates of tagliatelle to a four top who had all ordered the same thing. I of course groaned about this in the kitchen, but when I realized that it was for some of our favorite regulars, with some new friends they were introducing to their favorite restaurant, I quickly set my judgment aside. As I placed the steaming plates in front of them, one of them folded his fingers together in delight and exclaimed, *Oh my god, I LOVE this!* It was so sweet and sincere that I welled up with tears as I walked back to the kitchen. What an absolute honor it was to give people something they looked forward to. What a pleasure it was to be that part of someone's day.

...

WE CLOSED BRUCIE ON February 15, 2016. We had always been known for our over-the-top Valentine's Day celebrations, most notably the Beyoncé-themed one we threw in 2014, which went so viral, we ended up with over a thousand people on the waiting list, and Bey herself sent swag for us to give out to the lucky few hundred that scored a reservation. Any chance we had to celebrate we took as a challenge to push the boundaries for how much fun you could have at an Italian restaurant. It seemed only natural that we would end this chapter on this day, in the most extravagant way possible.

We threw a two-night event with a menu filled full of all the hits, like the tagliatelle, spaghetti and not-my-grandfather's meatballs, lasagna, chicken parm, and birthday cake. The first night was a wedding theme, and the final night was a funeral, which felt like a very Brucie way to represent the arc of beginnings and endings. I suppose the first night could have been a birth, but that didn't seem particularly appetizing.

For the wedding, we wore all white, and encouraged the guests to dress in their nuptial best. We decorated with big bouquets of flowers and *Just Married* signs, and listened to Tina Turner and Mark Knopfler sing us songs about love. The second night we all wore black, and we put on a playlist that was all about death, yet surprisingly upbeat. Jeremy the bartender stood on the bar and delivered a beautiful eulogy dressed as a priest. I got up there after him and cried my eyes out, thanking everyone for being the family that I had always dreamed of. For supporting us, for getting our weirdness, and trusting us enough to order things like fried shrimp with peanut butter aioli and pickled plums. I thanked my staff for sticking by me even when I may not have deserved it, and for teaching me how to be a real person, and for showing me what all the songs ever written about love actually meant. There were many other toasts from beloved regulars and staff, tearful embraces, and an ice luge. It was meant to be in the shape of a tombstone that read *Brucie 2010–2016,* but the delivery driver dropped it on the way in, and it cracked in half. Luckily, he had another one in the back of his truck that was shaped like a star with *CONGRATULATIONS CLASS OF 2015* scrawled across it, so we sucked down freezing cold shots with that instead.

The very last plate of tagliatelle went out just after midnight, to my dear sweet friends Paul and Zoe, who had been with us since the early days with the tractor seats and the clothespin ticket line. We sat in the backyard, under a rented tent and heat lamps, the crowd dwindling from hundreds to dozens to a few core crew members. We smoked and drank and went around the circle with *remember whens* until the sun started to cast a pinkish glow on the rooftops, welcoming a new day for the city, and the end of an era for us.

The Brucie Tag

WOW, I CAN'T BELIEVE I AM TELLING YOU THIS! I HOPE THAT this curious combination of ingredients comes together to be a pasta that you love and look forward to. The tomato butter is the star of this dish, and it is also wonderful toasted onto bread in place of a traditional garlic butter, served with eggs, spread on sandwiches, or just eaten directly out of the jar in the event of an apocalypse. *You're gonna love the way you look in this tag, I guarantee it!*

SERVES 4

TOMATO BUTTER:

1 tablespoon extra-virgin olive oil
2 tablespoons minced garlic
2 sticks (½ pound) softened butter, salted or unsalted . . . who cares!
1 cup finely grated Pecorino Romano cheese
1 cup canned crushed tomatoes
½ cup heavy cream
1 tablespoon tomato paste
Salt to taste

FRIED BRUSSELS SPROUTS:

1 quart oil for frying
½ pound Brussels sprouts, quartered and cleaned
Salt to taste

PASTA:

- *1½ pounds fresh tagliatelle (If you can't find tag, don't fret! This tastes amazing with basically all pasta shapes, fresh or dry, but fresh tag is my fave!)*
- *3 cups tomato butter (see above)*
- *1 cup corn kernels (optional)*
- *Fried Brussels sprouts (see above)*
- *½ cup finely grated Pecorino Romano cheese*
- *½ pound burrata or stracciatella*
- *½ cup thinly sliced scallions, green and white parts*

Start by making the tomato butter: Heat the olive oil in a small pan over medium heat, add the garlic, and sauté over medium-low heat for about 1 minute, until it just begins to toast. Add it to a food processor or blender along with the butter, cheese, tomatoes, heavy cream, tomato paste, and salt and process until a thoroughly emulsified sauce forms, about 3 minutes. It will be super thick, but worry not, this is what you want. The butter will become bright orange when it is ready!

Fry the Brussels sprouts: In a medium-sized, deep saucepot, heat the oil over medium heat for about 5 minutes, or until the oil reaches 350 degrees. Add the Brussels sprouts, making sure they are submerged, and fry until deep brown, just short of burned, but with light green still visible in the center, 3 to 4 minutes.

Remove the Brussels sprouts from the oil and drain on paper towels. Sprinkle liberally with salt and set aside.

To make the pasta: Boil the pasta until al dente. While the pasta is cooking, warm the tomato butter in a large sauté pan over medium heat, adding the corn, if using, just until the butter is melted and hot. Do not overheat, as the cheese in the butter mixture will start to burn.

When the pasta is al dente, drain and add it to the pan with the butter and simmer together for 1 minute.

Plate and top with the fried Brussels sprouts, grated pecorino, burrata, and, last, the scallions!

Not My Grandfather's Meatballs

MEATBALL LITERALLY TRANSLATES IN ENGLISH TO *"BALL OF meat,"* but I personally do not think this definition gives credit to how pillowy, fluffy, and succulent a good meatball can really be. Here's the cold hard truth about a good meatball, folks: a good meatball, the kind you remember and want to make for someone you are falling in love with, has a lot of bread in it. The addition of milk-soaked (or water-soaked if you simply refuse to tolerate lactose) bread is what takes the average orb on a luxury trip to meatopia! I cannot overstate the importance of a binder like soaked bread, breadcrumbs, or cracker crumbs. Here is a little secret: I have used all kinds of bread in meatballs over the years. Seeded Italian is definitely preferable here, but I have even used a baguette, which has a thick crunchy crust, so sue me! Don't go running out in a thunderstorm if you realize you forgot the Italian bread and only have hot dog buns.

Meatballs are a great place to get experimental, and I love riffing on this recipe by adjusting everything from the protein to the spices, and adding in nuts, fruits, and vegetables to keep things interesting. Think chicken and sun-dried pepper meatballs studded with minced apricots, mint, and orange zest! Or lamb meatballs with feta, olives, and preserved lemon! The possibilities are endless, and I encourage you to get creative once you have nailed the basic principles of making the perfect meatball. Cooking, at its soft and tender core, should be fun, and this is a recipe that you will mush with your hands and speak to your heart! The only thing more important than having enough bread is being sure to enjoy your time making these meatballs. Have fun!

MAKES 20 (2½-OUNCE) MEATBALLS

2 cups torn (quarter-size chunks) day-old Italian bread
About ⅔ cup milk
2 tablespoons extra-virgin olive oil
1 small yellow onion, finely diced (about ⅔ cup)
2 to 3 garlic cloves, minced
1½ tablespoons plus a pinch of kosher salt
1 pound ground pork
1 pound ground beef
2 large eggs
1 cup grated Pecorino Romano cheese
⅓ cup finely chopped parsley
1 teaspoon crushed red pepper (more if you are a spicy meatball)
Finely grated zest of 1 lemon
¾ cup Italian-style breadcrumbs, seasoned or unseasoned

Preheat the oven to 350°F.

Put the bread chunks in a bowl and slowly add the milk (you might need more or less depending on what type of bread you use). Leave it to soak until it is the consistency of oatmeal, about 5 minutes. Some bigger chunks are okay too!

Heat the olive oil in a large sauté pan over medium heat and sauté your onions and garlic with a pinch of salt until translucent, soft, and just beginning to brown, 3 to 4 minutes. Remove from the heat and allow to cool for a few minutes so you don't burn your hands or scramble the eggs while mixing.

Once cooled, add the cooked onion and garlic to a large bowl with the soaked bread, the meat, eggs, cheese, parsley, crushed red pepper, remaining 1½ tablespoons salt, the lemon zest, and breadcrumbs. Here's the hard part: mix until thoroughly combined, but not overmixed.

Roll your meat mixture into balls! What size balls? Whatever size you like! The meatballs at J & J's were HUGE, like baseball-sized, which is super fun. Tiny ones are good for wedding soup or homemade spaghetti-o's! I like to do 2½ ounces of meat per ball, about the size of a ping-pong ball, but make the size that speaks to you. Just remember that the cook time will vary by size.

Line a baking sheet with parchment paper and arrange your meatballs on it. For 2½-ounce balls, bake for 25 minutes, or until they bounce back to the touch and reach an internal temperature of 165°F.

Or, for the full effect, simmer these babies in marinara (see recipe, page 26) over low heat for at least 1 hour. Can be stored in the fridge for up to five days or up to three months in the freezer.

JOHN TANGORRA'S POTATO SALAD

JOHN TANGORRA DIED ON FEBRUARY 1, 2018, AND REMAINS dead as of this recording.

I was sleeping in the guest room at his house in Asheville, North Carolina, when I got the call that he had passed. He referred to this room as the Purple Room since it was largely outfitted in purple furnishings. Purple carpet, purple drapes, a scratchy purple and maroon Indian-inspired bedspread. There was a purple lamp with a purple gem-encrusted lampshade, and even a purple enamel tissue box holder. He had been living on Social Security and food stamps after a bitter divorce, yet was still committed to respecting the modesty of his tissues. Puzzling. How many tissue box covers are there in the world? And why purple? And why didn't he just take better care of himself?

In the guest room there were also a few old blown-up photos of our ancestors on the Italian side of the family, and paintings and prints of scary clowns—a theme that ran throughout his home on Welsh Partridge Circle. Aside from loving purple, my father also loved clowns, and this made him a kind of goth Cathy cartoon. My parents had acquired a ten-foot painted wooden clown face at some point in their time together before I was born, and despite not having the same affection for harlequins, my mother had taken it in the divorce and hung it on the wall in her living room, cementing my role as *unique* among my friends, none of whom had any clown memorabilia in their family homes.

My father was dead, and I hadn't been there when it happened. I had missed the opportunity to pet his head as he drifted from person to ghost. I had missed the potential deathbed confession, perhaps even an explanation for the clown fetish. A few days prior to his passing, he made an attempt at atonement for his sins as a father.

Buddy, I'm sorry the life I tried to build after I split with your mother ended up being such a mess. I knew that there was cruelty you had to endure. None of it turned out how I had planned. I knew I should have just taken you, walked away, and started over. But I thought I was making a normal life, with a family. I know it wasn't normal, I know you were unhappy, and I'm sorry for that. He pushed the words out while shifting and grunting, trying to get comfortable in his tiny hospital bed.

It's okay Daddy, I understand, I said.

I meant it. My adult self did understand the tendency for broken people to make poor decisions, and that he had wanted a *normal* life for both of us. But he was far from fluent in normalcy, and thus, how could he ever teach me to speak it? I don't really even know what normal means, or use it as a metric for success, but what was missing from my upbringing, and what I believe he was trying to atone for, was a severe lack of emotional safety. The little girl sitting on the edge of his hospital cot wished she had been better protected, and here we all were, all the versions of ourselves having a long goodbye, like Philip Marlowe.

I wondered what it would have been like if he had walked

away from the debris of his failed experiment at the nuclear family, soot-covered and glowing yellow, but walking toward fresh air. If we'd had the courage to pack our bags and start a new life as two people unafraid to pursue joy. To be fair, my father could be incredibly difficult and was a damaged person who I have no doubt brought his own unsavory behaviors to the relationship between him and my stepmother, but it doesn't change the fact that my experiences sharing a home with her half of the week as a child were not ones I recall with great fondness.

She brought to the relationship a very sweet daughter, the same age as me, with straight blond hair to contrast with my frizzy brown tangle. My stepsister was and is a lovely person, but because she was "the good child," my stepmother rarely missed an opportunity to remind me that I was the polar opposite, the weirdo, the outcast, the reject. This did very little for my already tenuous self-perception.

She was disinterested in food and music, my father's two greatest passions in life. After they got together, what little enthusiasm he had left for cooking was extinguished and replaced entirely with low-cal processed foods, and he only enjoyed his vast record and CD collection via headphones or in the car. What would life have looked like if we came back to a tiny apartment, just the two of us, and listened to *Exile on Main St.* while making beef stew together on rainy November evenings? Or danced around in the backyard grilling ribs after he taught me how to make his famous Gruyère-laced potato salad, instead of coloring inside the lines of what a *normal* life was supposed to look like?

In fact, my mother was the one who taught me how to make his potato salad when I was thirty-seven, and she gave me his old cookbooks with pages crusted in cake batter. I learned a lot about my father's culinary legacy from her. It felt inaccurate, rude even, to call this dish potato salad, because it is, like John, filled with little surprises and so much more complex than anyone would think from looking at it. The trick is to fold shredded cheese into baby red potatoes while they're still hot and then when it's all melted and stringy, you add sour cream, mayonnaise, Dijon mustard, chopped-up pickles, and loads of fresh dill and chives.

My father was the best cook I have ever met (besides my mother), and it was as much of a shame as can be that my stepmother encouraged him to eat frozen Lean Cuisine dinners and boxes of SnackWell's cookies and sip SlimFast. I would only discover his culinary genius in small ways growing up when he was allowed to cook. He would make a beautiful Christmas dinner every year, beef Wellington with homemade puff pastry, potatoes dauphinoise, and carrots caramelized in cognac and molasses, accompanied by gougères and gravy made from veal stock he had been simmering for twenty-four hours. My stepmother wouldn't eat any of his offerings, and she would make fun of John for *going overboard,* laughing at the overabundance of food as she sipped Crystal Light and pushed around some scrambled eggs on her plate. My father couldn't be his wildly creative self, so he adapted it. He fit his passion into a suburban mold by buying every decoration that was sold at the local big-box store, and punching up Hamburger Helper to a Michelin level. But even in hiding, John was a savant in the kitchen, and I knew it at Christmas, and I knew it in my bones, the way you know if an avocado is ripe—you can't see it, but you feel it.

My father digested life sonically, even if he was only allowed to hear Mick's voice through his Kloss Quadraphonics. Music was as important to him as food and water. He had thousands of vinyl albums, and he particularly loved the blues. His food tasted like a Muddy Waters record, powerful and rootless and layered. It relied heavily on emotion and slide, as did he. It was where he put his pain, and you could taste that, in the best possible way. John's pain was like a B.B. King record, authentic, rich with vibrato.

He had been an only child until age eleven, when his three cousins moved into their tiny three-bedroom house after their mother died and their father, my grandmother Helen's brother, was too consumed with grief to care for them. This was a benevolent act on the part of my grandfather, who could be both a terrible man and a tremendous softy. He would beat my father, and when John became tall enough, he would beat back, and this all came to a head shortly after the cousins moved in. And so John was sent away to a school for boys, the type of place you see in movies about dysfunctional families in the 1960s and think, *My god, how could anyone send their children to a place like that.* A lot happens to a child in *a place like that,* and from then on my father became an electric guitar solo that could shake your soul. He came home at seventeen and became obsessed with music as a means to escape. He ran around getting into knife fights and selling acid. He became determined to be the most creative person to ever live, and I believe he mostly succeeded in this effort.

When he met my mother, he began a lifelong obsession with food and art. He was too afraid to fly, so he traveled all over the globe via LP, cookbook, and literary magazine. After it fell apart with my mother and he got together with my stepmother, he tried with all of his might to be a boring white man in Men's Wearhouse suits, and on the surface he succeeded. He grew a conservative-looking mustache. He traded his retro wood carvings of people having gratuitous sex for seasonally appropriate flags to hang above the front door and a train set with a snow-covered miniature town that lined the perimeter of the living room every Christmas season. He put in an aboveground pool. He wore loafers most days of the week and even matched his belts to them. He furnished his new house almost exclusively from Pier 1, as this was the closest mainstream option to his authentic self he was allowed to embrace, which explains the purple and maroon Indian-inspired bedspread that I was wrapped in when I got the call that he was dead. He had gone from delinquent child to eccentric twenty-something, to genius cook, to prolific artist, to abusive husband, to loving father, to negligent father, back to loving father, and all the while maintained his firm stance as a clown lover. And now he was dead.

. . .

MY PHONE RANG JUST after seven a.m. on February 1, 2018, and when I saw the 828 area code, I knew something was wrong. He was supposed to be transferred to a hospice that morning, there was supposed to be more time. There were supposed to be more dinners where we got a little too drunk on Manhattans and played *The Last Waltz* so loud our ears hurt when we went to bed. I thought at the time that there was a real possibility that he would get better and come home and see the dogs again, or thumb through the shirts in his closet deciding which one to wear, use one of his Q-tips, or flush the pee he had left in the toilet when he left the house to drive himself to the hospital six weeks earlier. I thought I would hug him again, us both standing upright, feeling his big hand on my cheek as he said, *Love you buddy.*

I had been woken up by the sound of the phone in the middle of a dream of him and me at the beach. He was younger and more able-bodied, and we were splashing around in the waves. And then he wasn't. Then he was gone, slurped out into the abyss, and I was on shore. And when I woke up, he was dead and I was on a free-falling elevator. My heart plastered to the top, my body not yet feeling its absence. On the other end of my telephone was a nurse that I had not had the privilege of meeting in my six weeks as a fixture on the eighth floor of Mission Hospital, a complete stranger.

Ms. Tangorra, your father has just passed away, I am so sorry.

Okay, I replied, and thanked her very matter-of-factly, like I was asking for directions and she had just told me I was walking in the opposite direction of the Sagrada Familia.

She asked, *Would you like to see the body before we bring him down to the morgue?*

No, thank you, I replied.

No, thank you is what you say when someone asks if you want another helping of baked beans, or how you reply to one of those people on the street asking if you want to *save the children.*

After the words came out, I wished I could have breathed them back in and said instead, *I don't know if I can. I'm afraid. Can I think about it?* The thing about bodies is that they don't make baked macaroni and cheese with a crunchy breadcrumb topping or brush your hair before school or take you ice skating and give you a thumbs-up from the side of the rink every time you get up after taking a spill. Bodies don't teach you that a big scoop of peanut butter makes chocolate chip cookies a thousand times more delicious, or why it's important to speak up when you see injustice in the world. They don't listen to you cry for hours on end when you're going through a painful breakup. They can't go to Bamonte's for dinner and order five different pastas to share, or tell you that you are the most beautiful daughter anyone has ever had, or pick you up from school early when you're having a bad day and take you for hot fudge sundaes, or cheer for you at a lacrosse game. A body can't send you thirty mixed CDs for your birthday, or not wish you happy birthday at all just to hurt your feelings. A body can't put its warm hand on mine and say, *How 'bout those Mets?*

I couldn't bear to see a version of my father that couldn't do these things, or at least the version that used to be able to do these things, and this response is the one regret I have in my whole life. Sure, I wish I had done some things differently. I wish I hadn't skipped school so much or gotten a Monroe piercing or said mean things to people or eaten that turkey sandwich at Ben's Kosher Deli that gave me the worst food poisoning of my life. But those aren't truly regrets, they are just poor decisions with unfortunate and embarrassing outcomes.

When I went to the hospital later that morning to retrieve his belongings and sign the necessary paperwork, I was led into the room where he had passed away. The *body* had not actually been taken from the room yet, and lay covered under a sheet, with only his large, lifeless arm poking out. This was a shock, and I screamed and slammed the door behind me, so this is the last image I have of him. I was completely terrified. I was embarrassed for us both. I ran away just like I had when I dumped spaghetti on that woman at Brucie, not only because I was scared, but also powerless in my panic. I had nothing to hold on to, nothing to cushion my fall. Seeing him like this, so broken and cold and deceased, dismantled every instinct that I have ever had to face my fears. We try to imagine who we will be in these unthinkable situations: I will fight off my attacker, I will turn in the suitcase full of money, I will be faithful and honest, I will have the perfect comeback. I was not the person I thought I would be at this moment, and I regret that. I regret not giving myself what I had believed to be the gift of jumping into the fire, but like Harry Nilsson suggested, this does not necessarily make us free.

I wish I hadn't fought with him the whole time he was in the hospital about the unpaid bills and the ATM pin that he couldn't remember. But we do, we mention the bills and pick fights, because these are the last fights to pick. Because living people have to remember their online passwords, and bodies do not. Because looking someone you love in the face and realizing you can count in hours how long you have left to see the light in their eyes is a heartbreak that can turn you to water vapor. So you fight about why they don't recycle, or you talk about how great next Christmas will be, or you make banana bread and picture wiping the crumbs off their face as they enjoy it.

What if I had seen his body? Would this have proved my love and devotion? I didn't actually want to look at my father's lifeless face, his closed eyelids and blue lips, but I've always thought I should have. I thought I should have been braver than him, someone who was so afraid to fly that he never left the country, and would yell and scream then hide himself away if anyone hurt his feelings. If I could not be braver, I would end up the same: a body with very few people who cared that I was gone. I am braver than he ever was, though, because I've traveled to Italy and California and many other places, despite the fact that I might drop from the sky into the Atlantic while sipping a gin and tonic, and because I don't hold grudges, and because I wear my heart on my sleeve even though he always told me not to. The truth is bravery cannot be quantified by how much you are willing to hurt yourself, but rather how you are willing to love yourself, so maybe my regret is actually not giving myself that grace.

. . .

DESPITE HIS INCREDIBLE LAPSES in judgment over the years, and an ego with the structural integrity of old receipt paper, my father was intent on raising me right. Manners and ethics were very important. Doing homework, keeping a clean room, learning to appreciate art and music and good food were all drilled into me as the metrics of a valuable person.

He met my stepmother in 1991, when I was seven years old, and they bought a house on Beverly Drive in Fort Salonga, Long Island, a few years later. I loved being around John, but when I was in that house I spent much of my time alone in my room upstairs playing *Sonic the Hedgehog* and drinking Pepsi, and feeling too uncomfortable and awkward to come downstairs and hang out with him.

Both my parents had picked partners who did not or could not understand me or want or know how to include me in a family. I lost a big chunk of my heart in those elementary years, the piece that held compassion and care for myself. *Why are these people who were meant to love me, and sometimes really do, so careless with my tender little heart?* Not knowing about mental illness, personality disorders, or how sometimes good people just stuff it because of their own trauma and baggage, I blamed myself. I told myself I deserved to be lonely, that it must have been my destiny.

When I mustered up the courage to be seen outside my room, I would nervously go sit next to my father on the couch as he watched TV and drank brandy.

What's up, buddy? he would say.

I wanted to tell him: *Oh nothing, I am just drowning in depression, but I don't understand what depression even is, but I know that there is no joy in this house, and I know I feel badly about myself every second that I'm here. Can we pack our bags and run away please? Can I skip school tomorrow and go with you to work and then after that we can move to Disney World and eat sizzling fajitas at the Rainforest Cafe every night for dinner? Can you please ask her to be nice to me, to not whisper behind my back? Can you take me back to Mom's? Wait, I hate it there too. Can you take me somewhere that I don't hate?*

But I would reply, *Nothing much, Daddy-O.*

Then we'd watch TV in silence until it was my bedtime. I was almost embarrassed to talk to him in fear that my stepmother would hear us being ourselves, and I think he felt the same way. So we sat there laughing at the same parts of Must See TV, like we were holding hands under the table. When it was time for bed I would walk upstairs, and I would wonder if the *Seinfeld* characters ever felt as sad as I did as I waited for John to come up and read to me and scratch my back. I would lay facing away from him, listening to him do all the voices as he read, and I would quietly sob into my pillow. It's sad to think about us as these people who neither of us wanted to be, both hoping that when we woke up the next morning everything would fall into place. That the life that he wished for so badly, that he had paid to make look nice, would actualize, painfully similar to how I initially approached things at Brucie.

But that is the thing about wishing: what we wanted never really materialized the way we hoped, like someone asking a genie in a bottle for all the money in the world, then being trapped beneath a staggering pile of currency when the wish is granted literally. Wishing leaves too much up to chance and interpretation. Wishing was all John really knew how to do, and in the end, his wish was granted, but it was Midas-like. This was the greatest lesson he ever taught me, albeit unintentionally. I do not wish anymore. I hope, I desire, but unlike my father, who was truly paralyzed by fear, I act. And action is so often accompanied by consequence, and deep disappointment, but it is living, and it is better than turning everyone you touch into solid gold.

. . .

A FEW DAYS BEFORE my father died, I learned that he had not finalized or signed his will, which was a patch in the quilt that was his own inability to accept his death. I had to call a notary and his only friend in Asheville to come to his hospital room and act as a witness. As I was getting the will ready, I looked over it. I had never seen a will before. Everything looked predictable, boring even, until I reached the page where he decreed who would get his ashes after he died. Naturally, being his only child, and the only family member he had any contact with, I assumed this would be me. I didn't see my name, however. I saw the name Carl Loomis, and I began to unravel.

What's this part here about you giving your ashes to Carl Loomis? Is this a mistake? Carl Loomis from the Crescent Club? The groundskeeper? Why does it say here that you want him to get your ashes? I said, feeling the tears well behind my eyeballs, burning like acid rain.

The last time I had seen Carl Loomis, my father's coworker and drinking buddy, was on a vacation to a resort called Woodloch Pines in the Poconos when I was nine. Carl was also there with his two daughters, and this was the first and only time I remember doing anything socially with the Loomis family. When I strain to remember Carl Loomis at all, I picture him as a taller version of Bruno Kirby, who talked a lot about grass and weeds. His daughters and I stole cigarettes from him, and when I smoked one I threw up. Grass, dad jeans, mustache, cigarette, barf: this was the space this man occupied in my head.

Carl called me on my birthday every year, I've known him for twenty-seven years, he never missed, my father countered. He rubbed his brow, looking toward the window as if maybe a bird would fly in the room and rip the paper from my hands before I could interrogate him any further.

So you think that means he wants a box with your human remains? Because he remembers your birthday? For what? So he can keep you on his coffee table? What about when he dies? You go to his kids? The Goodwill? In the trash?

I want him to take me out to Robert Moses and sprinkle me.

This answer pushed me over the edge. Moses was sacred. Thinking that he wanted to spend this most intimate last moment with Carl Loomis was such an affront to our entire relationship, I couldn't fully process it. *Sprinkle you? Sprinkle you?!*

I just didn't think you'd want them. I thought you would be grossed out. Can we please . . .

I cut him off. *It's your ashes, Dad, not a dirty diaper. Don't you think that perhaps this would have been worth, like, I don't know, a conversation before you put it in a legal document? "Hey Z, do you, my fucking only daughter, want my ashes or will you be grossed out?" And then I would have said, "Of course I want them, Dad, who else would they go to?" And then you would have said, "I don't know, I was thinking Carl," and I would have said, "Who the fuck is Carl?" and you would have said, "Carl Loomis," and I would have said, "Who is Carl Loomis? The groundskeeper from the Crescent Club?" And then you would have said, "Yeah." And I would have said, "I don't think he wants a big box of your ashes," and it would have never made its way into your will and we wouldn't be fighting about this now.*

It's just ashes, Zahra, he said, sucking on the grape Tootsie Pop in his cheek. I had taken to buying us each a Tootsie Pop every morning at the hospital gift shop as a little treat, a few minutes of joy we could share every day.

In that moment, once again I was reminded that I do not matter—not just to him, but in general. To anyone. How could I? In that moment I was fifteen, calling him a hundred times in a row with no answer because he was mad that I wanted to spend Christmas with my mother. I was twenty-two, opening the Get Well card he sent after the bus accident, with no message, simply signed *—John*. I was a rolled-up, squeezed-out toothpaste being tossed into the trash.

I'm going to rip this page up and when you die, I'm going to take your ashes and sprinkle you in the parking lot of the Walt Whitman Mall, I said, going in for the kill. Then I stormed out of the room and ran to the car to scream at the top of my lungs.

The next day, I was back in my father's hospital room, sitting on the thinnest sliver of his bed, trying to be as small as possible and not smell anything or look at the bedpan or the tubes or the hazardous waste cans, or directly into his face. Trying not to look anywhere. There is nothing in a hospital room upon which your eyes can take refuge. He was naked under the thin hospital gown, and every time he moved and shifted, I was consumed with the fear of accidentally seeing his penis and then needing years of hypnotherapy to remove the image from my brain.

I was attempting to calm him down after a difficult episode the night before. He had stayed up to watch the president's State of the Union address on TV, and had become so enraged by his ramblings that he had to be physically restrained, which led him, later, to pee the bed. In fact, one of the last words I ever heard him speak was a deeply disapproving and venomous *Trump!* through clenched teeth. His outrage was so deep that it forced out a blast of thick white spit, some of which hit me square in the eyelid. My father was far from being as hideous as the man on the TV, but he had deeply unsavory qualities of his own. He noted people's race when he didn't like them or approve of how they were acting. He also called overweight women *fatties,* and referred to my mother as a *cunt* when talking about her to me when I was too young to ride a roller coaster. But he also made dozens of pumpkin breads for all the nurses at Cancer Care when he was so sick that he could barely move, and spent his monthly Social Security check to buy birthday presents for the grandson of the woman who helped to clean his house because she said no one in her family could afford it. People are dodecahedrons. He hated the president in earnest, and I think this vitriol for him helped him feel better about his own shortcomings.

In an effort to lift his spirits, I asked him what he'd want to eat if he could have anything in the whole wide world. There simply had to be something to change things, to get him out of the hospital, to make him better, to make Trump not be president so he could at least die in peace. To make me seven again. To let us keep joking and bickering and shouting over the music. Anything to prolong the inevitable that was rising toward us like the high tide. If I could make something he would eat, life could go back to normal, and I wouldn't be left alone in this world without him.

What can I make for you to eat? I asked. *If I make it, do you promise to not leave me?* I added telepathically. As a chef, it's my reflex to treat people's wounds with food, to wax the waning with a stew or a roast or a plate of cookies.

Without any hesitation, he answered, *Roast beef sandwich with cheddar, tomato, and mayo.*

This surprised me, as he'd had almost no appetite for the past month. Every time I'd tried to feed him, he'd take a bite or two and then push the food away, or spit it out, or throw up. I'd go to the best barbecue restaurant in town and get hush puppies and honey butter and gooey mac and cheese. I'd wait in line for thirty minutes and spend fifty dollars at the artisanal doughnut shop, figuring that if I bought every flavor there would be one that he could eat. I made bone broth and congee at his house, and picked up strawberry milkshakes and egg and cheese sandwiches on my way to the hospital. One morning I tried so hard to make him eat a bagel that I found myself literally shoving it into his mouth, and only stopped when he bit me and said *what the fuck are you doing,* cream cheese smushed into his red mustache. But he knew he wanted a roast beef sandwich. Maybe he'd had the same dream I would have two nights later. A beach. A wave.

As he lay in the bed that was too small for him, sweating

and uptight and in utter contempt of the fact that he was dying, I went home to his lonely but beautiful house and made roast beef from scratch. He'd purchased a ton of ingredients from the fancy grocery store a few days before he went to the hospital in anticipation of my visit for a late Christmas celebration, but a day before my arrival he'd rushed himself to the hospital after having difficulty breathing. He never shopped at the fancy grocery store for himself, instead eating soup from cans and hot dogs that were on sale. But when I came, he bought butter from grass-fed cows and local cheeses and the good bourbon. He was nothing if not devastatingly considerate. There was already an uncooked roast beef in the freezer, so I stopped at the fancy grocery store for some nice cheddar and a tomato, and at the regular grocery store for Martin's Potato Bread.

As I roasted the meat, I turned on all the lights and watched reruns of *The Office.* None of his windows had blinds and, as a city person, I always feel exposed and a little afraid in the suburbs. I went to bed with all the lights still on, in front of the TV.

The next morning, I assembled his sandwich before I left for the hospital. I made sure the cheddar went all the way to the edges of the crust and sprinkled a little extra salt on the tomato. I spread softened butter on the bread first so it wouldn't get soggy from the tomato juices—he taught me that trick.

A few hours into our visit, I fed him the sandwich.

I tore the potato bread into tiny manageable bites, I wiped the mayo from the corners of his mouth, I moved the straw to his lips so he could sip Diet Coke. I noted the irony that a three-hundred-and-fifty-pound man with days to live was concerned about the unnecessary calories in regular Coke. I didn't mention it.

When my grandmother Violet got old, and it became harder for her to cook for herself, Bobbie would go to Florida a few times a year to fill her freezer with food. I interpreted this not only as the ultimate act of love, but more specifically how adults show they care. When you become an adult, you will have the means to travel to another state by plane, shop at the grocery store for three months' worth of food, and spend four days in your loved one's kitchen proving your dedication with every crab cake. Your level of devotion to their ailing beloved will be measured in quarts.

When I reached an age when I was capable of doing these things for John, I did so with the enthusiasm of Paul Prudhomme and the will of Jeremiah Johnson. This will make you love me, really, finally, it has to. This means I am a grown-up. This means you will keep on living for as long as this freezer remains full. A lasagna takes at least a month to eat, there's another month I can keep him in my universe. Twenty servings of beef chili, another month. Control. Casseroles. Twenty pints of beef barley soup. He was nothing if not conscious of food waste. Maybe if I had made a thousand sandwiches he would still be here, buying CDs with his Social Security checks and working on his *dollhouse from hell* (use your imagination), but I only made one sandwich. And he died the next morning.

When the phone rang a little after seven a.m. on February 1, 2018, I let go. I'd never be able to make a stack of sandwiches big enough to keep us together forever. I'd never be strong enough to keep both of us on shore. That is how the tide works. I am not a lifeguard, I am a chef. And so was John, and now he's a wave, and I think of him every time I see Martin's Potato Bread. I think of him most other times too.

When you are losing someone, you cry out to the open air,

Stay with me! Here's a sandwich, here's some money, here's a buoy, here's the world, it's all yours, just stay. Turn us to tall trees with our roots buried deep in the ground. Make us igneous. Freeze time, suspend the breaking of the waves. Stop the rising of the tide. Stay with me. And even when they go, even if the current gets the better of you both, they do stay.

I hung up the phone after the nurse told me my father had died, after I said *No thank you* to seeing his body, and walked into the kitchen. On the counter there lay a banana bread I had baked for him the night before and planned to bring him that morning. I put so many chocolate chips in it, it was barely passing as a bread of any sort. I thought this would make him eat it, or possibly put him into a diabetic coma, or both. I grabbed it and squeezed it in my right hand, my bad hand, and watched the mashed bananas and melted chocolate and pecans squish through the space between my fingers like wet sand. I flung what was left of the mess onto the counter and walked over to the sink to wash its gore from my hands. I walked into my dad's bedroom, the dogs following behind me. I sat on his bed and bent my head down and pressed my face into his pillows to inhale the last whiffs of him, and I screamed into the pillow until my throat began to burn. I opened the drawer next to his bed looking for nothing in particular, and when I found nothing in particular, I looked harder. I moved to his dresser, then the closet, then the file cabinets in his office, trying to find something nefarious or incriminating. Something to prove he was a deviant so I wouldn't be so sad that he was dead. A note confessing he had murdered someone, a piece of bloodied clothing, weird porn. But the harder I looked, the less I found. I landed back on the bed confused and exhausted. What was I doing? I looked around his room, which was covered in clown paintings. I laughed.

. . .

AS PER HIS WISHES, I had him cremated. I did not sprinkle him at the Walt Whitman Mall, and I did not send him off to live with Carl Loomis. I considered phoning Carl to tell him of John's bizarre plan to move into his house postmortem, but reconsidered because I didn't know him at all, and feared he would not share my dark sense of humor, and we would end up in some sort of custody battle over the whole thing.

The day after his death, I drove up to the funeral home and called Bobbie from the parking lot, but she didn't answer. I called my boyfriend at the time, but he didn't pick up either. I turned on the radio and Blues Traveler's "Hook" was just starting. I turned it up to full blast. A cardinal landed on the hood of the car, and I laughed.

This is a dream. This is a heavy-handed script written by Zach Braff.

I start to sing and the cardinal flies off. I picture my father and me eating Kraft macaroni and cheese with ketchup on the couch in the cottage he rented when my parents first split, watching *Married with Children.* I sing so hard that my voice cracks like thin ice. I would sing this at Montero's Bar with my friends after a long shift at Brucie. How can this possibly be the same song? I remember what it looked like when he took a bite of food, the direction his eyes rolled. I hear his laugh. I smell his pizza rustica on Christmas morning. I spit out lyrics over the harmonica licks. I am entranced. My eyes bulge and snot drips into my mouth.

I am screaming Blues Traveler in my father's dinged-up Acura MDX. It is covered with dents and scratches because he would back it up out of the garage fifty feet to the mailbox to avoid walking, and he was a terrible driver who hadn't even tried until he was nearly forty. Fellow mourners pass by and stare at me as I loosen hinge by hinge. I imagine them thinking that John Popper must have died. The song ends and I fumble around in my bag for a cigarette and drop it between the seat and the center console. I reach down to fish for it and pull up a huge chunk of dried-up hamburger with plasticky dried orange cheese still affixed to its surface. I was on the phone with him a few months before when he said *Mother Fucker!* and when I asked what was wrong, he replied, *Half my god damned burger just fell into the void between the seat and the center console.* I laugh. How strange that this is how it was uncovered.

I walk into the funeral home and am as alone as if it's my first day at a new school. There is no one to protect me, there is no one to sit with me at lunch or listen to me tell them how awkward I feel. I miss my parents. I am wearing the wrong thing. I am sweating through my new clothes. I am bleeding through my white pants. I am at the bottom of a ravine in the desert crawling with poisonous snakes. Make me a hawk. Make me a shooting star. Get me a motorcycle. Throw me a life raft.

Hi, I'm here for my father, John Tangorra, I say, like I'm meeting him there for a steak dinner, my voice raspy from my recent karaoke session in the car. I am here for my father, who is now a pile of dust. I am a palm tree bending in half in a tropical storm. I am a polar bear on a free-floating ice cap. I am eight. *Look how long I can hold my breath, Daddy.* I am fifteen.

Please pick up the phone, I need you. I am thirty-two. *Hey Johnny, it's time for your medicine.*

The funeral director, a very large man in a royal blue suit, is kind. He absorbs the most guttural versions of strangers' grief all day every day. I think that mine is unique, and it is, and also it is not. It is shock. It is skin on hot coals. The pain of losing someone for the first time is as close to being born as we can get. Everything is on fire, it's all brand-new.

I think of saying: *You don't understand, my father was special. He used to send Ninja Turtle cupcakes to school on my birthday. He had over one thousand records. He knew how to bake bread, all kinds of bread! Bread with salami in it! He taught me to ride a bike. You probably cannot imagine how much pain I am in. It is the most pain anyone has ever felt.*

Are you married? asks the funeral director. I am thirty-four, and people love to ask women my age if we are married to suss out just what kind of woman we are. Should they feel bad for you, or is there someone to help you to the toilet when you're sick or jumpstart your car or whatever partners do? I am a squeezed-out toothpaste, twisted and empty with no cap.

I start to cry. I am not married, I am dating someone who makes everything hard, who doesn't seem to like me, let alone love me. Someone who suggested not too long ago that we start bringing our own books to restaurants so we can read at dinner rather than conversate. Someone who will leave me in two weeks because his dog will die and he will tell me he is in too much grief to be in a relationship. So yeah, I'm not married, and maybe I'll never be married. Maybe I will die alone choking on a carrot that I'm dipping straight into a jar of mustard while standing in the open fridge in my underwear because no one is there to stop me, or save me. Maybe I'll go on all my vacations alone because my father was so cruel to me at times that I haven't been very good at picking the correct people to love up until this point. And this makes it equal parts harder and easier not to feel totally devastated, sitting in this comically large chair, across from this comically large man on the worst day of my life. *No, I am not married,* I say.

Your father was a big fella, and typically we charge two hundred dollars extra for folks over three hundred pounds, but I'm gonna go ahead and waive that fee for you, the funeral director says in his smoky baritone voice. This is a pity savings for being single and in my thirties, and for having an obese father, and for having mascara running down my face, and it is the first time I have smiled in days, because I love a deal, no matter how somber the occasion.

He offers me a tissue, and I wonder how many boxes of tissues he goes through in a year. I have never bought a box of tissues in my life; it has never even occurred to me. I cry fairly often, but into rough paper towels and the sleeve of my sweatshirt or in the shower. This is when I think of the purple tissue box holder in the guest room at my father's house. I clench my teeth so hard that I feel like they will turn to gravel. *No thank you.*

Would you like to purchase one of our premium urns, or mahogany boxes for your father's remains? he asks.

. . .

REMAINS. WE CALL WHAT is left of the body after it has been charred to a crisp, and the burned bones and flesh and fat and eyelashes and squishy kneecaps and heart get swept into a little bag, and placed in a premium urn or mahogany box, *remains.*

What actually remains is the first song they ever played for you and all the times you said you were too busy to talk. The times they broke your heart, the times they sent you a corsage at school on Valentine's Day so that you would feel special. The times you said *I love you* to each other, or didn't when you should have. But what is actually funneled into a plastic bag that gets crammed into a premium urn or mahogany box are *ruins*. They become an artifact that we place on a mantel or release into the air blowing through the Grand Canyon, or try to give to a random friend they haven't seen in person in twenty-five years. They are lifeless corridors where a society once flourished. Remains are holding hands as you descend the peak of your first roller coaster. Remains are learning to make chocolate chip cookies. Remains are crying into your pillow, and a back scratch and *National Lampoon's Christmas Vacation* and *London Calling* and spaghetti and meatballs and John's heartbreakingly delicious, sweet and savory pea soup. Remains do not have edges.

I settle on the cheapest, plainest box that they have, one step up from a shoebox really. I don't know why I am being so thrifty about this, because despite loving a deal, my nature is usually to throw money at just about anything, despite whether I have it or not. John was the same way, yet I feel like buying the expensive box would have been too celebratory, so I go with the shittiest one to prove my devastation to the funeral director and my father, and myself.

I leave the funeral home in the early evening and drive to a local French restaurant in Downtown Asheville and have French fries and a Manhattan. This is what my dad would have ordered, and he would have also had a medium-rare steak, but I do not have the emotional fortitude for chewing, and it would be a bit dramatic to choke to death the day after him, even for me. I am in shock when I take my first sip of that drink, and by the last, I am just beginning to feel sad. I eat the cherry, and it makes me laugh. John loved the cherry at the bottom of a Manhattan, and he always laughed at things that were only amusing to clowns, things that were so sad that he had to find the smile in them.

. . .

A FEW WEEKS AFTER John's death, I was living at my mother's house in Long Island while I recuperated from my breakup and my immense grief. One very cold and gray day, I took a ride out to Robert Moses beach with Bobbie to hurl the wooden shoebox filled with my father's ashes and the song lyrics I'd written on slips of paper into the Atlantic Ocean. It was a windy February day, and I knew for certain that if I were to open that bag of dust it would fly back onto me. My father was a prankster, but I did not have the bandwidth to be covered in John powder, so I decided that I would fling the whole box in and let it sink like a buried treasure.

My mother and I walked out there together, me up to my ankles in the freezing cold water, and released him almost exactly as he had requested. More of a kerplunk than a sprinkle, but honestly, he wasn't a *sprinkle* in life, and we cannot outrun ourselves even in death. We drove home and I stared out the window as we listened to Tom Petty. Two days later a Suffolk County police officer drove up to my mother's house and rang the bell. The box of ashes had washed ashore, and some curious winter beach walkers had opened it, found the ashes, and called the police, who then collected the box, which I'd failed to realize had my name and mother's address in it, and brought the warped wood and soaking wet ashes back to her house. The officer, I'm quite sure, had not had this big of a case in years, and told her that this was illegal, but he wouldn't report it, *just don't let it happen again or you could face jail time*. How could it happen again?

This was so John, refusing to just make anything easy, but in a way that kind of just made him more lovable. Some people are ready to die. They find a way to accept the tide going out, the ending of their favorite song. But John did not want it to end, despite the fact that the record had already been flipped twenty times over, so this was his way of flipping it once more. The box was placed in a remote corner of my mother's living room for three months until it dried out and the weather warmed, and we once again drove out to throw John into the sea. This time we chose a Long Island Sound side beach in Eatons Neck, on a less windy day, and I carefully opened the bag and sifted the ashes, which had kind of clumped together like cat litter from the soaking and re-drying, into the water and watched as he washed away. He got what he wanted, a proper sprinkling, or as close to it as irony would allow. I wondered if Carl Loomis would have done a better job after all. Maybe so, but Carl Loomis never rode an elephant at the Bronx Zoo as John watched on with a smile only a proud father has, or maybe he did, but either way, I was the one to send him off, and this was how it was meant to be. After all, we were tangled strands of DNA, and I loved him the most.

John was a clown. Not because he was silly, although he was. Not because he was scary, although he was that too. He longed to be good. He longed to be happy and kind, and sometimes he would be. Sometimes he would light up a room, and other times he would smoke it out. Sometimes he would make eggplant parmigiana, and sometimes I would get to eat it, and other times he would throw it at the wall, but I would still try to eat the bits that I cleaned off the wall that didn't have plate shards in them, because it was that good. He was mysterious and tortured and hilarious, and ashamed, and he hid behind a face covered in paint. He hid behind peanut butter cookies and rare Bob Dylan B-sides. He hid under his thick red mustache. He hid in a handful of OxyContin and a tall glass of brandy. I wish I could have really seen the man behind the makeup. Canio as he was walking home and having a cigarette in his street clothes, humming "That's Amore."

John loved clowns for the same reason he loved the blues: they are both bittersweet, just like his food. A balance of chaos, comedy, texture, hysteria, and beauty. He could teeter on this razor's edge between melancholy and majesty better than anyone I have ever met. My father made me realize that you do not have to be wholly good to be loved. That you can be a little scary and filthy and insane and still be someone's everything. Until he died, I never really knew that to be true—either about him or about myself. But he was my hero in many ways. He was the one human that I felt truly understood me, and I am still not sure that is a good thing, but it is a real thing. He was one of my favorite people to ever live, and he was, like the blues, terribly messy, and totally perfect, and I hope that when I am a ghost one day, someone will think of me this way too. That my dissonant harmonies and crooked smile made me more lovable instead of less, and that I made the best something that they have ever eaten.

Potato Salad

I NEVER HAD THE CHANCE TO TASTE THIS POTATO SALAD WHEN my father was alive, but I feel connected to him when I make it. Just like I know he would be, I'm excited to share it and see the look of delight on people's faces when they try it. This is an *eyes roll back in the head* recipe, so just be sure to know you'll have a lot of new lifelong friends after bringing it to your next cookout. It really is so unique and special, and such a *John* recipe. If a little makes its way onto your hot dog, that's not necessarily a bad thing.

SERVES 4 TO 6

2 teaspoons kosher salt, plus more for boiling the potatoes
1½ pounds small red or Yukon Gold potatoes, whole, skin on (about the size of a golf ball)
½ cup sour cream
¾ cup mayonnaise
2 tablespoons Dijon mustard
1 tablespoon whole-grain mustard
3 tablespoons apple cider vinegar
1 teaspoon coarsely ground pepper
2 teaspoons onion powder
½ cup thinly sliced celery
½ cup sliced scallions, green and white parts
½ cup thinly sliced cornichons
¼ cup chopped chives

½ cup chopped dill
¾ cup shredded Gruyère cheese
¾ cup shredded Swiss cheese

Place the potatoes in a stockpot and cover with water. Add a few hearty pinches of salt, place over medium-high heat, bring to a boil, and boil until fork tender.

While the potatoes are boiling, combine the sour cream, mayonnaise, mustards, vinegar, salt, pepper, onion powder, celery, scallions, cornichons, chives, and dill in a large bowl and stir together.

When the potatoes are cooked, drain them and cut them in half, minding your fingers for the heat—I like to hold the potatoes with a fork and cut with a knife—since you need them to still be hot so the cheese will melt. Place the halved potatoes in a large bowl and toss with the cheeses. Let sit for about 30 seconds, then toss again. The cheese should be getting melted and stringy at this point. Add the sauce to the potato and cheese mixture and mix thoroughly.

Serve warm or chilled.

PEA SOUP

When something traumatic happens, there is a strange feeling of calm after, a safety in assuming, incorrectly, that lightning cannot strike the same place twice. After violently throwing up from a bad clam, there is a momentary stillness, a false and fleeting faith that the worst of it is over, it has to be, there's nothing left to give. Lightning can, and often does, strike the same spot multiple times, especially if said object is tall and sticks out, like, say, the Empire State Building, which is struck an average of twenty-three times per year. When you have just suffered a trauma, you are the Empire State Building: you stick out and are thus often more likely to be struck again.

John had died, and along with him, so did the parts of me only seen through his gaze. Our conversations about music and art, our terrible fights and long bouts of his silent treatment, our inside jokes had all died. Our genetically shared traits and strange sense of humor: *dead*. Our bumpy noses: *dead*. His big, freckled hands with cigar-shaped fingers: *dead*. Pea soup: *dead*. Bloody Marys spiked with A.1.: *dead*. Christmas: dead. Laughing: *dead*. Manhattans and rib eye steaks: *dead*. It was all dead, and what wasn't yet would die with me, as I was the last Tangorra branch in our family tree. I could describe my father, but no one else would ever be able to know how strange and silly and mean he really was. No one would have to protect me from him because he couldn't hurt me anymore, or so I had thought. There were things that I assumed I did not know about my father, and would never know for sure unless a family member made a deathbed confession, or I found a diary or a pile of bones under a creaky floorboard in his house, which all seemed unlikely. Surprises: *dead*. Truth: *dead*.

I would instead make up the things that I wished to be true or untrue about him. That he had mob ties. That he secretly ate chicken and fish, which he claimed he hadn't since he was eight. My father was a chicken-eating mobster, and I told myself that he loved me too. That he wasn't a narcissist or a psychopath. That he wasn't mentally ill and pathologically selfish. That he was good under it all. That you can act bad and be good. I told myself that I knew him better than anyone, that I knew him at all. I told myself that I liked him, even though to this day I am still not sure that I did. But I wanted to like him, and I wanted everyone in the world to know that even if I didn't like him, I did love him and was devastated over his passing. And more so, I was traumatized. I had not yet learned the different colors that come together to make the brilliant blue of grief. I was traumatized by the tubes and the murky-colored juices and the bright red blood that poured out of him at the hospital, and by the ease with which he had abandoned me over the years. I was traumatized by his rage, his own traumas that seeped out of him like bitter-smelling sweat whenever the heat of being alive was turned up a few degrees. Traumatized from the giving and taking away of his love, now gone forever: *dead*.

My father had died, I had been broken up with, lost my

apartment, and was living at my mother's house, which felt like a hellish but manageable amount of drama to endure at once. *I can do this,* I would think, people go through much worse, all day, every day. I had a caring and supportive mother and stepfather, and I was lucky enough for them to welcome me into their warm, safe home while I mustered the strength to get back on my feet. I had incredibly loving friends who checked in on me and made sure that I didn't give up, even when I told them to forget about me and move on. I had skills, potential, and a real shot at a good life, and for these gifts I was, and will forever be, grateful.

But pain is not a contest. I had already had several strikes with grief and was unsure I could move or breathe. Grief is confusing. When it was first thrust upon me, I didn't know where to put it. *It's too heavy to walk with, so I will just lie down. It crushes me when I try to sleep, so I will try to outrun it. It is faster than me, so I'll put it on someone else. That only makes it grow stronger, so I'll swallow it and hide it inside my stomach. It's making me sick, so I will medicate with tequila and cigarettes.* Then I came to realize that the best way to live with it is to let it hold me instead.

But I had not yet come to this realization on the evening that I got the message from Brad. I was still in the medicating phase, polishing off a bottle of cheap, oaky wine, sitting across from my mother in her therapy office on a white leather couch, and scrolling through Instagram when a message appeared. It was from a sender whom I did not know and it was long, so my first assumption was that it was an old Brucie customer asking for a meatball recipe. But as I read on, lightning struck my pointy metal spire once again.

Hi Zahra. My name is Brad Bertani, and I have a weird but hopefully fulfilling story for you. I was born on July 30th, 1969 in Kansas City, Mo. I now live in Columbus Ohio with my wife and 3 children. You can look me up on Facebook or Google me to confirm that I'm not some nut! Back to Kansas City. I was adopted at birth and have lived a very good life ever since. A few years ago when my adoptive mother died, I decided to do some searching for my birth parents. I hired an expert in such matters. Through her I discovered my mother's name was Lucie Morvan from Huntington, Long Island. She had me when she was very young and traveled to Kansas City to stay with her sister whose husband was stationed out there in the Air Force. I was able to find out that Lucie passed away in 2007 but found her sister, my cousin and my birth grandmother. They are all from Huntington as well. After reuniting with them they let me know that my birth father's name was John Tangorra!

My heart sank. This was not a meatball query.

I tried to connect with John through my searcher even sending a certified letter to his home in Asheville, NC, but he never responded. This morning I did a Google search for him and was shocked to see that he had passed. I saw you listed as his daughter in the obit and this is why I am reaching out to you . . . I believe that we are half brother and sister! I have been an only child my whole life, so to find you blows my mind. I would love to connect with you somehow. I totally un-

> derstand if that is completely out of left field and I respect your privacy, but I really hope that we can meet someday. I'm sick that I never met John. From your posts you seem a very beautiful and interesting young woman . . . I pray we can get to know each other. Take care, Brad. Btw my birth aunt and cousin knew John. I sent them some of your pictures from Instagram and they confirmed it was him. They also remember the Lovin Oven!

The color vanished from my face, much like it did when I had been electrocuted by the walk-in freezer at Brucie. *Mom,* I said in a lamb's voice, *Mom, something is happening.*

What is it, Zaz, are you okay? she asked, noticing my shaky voice and absence of blood flowing north of my clavicle.

I gave her the phone to read the message. *This guy is saying he is my brother. Why is this happening?*

Why. The age-old, self-pitying, terrified, defiant, confused, exhausted *why me?* Why me is because, why anyone? Why is life so outrageous and so wonderful and punishing and strange? I felt like I was on an episode of *Maury Povich.* I wanted life to just settle down, I needed it to. I was outraged. I didn't believe it. Clearly this person was out for an inheritance that didn't exist, or playing a cruel joke on a grieving person to get some sort of sick thrill, like people who falsely confess to unsolved murders.

I remember your father talking about Lucie. Oh my god, Zahra, this is incredible! Bobbie said, beaming with wonder and excitement.

Incredible? Of course she would say this, defining how I should feel without asking me first. What was incredible is how I made it through my childhood alone with you two freaks for parents, desperate for a companion, an older sibling to protect me and be my forever friend. And now I apparently had one, and I was meant to embrace this chaos with only a quarter of my brain cells functioning and a smashed-up heart and a perpetually empty stomach? It was not incredible, it was horrendous.

Without the reality of a sibling, I had turned the emptiness of being alone into a strength and a point of pride, and now I had a fucking long-lost brother. It wasn't true. It couldn't be. If I was to have my DNA tested, the results would not come back saying one half Ashkenazi Jew, one quarter Irish, and one quarter Italian, it would say *100% only child,* because that is my true heritage. Grief had narrowed my reality to only my direct surroundings as I tried to put one foot in front of the other, and now I was meant to picture a human brother—WHO LIVES IN OHIO???? Where even is Ohio? Only child: *dead.*

Grief has a way of making you feel both invisible and dayglow all at once. The pain feels so unique and singular, despite its universality, and you feel like a silky gray apparition, floating among the living who have blood in their veins and joy in their beating red hearts. But grief also has a way of following you like a neon arrow pointed at your head, alerting everyone that you are an inconsolable, wild banshee. You are different and changed. Damaged, bruised fruit, when all you wish to be is a glistening strawberry in a pint of other identical glistening strawberries. You are desperate both to be seen and to disappear. I wanted my sadness to be validated, as it meant that I had loved and was loved in return, and that I was tortured by the loss of it. And at the same time, I was running in zigzags trying to outsmart the neon arrow above my head that pointed out that I was emotionally defective. A long-lost brother would double the arrow's size and brightness. *That Zahra, it's always something with her*. Make me a fucking strawberry, one without fuzzy mold or a wormhole in it. Make me alive again. Make me an only child again, it's the only way I know how to be.

I called my aunt Susan and my uncles Frank and Steven to tell them what had happened. Surely they would confirm that I was being extorted, and just like an episode of *Maury,* this would end and it would be time for the news where other people's horrendous problems would usurp mine and I could go back to haunting. But no.

Lucie was your father's girlfriend, Steven told me. *She had a limp, and he was embarrassed to admit that they were together, so he would make fun of her and put her down in front of other people, but she was definitely his girlfriend for a little while. She was a really sweet girl, I always really liked her. One summer she just up and moved away, and we never saw her again.*

Do you have a picture of Brad? Susan asked.

I did. There were a few on his Instagram page, and he looked exactly like my father—*exactly*. Same auburn hair, same hairline, same chin with same amount of chin fat that John had had when he was Brad's age. Same pale, freckled hands with cigar-shaped fingers. Icy blue eyes, slightly turned down at the corners, just like mine, except mine are green. Squishy bottom lip, slightly bigger than the top one, same bumpy nose (*not dead*). I resemble my father, but Brad looked like his son.

What is a sibling to an only child anyway, but a fantasy? But what is a fantasy that comes true?

I dialed the number with the Ohio area code with that strange feeling of both hypervigilance and dissociation that we get when we hear a strange noise in the middle of the night and walk downstairs to investigate. A man answered who had a different voice than John's, which surprised me; given how much they looked alike, I figured I would hear my father's voice again at the other end of the line. Brad's voice was sweet and warm, but higher than my father's. It was an earnest, midwestern voice. It sounded like baseball and small-town parades in the best possible way. I was nervous. It had all happened so fast. Within the span of two hours, I went from one kind of person to another kind of person. The accident flashed through my mind. That moment when I felt the tires hit the rocks, and then the air. There was no going back, and no seeing forward. I hoped this nice baseball voice was coming from an equally nice person.

Brad was nervous, yet curious and brave. He was sincere. He was an orphan who had wanted to find his parents, and his sister. By the time he had figured out who they were, his mother had died, and his father would not respond to his letters.

I later confirmed this with my father's only real friends, a husband and wife in North Carolina who John had told about Brad contacting him. According to them, my father had called Brad's mother a *slut who slept with all the guys in his crew, but not him*. Imagine the level of insecurity and self-hatred it takes to make a statement like this and believe that it's true. A sixty-nine-year-old man calling the seventeen-year-old girl in his memory a *slut*. A *slut* he got pregnant. A *slut* who he ran from and forced to deal with an unexpected pregnancy on her own. This made me dislike my father, and also his friend who repeated the story as though it were true: *She was a slut. He didn't want to upset you. He didn't think it was worth telling you because it wasn't true.*

I was unable to leave my bed for twenty hours of the day over a man who called women sluts. Who called *girls* sluts. Who refused to return a letter from a nice, baseball-voiced midwestern man with a sweet wife and three beautiful children who also looked just like their grandpa, because he didn't want to face the truth. He would have kept me from the older brother that I had begged the clouds for my whole life just so he didn't have to deal with it. We could have had barbecues together. He could have heard human beings call him *Grandpa*. He could have pressed his big body into Brad's for a tearful hug. I could have had someone at the hospital with me while I watched him die, someone to hold my fucking hand for once.

But this was my father. The parts of him that I didn't share in heartfelt social media posts. *I miss this selfish fucking asshole so much, he was a legend.* He deprived me of love when he felt incapable of doing the hard work that love required for my whole life, and here he was doing it again, in death. Had he been alive, I would have yelled at him and banged on his chest, something I was almost always too scared to do. But he was dead, and I was furious, and the closest I could get to expressing that would be shouting at the warped wooden box of waterlogged ashes, so, like always when he made himself unavailable to face the consequences of his bad decisions, I would beat on my own chest instead.

...

DURING THAT FIRST PHONE CALL, Brad told me he was the athletic director at a high school. He had married his high school sweetheart. He beamed with pride telling me about his three teenage children: *Joey is a baseball star, Lindsey is a cheerleader, and Lidia is just graduating and going to move to Arizona, she's a real creative, free-spirited type*. Just like her aunt, just like her grandpa.

Brad referred to John as *our dad*, which felt strange at first, but it also felt like a kindness to Brad and me both to expand John's role as a father of two. Our father was a song that I knew all the words to, and Brad had never heard, and so I played it for him that night, and many nights that followed, and he learned to sing along. Describing John to Brad was like telling a wide-eyed child a fantastical bedtime story as they cling to every word. A father is a mystery and a heartache and a best friend. Can a father be someone you have never met? Can a father be someone you are not related to?

I explained my father's politics to Brad, how he was a leftist, but he still watched MSNBC because he claimed the voices calmed him while he rolled around in bed at night trying to escape the insomnia brought on by the steroids he took to treat his cancer. At the end, he was addicted to opiates, he ate OxyContin like they were Peanut M&M's. He knew everything a person could know about music. He used the word *funk* often and put immense pressure on the *K*. *I'm still in my funK. That baseline has a tangy funK on it.*

Hah, funK, wow! I don't really say funk that often, but maybe I'll try to now, Brad replied, and my heart split for how tender human beings can be.

That's another thing that we do not see in each other, when we are in our grief bubbles, or even when we're out of them. It is hard to remember to look for the tenderness in each other. To remember that almost all of us have it. Had I simply passed my brother on the street, I would have made assumptions about who he was and was not. What a person like him, a middle-aged, white, midwestern man would care about, what he would cry about, and how he would regard tenderness in general. A wiser way to move through this world is to assume anyone could be an orphan, or a cancer patient, or a grief survivor, because everyone is, in one way or another.

When I told Brad the story of our father, the legend felt truer to life than it had ever been in my memory—he actually was a fascinating and complicated person, and the certainty of that was freeing. There was a letting go in telling Brad who his father was, because it was who my father was: a perplexing man ruled by fear and shame, and none of that was my fault. John thought of fear and shame as weak traits, and he wished to be tough, so he compensated for these undesirable qualities with worse ones like avoidance and rage. And John was also very silly. He made every holiday and birthday into an extravaganza. He overate. He was a fantastic cook. I try to be like him in all his best ways, and occasionally I am like him in his worst.

I did not feel comfortable yet asking Brad if he had a tendency to lash out when his feelings are hurt, and if so, what it has cost him, but I wondered in what ways he was like our father. Instead, I told him everything I could, so he could put the pieces together like a jigsaw puzzle. But there are no words to describe the weight of someone's hug, or the way they move their hands to wipe away their tears or yours. As many stories as I shared about our dad, Brad would never know what he smelled like, would never hear the strange noises that he would make while dragging his large, cancer-riddled body around the kitchen. He would never see how John watched him open a gift on Christmas morning. I could never have described the taste of John's pea soup, but if I were to try, I would say it was sweet and salty and how he was most honestly able to say, *I love you*. I could describe the softness of the large chunks of vegetables that would melt in your mouth after hours of slowly simmering on the stovetop, but I could never properly describe the strange softness of the man who made it.

In retelling the legend of John, I remembered that there was a lot to genuinely like about him, and that was where the grief grew out of, the seed that was his absence in my life. I was angry at my father for dying and leaving me with a mess to clean up after him. I was angry about the bedpans and the tubes. I was angry at his feeble, sick body, and for his inability to stay alive. I was angry to have a dead father and to be a weird grieving ghoul, trying to fit in with the shiny red strawberries of the world. I was angry at having to see his terribly white, limp dead arm poking out from a shitty low-thread-count hospital sheet. I was angry at the things he did to crush my heart like a fistful of potato chips, and the expectation to remember him fondly because he had died.

He died without understanding how much he had hurt me, or explaining why he was so fond of clowns. He died without meeting Brad, or telling me about him. And yet, there were things that made him extremely likable. John was a true antihero, his strengths so potent that they often hypnotized you into forgetting his weaknesses and abusive behavior. My father was like Tony Soprano, not because he was actually mob affiliated as I liked to believe as a teenager, and as I imagined after his death, but because you would find yourself physically unable not to love him, despite the fact that he was probably a sociopath.

Seeing goodness shine through in someone with so many

unsavory qualities is a kind of hope, a hope that's inextricably linked to the desire for others to see the best in us too. I saw the mica in the soil that was my father because I needed to know that the grimiest parts of myself also held the potential to shimmer, and that this is true for almost everyone should you hold them to the light, and pay attention as you dig. There was a transformation in passing along the mythos of John Tangorra to his son, a shift within myself from the stark black and white that had colored our relationship like a film noir. In the verbal sculpting of this man, from stranger to father, I started to accept the truth that he was composed of many shades of gray, and this helped me to realize that I did not need to come to a conclusion about whether he was a good or bad man in order to have loved him, and I am trying to be comfortable with the fluidity of his nature in our postmortem relationship.

These are complex notions to talk to a stranger about, even if the stranger is your blood relative. I wondered if Brad had merely hoped to know if John preferred the Mets or the Yankees (Mets), or what his favorite food was (rib eye, rare). I wished that I could have told him about a less complicated man, but I suppose a less complicated man would have been able to tell his son who he was in his own words. I may have said too much or not enough, but I knew I told the truth, and told it as kindly as I could. I think when it was over we both had a deep affection for our protagonist.

. . .

A LIGHTNING STRIKE IS always followed by the sharp crack of a thunderclap. One can estimate how close the lightning strike is by how much time passes before the roar of the thunder, generally one second per mile. When Brad and I ended our two-hour conversation, I said, *I love you.* He said, *Love you too, sis,* and this is how we have ended every call in the years since. I set the phone down on my mother's kitchen island and stared out the darkened window, tingling with exhaustion, hoping to see my father's ghost.

Five seconds later, a peeling clap of furious sobs shook me. It was like the crescendo of a thunderstorm, when the rain beats down like bullets into the ground below, and you say, *Holy shit, it's really coming down out there.* When you wonder how nature can be this unrelenting in its madness. Tears surged from my face like a flash flood. Gale-force howls, my fingers like branches trying desperately to grab something to just stay attached. When the tempest passed, and the earth began to soak in the rain, I was left with the same choice my father had had twice before—run from or run to—and I chose the latter.

Running from keeps us in a constant state of paralyzed motion, like trying to escape a killer in a dream, using all your energy but going nowhere. So I ran toward Brad, and toward many an opportunity after that, some of which remained forever out of reach, but I am glad for my efforts nonetheless. When my own life is over, I wish for it to be filled with as few *what ifs* as possible, and that means perhaps skinned knees and busted heartstrings, but at least I will never have the gifts I was too scared to open chasing me into the afterlife. John's weaknesses may have been strong enough to keep Brad and me from each other in life, but his death made way for new beginnings. I chose the latter, because however strangely timed our introduction may have been, we were family, and not just by blood, young love, or happenstance: by choice, our choice to stop being only children.

Pea Soup

PEA SOUP IS ONE OF THOSE FOODS THAT I THINK MANY OF US have strange feelings about. It is often associated with prunes, cottage cheese, melba toast, and other dishes that we grew up thinking were meant for people over the age of ninety-five. But you will never look at pea soup the same way again after trying this hearty, cozy, silky PEA-licious soup. This recipe cooks like a soup, but it eats like a meal, and if you have some peas, and some patience, you are going to realize pea soup is for everyone, not just the sick and toothless!

The key to my father's beautiful pea soup is patience. Patience and comically large chunks of vegetables. He put almost-whole veggies in here and let them simmer low and slow all day long, until simply looking at a carrot inside the pot would cause it to melt like a stick of butter. This recipe includes a meaty ham bone, but you can also use shredded ham or—if you are NOT the ghost of my father, who hated poultry more than flying even—smoked turkey wing pieces! Or leave it vegetarian, see if I care! Meat or no meat, this soup is going to wrap you up like a warm hug from a big, friendly spirit.

SERVES 4 TO 6

⅓ cup extra-virgin olive oil

2 large carrots, peeled and cut into 3-inch chunks

3 ribs celery, cut into 3-inch chunks

1 large leek, cleaned and cut into 3-inch chunks

4 small Yukon Gold potatoes (about the size of a golf ball), cut in half, skin on or off
10 cups stock (I like to use chicken, but John used veggie)
1 1-pound piece of ham bone with meat on it
1 (16-ounce) bag dried split peas, soaked at least 4 hours, then drained and rinsed
2 bay leaves
2 tablespoons honey
1 tablespoon apple cider vinegar
¼ cup minced dill
½ teaspoon ground nutmeg
1 teaspoon coarsely ground black pepper
1 tablespoon kosher salt

In a large stockpot, heat the olive oil over medium heat for 1 minute. Add the carrots, celery, leeks, and potatoes and sauté until just starting to soften, about 3 minutes. Add the stock, ham bone, soaked and drained peas, bay leaves, honey, vinegar, dill, nutmeg, salt, and pepper.

Bring to a boil, then cover and simmer over very low heat, stirring occasionally, for 2 hours, or until the veggies are mushy and all the ham is falling off the bone.

Remove the bone, taking off any meat and saving it to add back into the soup. Discard the bay leaves.

Serve with a dollop of sour cream, a drizzle of olive oil, and a hunk of crusty bread.

CHOCOLATE MOUSSE PIE

My mother, Bobbie, is a chronic mispronouncer. She says *karocheekan* when referring to cornichons, which always makes me think that she is describing a guerrilla pickle army. *Sir, we just got word that the karocheekans are planning to invade from the south by morning. There look to be thousands of them, and they are heavily armed, tiny, and very sour.* She says *rigoutta* instead of ricotta, *fraheetraz* in place of fajitas, and she calls America's sweetheart, the Bubble Boy, *Jake Gyleninthtcall.* I cannot find a proper way to spell how she pronounces Kazakhstan, and my cousin Rory's beautiful wife, Aigerim, is from Kazakhstan, so she says it often, and when she does it sounds like she is talking while chewing a lacrosse ball.

My mother has an incredible sense of humor. She not only tells good jokes, but truly appreciates good jokes, and she knows how to laugh. Her laugh is well-fed and genuine, and I make myself hear it after we have a fight so I can remember to like her again. She is shy, but not afraid of a little argument with a stranger at the supermarket here and there. She dances by bending her knees and swaying from side to side and jabbing her thumbs toward her mouth, getting lost in the joy of the moment. She makes an excellent toast, and will find twenty different things to celebrate and raise a glass to during any meal. She knows how to have fun, and is the absolute best celebrator walking the earth's surface. She has a childlike quality about her that she has passed down to me. And she has inherited from her own mother, my grandmother Violet, the ability to notice the small beauties in life, like a single golden leaf on a treetop swaying in the breeze, or lobster guts, which she loves. When we gather round with friends and family in the summertime for a lobster dinner, she laps up the tomalley from her carcass, and then moves along like a pool vacuum to everyone else's at the table. *Gotta have guts,* she says, licking the remnants off her fingers. Truer words . . .

Bobbie has become, later in life, the mother that I needed growing up. She calls to warn me about the weather, as if I do not have access to the forecast. *Chicken Little calling to tell you to watch out, the sky is falling.* She checks in with me every night when she gets off work at six-thirty on the dot, and makes sure I have a plan to eat dinner, and that said dinner is hearty enough to meet her approval. *A salad is not dinner, Zazie, you need protein. Why don't you go get yourself a nice hamburger?* I don't want a hamburger, I'm depressed, and she knows that, but she will keep *suggesting* it until I crack and get one, so I do, and it helps me feel better. If I have a sniffle, she is dialed in one hundred and ten percent until my nasal passages are dry. When I am against the ropes, she is dabbing my smashed-open eyebrows and pouring water into my bloodied mouth.

Sometimes I run from her kindness, because it makes me ache for how much I needed it when I was small. There were many times when she tended to me as a child. Cold rags for a fever. Lunch boxes packed with overstuffed turkey sandwiches and little bags of Doritos. Birthday parties with ice cream for breakfast, and bandaged wounds. There was sweetness, but there was little in the way of a recipe for trust, and a recipe really comes in handy when you are just learning to cook.

When I was little, we would get into fights about small things that would sadly come to leave big scars. We would start to argue about something banal like having a friend sleep over or going to bed, and as soon as I would start to have an emotional reaction, she would lock herself in her room. She would stay in there for hours, so long that, looking back, I realize she must have been peeing into a jar. I would scream, sob, beg to be let in. But she was afraid of me—tiny, furious me—and no matter how hard I tried to bargain, the door would remain locked, her only response an occasional scream telling me to go away. My tiny fists would bleed from hours of banging, my brain would throb after all the yelling. But my perception of myself was hurt worse than my physical body. I felt like a hideous monster. I would write ten-page notes apologizing for how horrible I was, cover them in Lisa Frank stickers, and shove them under the door. *Mommy, I am sorry I am so bad, please come talk to me. Please make me dinner.*

Please help me understand that I am not actually vile and unlovable, you're just overwhelmed and unsure of how to do this, I would think. Hours later, when I had fallen asleep outside the door, she would finally emerge. She wouldn't talk to me. We wouldn't discuss what happened and come to a resolution or understanding. Just the silent treatment, and when I would ask why she was so upset, she would give me only short responses, and threaten to go back to her room if I kept this up.

We are not born knowing how to regulate our emotions, we are born feral little wild animals. We learn through comfort and stability and guidance. We grow with regularity and consistency, and become stabilized with boundaries. We feel safe when our parents show up to teach the hard lessons the right way. It requires a lot of emotional strength to deal with a child throwing a tantrum. It has taken me decades to learn to stop banging down people's doors when they reject me. Not in a literal, Glenn Close bunny-boiling way, but in a way where rejection or toxic, emotionally abusive behavior makes me write the proverbial note covered in unicorn stickers. *Please forgive me, let me in, I am horrible, I am sorry.* This pattern has taken precious years of my life from me, spent crying and being too sad to eat, smoking myself sick. The imprint left by the closed door, the shame and fear of being on the other side of it, feeling so deeply unworthy of love, has long had a stranglehold on my heart, and this is the wall of resentment that stands between me and my mother. We are doing our very best to take it down, but god damn is it built from highly durable concrete.

. . .

BOBBIE AND I HAD adventures when we were in our halcyon days. Things didn't really start to unravel between us until I was twelve or so, although the door locking had been in her repertoire since I was in kindergarten. When I was in grade school, we lived behind a golf course, and we would journey out there during snowstorms and hide underneath trees, pretending we were wild animals, watching the wind blow the snow into steep hills all around us. *Do you think when we die, we will come back as mother and daughter?* I would ask.

I hope so! she would answer. *But maybe we will come back as two waiters working in a restaurant, like Tung Ting, wouldn't that be fun?*

We loved Tung Ting. It was an old-school Chinese restaurant on the water in Centerport, complete with a red and gold carpet, big banquet tables, a giant fish tank filled with exotic fish, and a piano player at the bar. The waiters were always joking to each other, acting like best friends. I think that is what I liked most about the idea: that Bobbie and I would come back in another lifetime as best friends. It felt, even then, that was how our relationship was meant to be. Neither of us responsible for the other's well-being, just happy to know each other, without the pressure of her having to be responsible or explain the world to me. I laughed hysterically, comforted by the idea that no matter what, or who we were, we would know each other forever and ever.

As much as we loved each other, I think that being a single mother was very hard for Bobbie, because it is inherently one of the most challenging things a person can be tasked with, especially when your co-parent is dead set on being your opponent, but also because at thirty-two, she wasn't ready to be a mother, a feeling I didn't fully understand until I got pregnant at age thirty. I had an abortion because I knew I had not matured enough to handle being responsible for a child. I was with someone at the time that I actually really loved, but I also knew we weren't ready: he struggled with alcohol and I was still very emotionally immature. There was a part of me that wanted to start a family, but a much stronger one that knew I needed to grow up before that could ever be an option. There were some really interesting ways in which I was following in my parents' footsteps, but bringing a child into the world with an unstable career and partner was not one of them I wished to imitate.

When I was born, my mother had terrible ulcerative colitis, which nearly killed her, was in a broken marriage that was barreling toward divorce, and would soon lose her business and go bankrupt. With age I have come to understand and find empathy for how hard this must have all been for her, and how the pressure of being a *good* mother may have at times felt impossible. I lived most of my life thinking how she would have had an easier time without me, and in my most turbulent times I have set out to prove it. But Bobbie was a good mother, and has grown into a great one. *Both things can be true,* she will say when I come to her with a problem that I am struggling to untangle, and it always fits, the duality of seemingly contradicting emotions sharing the head of the same pin. Both my parents were complex stews, and while they were and are tremendously unique, this simply makes them human. My mother did and does love me, *and* it would have been easier for her to move through that very rocky time in her life untethered to a small child. And it is now my work to truly believe that this childhood script of being unwanted and unloved no longer needs to be the narrator of my life as an adult woman.

After my parents split up, my mother and I moved to Northport, a few towns over, and she started cooking here and there again. Simple things like spaghetti, vegetable soup, and roast chicken with *magic sauce. Magic sauce* is equal parts ketchup and mayonnaise, and a little lemon. It was magic because it made a picky eater like me enjoy roasted chicken and steamed broccoli, and because it was the first time in our lives that we sat at a table in our home and ate dinner together.

In that new house on Conifer Court, she began a spiritual awakening of sorts. She joined a bohemian women's group and danced naked with them in the moonlight. She went on Outward Bound excursions, joined African drumming circles, and went to study at the Gestalt Center to become a psychotherapist. She dated a schizophrenic artist who would drag dead swans and old toasters that he had stabbed with kitchen knives into our new home and hang them from the rafters. Had we been the same age, Bobbie was someone I would have maybe sought out as a friend. We could have tripped on mushrooms and unpacked *The Undiscovered Self* together, while eating Tofutti Cuties and polishing our Birkenstocks. But as a little kid, I needed a mom who wanted me more than she wanted to explore the world, and so we began our journey away from one another.

My mother would sometimes do *mom* things, but always in a signature Bobbie way. When I was in the fourth grade, I had a part in the Christmas pageant at the ridiculous private school she had gotten me into on a full scholarship, because we were broke and lived in a not-so-great neighborhood. We kids were told to wear something fancy, and I had seen a dress on *Blossom* that I really liked, short with big bell sleeves and made from shiny satin, so my mother decided that she was going to make it for me. She got the old Singer sewing machine out of the hall closet, and we went to Zarin's to buy the fabric. The dress would be red with big white sleeves. When we got home, she had me hold the red sheet of fabric just below my chin, and she drew a free-form outline of my body from which to work. No pattern, just a squiggly cone shape of a child's body. The free-wheelin' sheets of fabric were quickly stitched together, and in under an hour, I had something that could have passed for a dress if one was to use the word as a concept rather than an item of clothing. It was oversized in the waist, and extremely tight in the armpits, with visible seams and errant threads trying desperately to escape. *I love it, Mommy,* I said, which was true. I love anything someone makes for me, regardless of its quality.

On pageant day, I got up onstage to sing Christmas carols with my classmates, who were all clad in Ralph Lauren, and just as the very first notes of "Jingle Bells" echoed through the gymnasium, the dress fell apart, rendering me half naked in front of the entire school and all their parents. It turns out Bobbie had used satin dress lining, and while it was shiny, it was not sturdy, and I was kindly ushered off the stage by one of my teachers.

Bobbie doesn't follow directions or recipes, but she is an amazing cook, and if I ate her food blindfolded, I could tell it was hers, because everything she makes tastes vaguely the same. I mean this as a compliment; everything she makes tastes like her: salty, soft, sweet, and very pushy. Bobbie cooks beautifully, effortlessly, and wild. To watch her cook feels to me the same as watching her walk, or talk on the phone, or drive to the grocery store—so much a part of who she is that it is easy to take for granted how her subtle movements in the kitchen add up to such mastery. She has things she makes that are *hers*. *Her* spanakopita, *her* chicken "bambazini." *Her* apple strudel, which was once her mother's apple strudel, passed down genetically like the smile in her eyes.

My favorite thing that Bobbie makes is *her* chocolate mousse pie. For all the different and often extreme seasons of our relationship, there has been chocolate mousse pie. Melted chocolate, bittersweet of course—two words collocated to explain the essence of the human experience, the wild juxtaposition of life on planet fucking earth. Sugar, stiff-peaked egg whites, fluffy whipped cream, Oreo cookie crust. If I were to die and find out that heaven was real all along, the streets of it would surely be paved with *her* chocolate mousse pie. Unlike spanakopita, she only tends to make chocolate mousse pie once per year, on Thanksgiving, which was always a truce day for us. Even when I was in high school and things were at their absolute worst between us, we would look forward to Thanksgiving, like we had been separated by war and had one day to spend with each other before redeployment. We would wake up at the crack of dawn to dance with the turkey before roasting it for three hundred hours, and then make *her* fabulous corn pudding, Violet's chestnut stuffing, and, of course, the chocolate mousse pie.

. . .

I HAVE DEEP SADNESS about what feels like wasted time in my relationship with my mother, and these laments of our past have a way of making even the sweetest moments present day sound out of tune. Lovely meals and special days hold within them a heaviness made so by my frustration with how many times weren't like that, but could have been. Sometimes when she says something painfully caring, or helps to free me from a terrible bind, I cannot appreciate it because all that I can think is, *Where were you before?* The choice to love or to punish is mine now, and I have to walk down the thickly wooded path to avoid the reaction that ultimately steals more rapidly fleeting precious time. I don't always take this path, but it is becoming more worn with the passing years. The simple truth is that I love my mother so much that I struggle to find the words to describe what she means to me, while I also have words in my vocabulary that I wish I did not for how badly she hurt me. I have an almost paralyzing fear of how much I will someday regret the ugliness that we have shown each other. I know there will come a time in the not-so-distant future when I would kill to hear my mother exaggerate a story, or even say something mean that hurts my feelings, because her voice is my favorite sound.

But here is the thing, the really true thing about love that deep: it can only exist amid its imperfections. Bobbie and I could have both done things better, and if we had another lifetime to do it again, I bet we would, and who knows, maybe we will be those two waiters at Tung Ting after all. But in this life, we fought because sometimes that happens when two people who are tied to each other cannot figure out how to swim with three arms. Our relationship was and is flawed and incredibly rich and textured, and if I am to be honest, I think what I would have regretted even more, what would really break my heart, is if I never tried to get to know her, and ask her to know me. Perhaps this struggle was the price of admission to a deeper relationship than we would have had without it, or maybe not, but either way, that great fortune is what makes the sun glow. The boldness that made me say mean things that I regret was the same boldness that demanded she do better, and she did do better eventually, and so have I. Reclaiming and repairing our relationship has been a very painful process at times, and it has required a humongous sacrifice on both our parts. But I will leave this world one day knowing that we both dug until we hit oil. We could have given up on each other a thousand times in our lives, but we didn't, and we have the scars and gorgeous memories to prove it.

Recently, when I was at a particularly low point, lost in the murky waters of a terrible heartbreak, I found myself lying on the white leather sofa in my mother's therapy office, among the dozens of little turtle trinkets and color-coded psychology books, and I sobbed from my bones, the way I had when I was a little girl. *Tell me that it all works out,* I begged her.

She replied, *It all works out, Zazie.*

Tell me I will fall in love one day, the good kind, the kind that doesn't hurt so much.

You will, she said, a kind lie, or maybe not, we will have to wait and see.

Do you love me? I asked.

More than anything in the whole wide world, baby.

The truth. And the truth hurts because that impenetrable kind of love made from diamonds is so much messier than we are led to believe. And of course there is a fine line between messy and toxic, and we have to be conscious of not poisoning ourselves, but we don't talk enough about the unkempt nature of a lifetime of unconditional love. Sometimes it can be just that, a lack of parameters that allows you both to experiment being your worst selves. Love is like eating a lobster: gotta have guts.

Do you love me on my worst days? I wonder. I already know the answer, and I think that is the deepest part of grief, whether it is present or anticipated. It's not the fights and shitty things you said to each other, not really. It's the fact that you have lost, or will someday, one of the few people who loved the worst version of you.

My mother takes pride in the fact that she doesn't follow recipes, and while I also have a soft spot for the bacchanalia of nonconformity, I also wish I was better practiced in specific methods. I believe that being able to follow a recipe makes you better at being able to write one, and while I might never have a child to pass any wisdom or culinary lore down to, I do wish to one day be equal measurements of head and heart. Being a student is more important to me than being a teacher, and I have come to realize that it only strengthens one's creativity to never stop learning from others. So maybe I don't follow a recipe when I make chicken cacciatore, but I do treasure the cookbook that is my mother. I transcribed the good parts and left the recipes out that called for three times too much salt, or too little sugar. My mother's greatest recipes are for compassion, whimsy, warmth, and forgiveness, and my deepest hope is to master these classics well enough that I may one day be qualified to truly replicate them with my eyes closed.

Chocolate Mousse Pie

BOBBIE HAS MADE THOUSANDS OF CHOCOLATE MOUSSE PIES in her life. The original recipe was adapted from Maida Heatter, but honestly she makes it a little different every time, and somehow it always comes out tasting exactly the same. I asked her to write me the recipe, and she said, *Zahra, you know I don't write recipes.* I said, *Neither do I. Let's try doing it together and see how it turns out.* This is her official recipe, and it is superb! It is also great served without the crust, in cups with whipped cream and fresh berries!

SERVES 6

CRUST:

(You can make yourself, but Bobbie always used store-bought, Nabisco brand and it is honestly perfect):

⅓ cup plus 1 tablespoon melted salted butter

2½ cups chocolate wafer cookies, crushed

2 tablespoons granulated sugar

½ teaspoon kosher salt

FILLING:

3 large eggs

2 tablespoons granulated sugar

1 cup heavy cream

8 ounces bittersweet chocolate

½ teaspoon kosher salt

WHIPPED CREAM TOPPING:

1 cup heavy cream
2 tablespoons powdered sugar
1 teaspoon pure vanilla extract

Preheat the oven to 375°F and lightly brush the sides of a 9-inch pie pan with 1 tablespoon of the melted butter.

Combine the chocolate wafers, sugar, and salt in a food processor and process to crush the wafers. Drizzle in the remaining ⅓ cup melted butter and process until mixed thoroughly. Press into the greased pie pan and bake for 12 minutes, then let cool on a wire rack for at least 1 hour.

To make the delicious mousse, start by separating the eggs into two bowls. Whisk the egg yolks (preferably with an electric hand or stand mixer with the whisk attachment) with the sugar for about 2 minutes, until fluffy. Set aside.

Heat ¾ cup of the cream in a medium saucepan over low heat until steamy, then add the chocolate and salt to the hot cream and stir to melt. Once melted, remove from the heat and let cool for 10 minutes.

Slowly whisk the melted chocolate and cream mixture into the whipped egg yolks, then let cool for 5 to 10 minutes.

In the meantime, beat the reserved egg whites with an electric mixer until stiff peaks form, about 5 minutes. Set aside. Then, in a separate bowl, beat the remaining ¼ cup heavy cream with the mixer until firm.

Fold one-third of the whipped egg whites into the chocolate, cream, and egg yolk mixture, then continue with the next third, and then the final third, being mindful to not stir too aggressively. Fold in the whipped cream.

Pour this mixture into the chocolate pie shell, then chill in the fridge for at least 6 hours or overnight.

To make the whipped cream topping, beat the heavy cream, powdered sugar, and vanilla in an electric mixer until stiff, about 2 minutes. Top your cute little pie with the fluffy whipped cream and eat immediately, then have a second piece!

ALLA GRICIA

I RECENTLY READ AN ARTICLE ABOUT A NEW JERSEY WOMAN who bought a small home on a private island in Maine, and lives there in solitude from May through October. I wondered if she got dressed and put on makeup, if she made herself nice meals and set the table and lit a candle, or if she talked to herself. I wondered if she laughed, and hoped the answer was yes.

When I am lonely now, at age forty, I often put on makeup and dress nicely even if I know I will not see anyone. I spray expensive perfume on my neck and clothing for no one to smell. I eat weird dinners that my mother wouldn't approve of because they contain no protein or carbohydrates, sitting on my couch watching episodes of *The Sopranos* that I have seen so many times I can recite all of the lines. I sit at the bar at local restaurants and order the same things, and read a book, or look at the same page for forty-five minutes because my frontal lobe is clogged from stewing in my latest failed relationship. Sometimes I cry because I can't imagine ever escaping loneliness and being held, and it feels like I am stranded on a freezing cold remote island off the coast of Maine, even though I can hear my upstairs neighbors having sex. I wonder why this New Jersey woman would choose such dramatic isolation. She must be very brave.

Because I was an only child until I was thirty-four years old, my relationship with loneliness is my longest and most intimate to date. When I was small I talked to myself in the mirror in different voices, and maybe I still do, so sue me. I learned a Cockney accent from watching *Mary Poppins,* and from age seven to ten I was a part-time chimney sweep from turn-of-the-century London. I looked at myself for hours as I made strange faces, and when I got older, I obsessed about plucking all the hairs from my eyebrows except for a precious few that lay in a pencil-thin arch, which as a result have never grown back in a meaningful way. I delivered long, improvised monologues to the wall in my bedroom, and had imaginary fights with those who I felt had wronged me. I would linger in the linoleum-tiled kitchen and rummage through the junk-food-stuffed cabinets for something to suppress my anxiety and keep me company.

I was a latchkey kid at my mom's house, where I spent the majority of my week. She worked full time, so I welcomed myself home from school and had the run of the house. I was scared of everything as a child, because being alive is scary, and so is being alone, and it becomes clinically so when the unknowns you are learning about from the harsh and confusing world you have been thrust into aren't explained. I saw the movie *Outbreak* when I was nine and spent the next four months convinced that I had Ebola, constantly checking my face and body for pustules or blood seeping from my eyes. This could have likely been avoided if my parents had told me that you cannot contract Ebola visually, but I learned the hard way.

I would hop off the bus and walk up the steep hill that led to the house on Conifer Court, open the always unlocked front door, grab a kitchen knife in desperate need of sharpening, and immediately check for a murderer in every closet and under each bed before finally settling in front of the TV with a Tombstone pizza, a Twix, and maybe some Dunkaroos. I never felt settled, and I was uncomfortable in my body, but the junk food made me feel less alone because it was something to focus on. I would hear a noise over Jerry Springer's opening statements and check again for the killer who had obviously outsmarted me the first go-around, but it was just the cat. I'd turn back to the TV and watch Jerry questioning a panel of guests who are afraid to wear clothes, and their breasts and genitals are blurred out. Then I'd three-way call my best friends Jen and Madi to talk about our crushes and what teachers we thought were potentially a part of the Illuminati, and after hanging up, I would grab my knife and check the house again. Around nightfall I would hear the garage door opening, and the relief that my mother was home and alive was like warm milk filling me from head to toe. She would walk in the door and say, *I didn't mean to worry you, I was working late.* I never questioned it, I was just so thankful to have her back. I think of these times and wonder how the woman in Maine could pay over three hundred thousand dollars to live like that for six months at a time.

When I was nineteen and enrolled at FIT, I moved in with a boy I had been dating since my senior year in high school. Ryan and I lived in a studio apartment on 106th Street and Riverside Drive that had been passed down from my older cousin Elana. There was a homemade lofted sleeping area, a bathroom so small that you had to leave the door open when you sat on the toilet, and a porch equal in size to the apartment itself that faced the backs of the adjoining buildings. In the evenings a man in another apartment across the way would sing opera, and we would sit and listen, chain-smoking Camel Lights and drinking Jamesons and soda.

Ryan was very sweet, and we had the kind of relationship that one would expect from two nineteen-year-old kids pretending to be adults in New York City. Loud and awkward sex, frequent but innocent arguments about things that felt very important at the time. I loved Ryan the best that I knew how, but like Ebola, no one had ever explained love, and I did not yet know how to properly give or receive it. I was wild and just learning to be a person, and we split up about a year into living together.

I was lonely again, but this was a different brand of loneliness. This loneliness made me feel plucky and mature, like Carrie Bradshaw. I bought a vintage fur coat that shed tufts of rodent hair when I moved, and a gold nameplate necklace, and then I *was* Carrie Bradshaw. Loneliness felt very different as Carrie. It felt powerful, and it came naturally from my training in the *Jerry Springer* days. It felt intentional and chosen. I would paint and blast Joy Division and stay out until six in the morning with my friends, then sleep until noon and get oversized Italian sandwiches from Milano Market to ease my hangover while I watched Criterion Collection DVDs that I'd rented from Kim's Video. I felt like the king of my very tiny castle. I still checked behind doors for a killer, but this took much less time in a three-hundred-square-foot apartment.

I have had a half a dozen or so serious relationships, many of them with people I've shared a home with. They have left, or I have left them, and again I am lonely. Most of them were poor matches. I think I picked them so I could tell myself that if I fixed them, I wouldn't be destined to be lonely, while knowing that I couldn't fix them, and eventually would just go back to my spot on the brown corduroy loveseat in my mother's house, convinced that Joel Rifkin was hiding in the closet. This is the ease of walking down the well-traveled path to a place that scares you, yet the door is always open so you can sleep there rent-free as long as you like.

I think of this woman in Maine and I wonder if she hugs herself. I wonder if she avoids intimacy like I do. I wonder if she pretends to want togetherness, but can't seem to place it on a map. I wonder if she puts on plays and does all of the parts. I wonder if she cries, or if she went there to stop crying, and if so, did it work? I wonder what happened to her that she chose solitaire over gin rummy. Maybe she's a misanthrope. Maybe she had a nervous breakdown. Maybe she just likes the roaring silence of the smashing breakers. I wonder how often she checks behind the doors, and if she has a very long knife underneath her pillow.

. . .

IN 2018, SIX MONTHS after my father died, I went on a ten-day trip to Rome by myself. I had been to Italy a few times before, but never to the Eternal City. I made my reservation at Roscioli, re-watched *8½*, and I was on my way to a tiny but sun-drenched flat in the heart of Trastevere. I was awestruck by the charm of the winding cobblestoned streets and pastel buildings smothered in kelly green ivy, the dark wooden shutters thrown open with freshly hand-washed linens drying in the breeze like sails. I would walk upward of fifteen miles per day, stepping into churches and lazing about under rows of cypress trees in the Borghese Gardens. My aloneness had informed me to pay close attention to the gentle wind and how it swayed the branches of the broccoli-shaped stone pines on Palatine Hill. I heard the hiss of every espresso machine, and came to realize that my favorite sound on planet earth is that of plates clanking in the sink of a kitchen in a quiet alley, while the smell of toasting garlic, cigarette smoke, and nutty coffee hangs in the air like perfume clouds.

I would crunch into thin, crispy squares of pizza rosa with tangy tomato sauce, salty anchovies, and peppery olive oil and the pleasure was all for me. No counter opinion, no concern for someone else's expectations or disappointments. I would eat long lunches of cured meats and various types of pecorino cheeses, washed down with crisp white wine and a few Italian Marlboros, watching tourists get frustrated about being lost and ordering a cappuccino after eleven a.m. I'd pretend that I wasn't one of them, that I was Roman, or at the very least, not American, because I'm not really, I'm a New Yorker. I knew that cappuccino was for breakfast only, and how to politely order dessert without it sounding like a demand. I felt liberated not to have to negotiate what to do after lunch or think of things to talk about.

When I wanted to share my experience, I called my mother and beamed about how Rome was the most amazing place on earth, and we promised each other one day we would go there together. At this moment, though, I was grateful to be there alone. I was sore all over from the grief of losing my dad, looking everywhere for his ghost, for a sign it wasn't over yet. I was heartbroken from being dumped by my boyfriend two weeks after John's death, and I did not have the emotional strength at the time to worry about anyone but myself. If I wanted two pastas on the menu, I didn't force myself to choose, I ordered both the cacio e pepe and the pajata. I did not want to leave this city or this life without knowing how both these dishes tasted at Armando al Pantheon, one of the city's best and oldest restaurants. I ordered bottles of wine, not glasses, because the wine lists at the places I was fortunate enough to go to were mind-blowing and I wanted to drink the La Stoppa 2012 Ageno with the saltimbocca alla romana. I wanted to get lost in the symphony of my isolation, on my private island, surrounded by millions of people.

One evening, I made my way to La Tavernaccia Da Bruno, a family-run trattoria on the outskirts of Trastevere. I had read Katie Parla's glowing recommendations of this spot, and knew that if she loved it this much, it had to be something special. I walked into the brightly lit, stone-walled dining room around eight-thirty and was shown to my table for one by an incredibly friendly server, who would take care of me for the rest of the evening. Italy doesn't really do bar seating at restaurants, not the way I was used to in America. In New York, where I go out to eat alone all the time, I saddle up to the bar, open my book, and blend into a half dozen other folks doing the same thing. When I first arrived in Rome it was a little intimidating holding court over an entire table, ordering a meal for two for one, but by the time I arrived at La Tavernaccia, I had acclimated, and even started to prefer it.

I spotted Walter Massa's salty, tropical Derthona Timorasso on the wine list, and ordered a bottle. My best friends Mary, Becky, Dan, and I had fallen in love with each other over this wine back in the Brucie days, and now the wonderful waiter and I also bonded over our shared reverence for this perfect bottle, which bursts with the flavor of salty mango and pebbles. The menu was small, and everything sounded incredible. He recommended that I start with their classic tomato bruschetta, and then the rigatoni alla gricia. I had never had pasta alla gricia before, a creamy cacio e pepe / carbonara hybrid, made from crispy guanciale, loads of cracked black pepper, and Pecorino Romano cheese. The alla gricia preparation wasn't on the menu, but he told me that I had to try it, and he would have the chef make it special for me. I was almost ashamed, as asking a chef for special anything (with the exception of extra sauce) is against my religion, but the server, who turned out to be the chef's son-in-law, had given me his blessing.

The bruschetta was phenomenal, the quality of the ingredients making the dish far better than I could ever have imagined diced tomatoes, garlic, and olive oil on toasted bread could be. Then the rigatoni alla gricia arrived, simply adorned with a sprinkle of pecorino, the quarter-sized chunks of perfectly crisped guanciale jutting out from the al dente pasta, glossy with salty cheese and hot pork fat. For dessert, my caring new best friend sent me pistachio mille-feuille and grappa. The table next to me, a couple my age on their honeymoon, glanced over to me and said, *You look like you're having the best time,* and they were right.

I walked home along the Tiber in love with life, the beautiful ancient city, and the aloneness that had been so painful to cultivate but finally made sense. I was in Rome on this extravagant vacation because my father had passed away and there was a few thousand dollars left over from the next to nothing he had left after he died, so I used it to be better at being lonely than he was. My father was the loneliest person that I have ever known. He was good at being alone, but in a bad way, and I am glad that I do not have to be afraid of living the way that he was.

. . .

THERE ARE PLACES WHERE we are stranded and others we travel to by choice. I wonder if I had not spent so many hours staring at myself in the mirror perfecting a Cockney accent, would I have ever had the courage to travel alone? If I had a partner with me in Rome, perhaps I would have never heard the plates clinking or noticed the shape of the shadows cast on the pale pink buildings, or the subtle sound that clean laundry makes when it flaps in the air. Maybe I would have been too shy to eat gelato every night if I was with a lover or a friend, and what a shame that would have been, because this is the only life I will ever have, and nothing is more luxurious than an ice cream cone, or ten. These moments are life rafts. I go back to them and remember this is the pact I have with myself, and while it is hard, it is also quite beautiful. And one day I will have to make a different trade, someday I might wish to be lonely, maybe even the bad kind of lonely because it feels safe even though it is haunted. Someday I will go to Rome with a man I am madly in love with, and I will be forced to share my silence. I will savor the times I wished for company, because they were already everything.

It is possible that the woman in Maine chose to live in solitude because she actually prefers it. That she is held in the company of nature and the sound that her breath makes in the absence of conversation. There is a distinct power in loving yourself enough to do something that makes you lonely. To buy a house on a remote island and spend the days reading and digging for clams and tending to the garden solely for your own amusement. To sit with the knowledge, no matter what has brought you there, or where *there* is, that you are enough, maybe not everything, but completely and totally enough.

In the article, the woman talked about staying on her island through a mighty storm one fall. She told the paper that she could hear the winds whipping around her, but her home remained intact throughout. *A lot of people are like, "Wow, you're really brave. You're on that island by yourself." And I was like, "No. I just always felt very safe there."*

Loneliness can be a gift, not just something to be endured, but to be wholly enjoyed. It is a survival skill that allows you to see more of the world instead of less. To see the Colosseum and keep its majesty all for yourself. To eat ice cream every night and dance yourself home to the sound of plates clinking. If we are lucky, learning the hard way makes it possible to experience joy the easy way. It is not a full turn all at once, or a permanent one, but a practice and cycle that we metamorphosize through over and over again in the span of a lifetime. I will try, like the woman on the island, to use what I have learned in the cocoon, then burst out and live, and return when the wind has tired me out and I need to remember how to fly.

I am alone. I am lonely. What is the difference? The difference is in how we write our own profile of solitude.

TUSCAN WHITE BEANS

When I was thirteen, I would write love letters to Leonardo DiCaprio, and hand them off to my father because he was an adult and knew how to use the mail. I was obsessed with Leo and would fantasize about spending our lives together. I was certain that after he read my letters, he would make his way to the home of a strange child (me) and take me back with him to California to be his bride. I would have what I imagined to be adult conversations in the mirror. *I think we should put the pinball machine in the dining room so we can play while we eat dinner and drink red wine.* I would fall asleep practicing kissing him using the back of my hand.

When I was cleaning out my father's house after he died, I found a stack of the letters, still in their envelopes, addressed to *Leonardo DiCaprio,* with no mailing address. He hadn't sent them, opened them, or thrown them away, a series of choices so sweet it hurt my teeth.

Dear Leonardo DiCaprio,

I call u by ur full name because I don't really know u (unfortunately). And furthermore, on the subject of not knowing each other, I would love 2 meet you some day 'cause (this sounds really stupid) I think (by what I know of you) we would really get along! I'm not really the 1 to write "fan mail", but I really "cosmically connected" or "whatever".

Anyway, let me tell u a little about me. I'm hoping 2 be a movie actress in the near future. I love to play basketball, lacrosse, ice hockey. I'm a funny, punky, spunky kinda person. I love to be wild and different, or maybe I just am. By the way, I heard that you write poetry, so do I. Here's 1:

'As I sit and wait for my soul to come forth, I'm suddenly awakened by an unsettling wave of uncertainty. It boggles me how such tension can build within such a calm person. For when life is at it's best, I am only partly hole. But I suppose I am always partly hole, because I am lacking my final part. I need something to complete my soul. I am happy but some what empty. But he, he who's face is as pure, and hair and body as sweet, dear perfection, it's self, he who knows not who I am yet I yurn for his sweet, soft lips to caress mine, he who I long to see or talk to for only a minuet, he who would fill my gap.'

Done! (that's not even one of my best)

You like it? Good. I would love 2 hear one of yours some day.

Oh, by the way I don't know if you know the girl who was gonna play opposite of you in Romeo and Juilet before Claire Danes got the role, but she is an acquaintance of mine. So I got 2 go. See ya bye.

Love Zahra Tangorra

PS whoever gets this please!!!!!!!!! Send this letter 2 Leonardo himself. I would appreciate it. If you have a heart please do it.

PPS Leonardo call me if you get this 516-555-5555

Write me 15 Conifer Court, Northport NY 11768

PPPS Please send me a poem or something

Before my very long affair with Leo, I fell in love with the cartoon voice of Raphael, the Ninja Turtle who wore a red bandana. Ever since the year 1991, I have been in love, the kind that makes you frenzied and uneasy, and is often unrequited. After Raphael came Christian Bale, Brad Pitt, and Christian Slater, and then of course Leo. After that I transitioned for the most part to people I knew in real life, with the one exception of Kevin Costner, who I, much like Whitney Houston, will always love.

. . .

TWENTY YEARS AFTER MY unrequited passion for Leo, all my childhood fantasies of love came to take shape in my adult body at a house atop a hill in a tiny Tuscan town. It is a classic villa, perfectly smothered with ivy in all of the right places, and it crumbles in parts, which only makes it more charming. To reach it from New York City, you must take a taxi cab to John F. Kennedy airport, then fly to somewhere in Italy, preferably Rome, so you can spend a few nights eating carbonara and slurping water from two-thousand-year-old spouts. From Rome, you take a train for three hours, up to Montevarchi, a large commercial town nestled conveniently between Florence and Arezzo, and then a twenty-euro cab ride from the station. Or you can rent a car and speed your way two and a half hours up the autostrada, stopping once or twice for gas, an espresso, and a pack of Italian cigarettes. The drive up to the house from town winds up a thickly forested hillside, and when the foliage breaks, there are sweeping views of the Tuscan countryside, which looks like it is a movie set of the Tuscan countryside, the hills rolled in shades of green like something I saw when my brain was ablaze with acid.

The first time I went to the house on the hill, it was late August 2019, and the wavy landscape was brownish green and bone dry. I was in the backseat of a stick shift Panda driven by a friend of a friend, feeling the gears switch and my heart pound hot blood to my cheeks as the car pulled its way up the hill. The road up to the house was lined for about a hundred yards with pointy cypress trees that made it clear that you are arriving somewhere supremely special. From afar, they looked smooth, like dark green torpedoes shooting up into the crisp blue skies, but when I passed them in the car, I saw that they were shaggy with branches that poke out at strange places, and this only made them more majestic, because it was evidence that they are in fact real, and I was actually in a place this beautiful, and not tangled in my sheets having a dream.

I didn't talk much on that drive, because I was carsick and nervous to see David. I was, and always will be, nervous to see David, but not because he is intimidating. He is warm and friendly, and always greets me with a big hug and a smile that melts me. I was nervous because I loved him, and I have since the moment I saw him two years before, and I suppose, in some way, I will until I leave this world. I was nervous for the smile that I knew was coming because I am shit at being melted. When my heart flutters fast, my armor dissolves, and without my armor I feel naked, and to be okay with being naked I need to have thirty-seven glasses of wine, which is what I planned to do as soon as we parked and walked our way up the path, following the smoke from the wood-fired barbecue to the stone-paved garden enclosed by fig trees.

I had been in love with David since the summer of 2017, when I got a message from my chef friend Carolina asking if I wanted to go to Tuscany for two weeks to cook for a yoga retreat. She had met Alix, a woman who ran an amazing fitness retreat in the heart of Tuscany, a few years earlier at the wedding of a mutual friend, and Alix had asked her to come cook for her clients, but because of a scheduling conflict Carolina was looking for someone to replace her. All of my expenses would be covered, and I would have to leave in three days. At the time of this proposition, I was in deep need of a fantasy, and in my mind, red wine flowed from the faucets in Tuscany and wild boars poured their milk into your cereal. I was in a dead-end relationship, and without Brucie, the total lack of purpose in my life made my eyes feel heavy and half open. My heavy, half-open eyes needed something new and beautiful to look at, and so, with less than seventy-two hours notice, I was off to Tuscany.

When I arrived, I was whisked from the station to the agriturismo, where the retreat was held, by a bubbly and slightly unhinged American yoga teacher in her early twenties who drove like Popeye Doyle. When we fishtailed into the parking lot, I thanked my dead grandparents for sparing my life, and decided that I would rather walk the ten miles to town for the next ten days than get in a car with this psychopath again. She ran off, leaving me to lug my suitcase by myself. It was a hot day, over one hundred degrees, and I was feeling regret mixed with jetlag, making my nose tingle like I was about to cry.

Hello there, said a man with a cheerful British accent as he walked down the path to greet me. I would soon come to learn that he was Australian, but he and his siblings were raised abroad in Western schools, so he does not say *barbie* in place of *barbecue,* or end every statement as though it were a question. He was once kicked by a kangaroo, but this really could have happened to anyone. *Let me get that for you, you must be exhausted,* he continued, only partially visible with the sun beaming strongly against his back, shading what would come to be my very favorite face, a face that was often split into a wide smile that showed the gap between his front two teeth, the most precious bit of real estate in the entire region of Tuscany.

He grabbed my suitcase with his brawny hands. I noticed his arms were tanned and sturdy, covered with sun-bleached hairs, and he was wearing a navy blue polo shirt caked in a thin layer of dust. When he introduced himself—*I'm David, Alix's brother,* flashing that gap-tooth smile—I pictured what our children would look like.

I was not prepared for this. I was told there would be roads lined with cypress trees, two pools, dozens of hectares of Sangiovese grapes, and groves of olive trees from which the hotel pressed its own oil. I was told that I would be cooking for twenty guests for ten days, breakfast, lunch, and dinner, and that my boyfriend Luke could join me for the last two days of my stay free of charge. I was told that I could shop for ingredients at local markets and pick fresh herbs from the hotel garden. I was told it would be very hot and that I could cool off in the pool whenever I had time. I had brought important books that I never had time to read at home, and trashy magazines that I bought at Hudson News at JFK. I brought SPF 50 for my face, comfortable footwear for work, and elegant dresses for the vacation that was to follow. I had failed to anticipate falling in love the moment I arrived. What do you bring to be ready for something like this? There is simply no way to appropriately pack for love at first sight.

Love at first sight is like seeing a ghost, and I have experienced each of these phenomena only once. When my father died, my friends Becky and Bretton and I went down to sort out his house, and on the last night there, we were all awakened in separate rooms at the same time by a cold wind, and then seconds later, dozens of tin toys in his collection went off in unison. I tell people this and they say, *Oh my god, that's crazy,* but I doubt anyone truly believes it happened. There must be an explanation for why fifty-plus vintage tin toys started marching around at three o'clock in the morning. Perhaps they were just stretching their legs.

The same goes for love at first sight: spectral, unexplainable, occult love, that is almost scary to admit could exist, because to do so would imply the possibility of past lives or alternate realities. It would imply that it could happen to anyone, against their will, like being struck by lightning, and we are meant to be able to control our hearts better than rogue electric currents exploding from the sky.

David was easy to love, both at first sight and even more when I got to know him. He came off like a dreamy lead in a rom-com, but he was also a brilliant and interesting person, with a fascinating life story, and very good manners. His voice was soothing and his laugh so intoxicating that you would do anything to keep yourself drunk on it. He was warm like sun-ripened figs, and just as sweet. He was genuinely interested in everyone's stories, and I love this about him, how generous he is with his time and his eardrums, and how he leads with his gap-toothed smile. How every living creature he encounters, from a salamander to a server, gets genuine time, attention, and respect. Sometimes this made me question if I was special, or if I had imagined our connection. *Maybe I am no more special to him than a salamander,* I would sometimes think. But no matter how many people or lizards have basked in the glow of his charm, something rare burned between us over the time we spent together that summer, and all the summers since. I saw the cabinets open and close on their own, I'd bet my life on it.

I started skipping time that could have been spent lounging by the pool to go on the hikes he led for the guests, and this was all the proof I needed that I was in fact in love, because it was hot enough to cook an omelet on the cobblestones, and hiking through the rocky, arid hills midday made me wonder if blood can in fact boil. But those hikes were magic, and I return to them often when I am fighting with my brain to find happiness. He would stop along the trail to pick wild herbs and crush them into my hand for me to smell, and only a fool would fail to realize that a palm full of wild juniper wields more power than a cheesy pickup line. I fell for the juniper, telling myself it grew just for us, to be a part of our story, maybe one we would tell in our wedding vows.

When I fell in love with him, it smelled like that juniper. It smelled like garlic frying in olive oil. It smelled like dry dirt and sun-scorched bay leaves and musty old stones that the houses are built from. It smelled like spaghetti limone, chicken with hot peppers and eggplant, and fig tart, frittata with squash blossoms and mozzarella, and all of the other bright, homey dishes I made for the guests while I was there. It smelled like Italian Lucky Strikes, Ichnusa beer, and salty dried sweat from a day's worth of hard work. It sounded like dishes clanking in the distance, and Italian ladies complaining about their husbands. It sounded like church bells and wine pouring into short glass cups, and wind blowing through olive trees and making the leaves click like crickets.

At night, when the dishes were sorted and the guests had retired to their rooms, we would sit on the cobblestone path in front of the two-bedroom apartment we shared. We never crept into each other's beds during the night because I had a boyfriend whose impending visit loomed over our bonfire like a pitch-black storm cloud, but we did get to know each other, and ten sunsets felt like ten years. He told me his mother had passed away unexpectedly not long ago, and I told him about my dad's cancer, and practically every interesting thing that has ever happened to me in my life. I had never felt like opening up that way with anyone else. Not with a friend or a lover or even a therapist. It was exactly the feeling I had imagined as a young girl, writing letters in my room to Leo, that childlike, innocent longing for connection. Somehow, here that connection was, with David, at midnight, on the stones warmed from a day's worth of sunlight and smoothed by thousands of other people's stories that came before. I let the power of each and every star from the blue-black sky electrify my dreamer's brain. I let myself believe in all the love stories I had ever seen and imagined, hoping that this would be my salvation from so much disappointment and loneliness. It felt like someone, somewhere, had opened my letters.

My boyfriend Luke was coming in a few days, and the ripe, juicy peach I had been eating would be nothing more than a hard pit that would break my teeth. I was hoping that maybe I would get lucky and Luke would fall into a sinkhole, or join the Peace Corps and be unable to make his flight. Luke and I were two good friends, decent people who made a terrible couple, and this only became more evident the more time David and I spent together.

Much to my dismay, Luke had not been abducted by aliens, and showed up as planned, and we had a very uncomfortable, albeit beautiful, trip through the Tuscan coast, then broke up right after my father's death. When we got back to America, I tried to explain to my friends what had happened, how I had met the man I wanted to spend the rest of my life with, and they reacted how anyone would: *Wow, that's nuts.* When I told my father, he told me to move to Italy. It's funny who believes a ghost story.

. . .

DAVID AND I KEPT in touch as friends, and he was the first person that I called when my father died. I knew that the romantic infatuation was largely one-sided. I thought the reason for that was me, that I wasn't pretty enough, or that I was lacking in some way that kept him from hopping on the next plane to New York. I hadn't considered that he met hundreds of people each summer who came and went, and most of them became a nice memory, as people do in these situations. I hadn't considered that he had a hole in his heart shaped like his late mother, that no lover could fill, or that there were parts of his story he hadn't shared that made him terrified of love. But this is the only math I knew at the time; he was plus and I was minus. Anyone else I dated felt like a taped-on side mirror. But as the years of long WhatsApp messages continued, we really did start to develop a relationship that was much deeper than pen pals.

At the same time, I became very close with Alix, who

owned Tuscan Fitness, and she asked me back the summer of 2019. Which is how I found myself in the back of the Panda marveling at the cypress trees as I drove by, then stumbling into the garden for the first of many barbecues at the house on the hill. I had brought a platter of beef carpaccio with bitter arugula, anchovy aioli, and parmigiano, and had burned the back of my right hand with hot beef fat while quickly searing the outside of the meat, leaving a blister in the shape of a heart. It had been two years since I had seen David, and despite the thousands of messages and phone calls, it felt like we were meeting again for the first time.

Alix's children were playing and running around, and David's giant Portuguese water dog, Cencio, was barking and trying to see through the tangled fur that covered his beady black eyes. There were a dozen and a half people in the garden speaking in both English and Italian. They were calm and casual with each other, moving like silk scarves blowing in the warm evening air. There was a perfect chaotic energy, an energy that I had waited my whole life to be a part of. I had thought my potential to be a part of a big family had ended with Brucie, but this moment filled me with hope that the dream was still alive.

I spotted David by the wood-burning barbecue, flipping sausages and drinking a beer. He smiled at me, and I had to excuse myself to run upstairs and go to the bathroom. I closed the door behind me and breathed out for the first time in ten minutes. I looked at myself in the mirror and held back tears. *Where was I? How did I get here? How could I ever leave and go back to my old life?* Ever since that night, this suffocating feeling wraps its beautiful fingers around my long neck whenever I return to Tuscany. I find myself inside the fantasy, and it snatches my breath away knowing that time will soon take it from me.

I fixed my hair and went back outside to take my place under the shade of the fig trees with a glass of homemade wine to watch the revelry unfold. Dinners in the garden were unwieldy, with food being plucked off the grill and laid out on Alix and David's mother's beautiful Rampini platters from Radda. Big salads would get eaten with hands while standing, and Alix was always finished eating before anyone else even started. *I'm full,* she'd say, *have we got any chocolate?* Her casual attitude toward eating has come to be one of my favorite things about her. Arty, Alix and David's father, also lived at the house on the hill, and would sit at the big table with the same smile his children had, charming everyone with his hand-tailored compliments and hilarious stories from a life well lived.

Before barbecues at the house on the hill, I used to have a controlling and uptight nature about even the most casual of meals. Everything was to be placed on the table at the same time, arranged just right, so that the table looked balanced and colorful. Everyone needed to sit all at once, pass around the bounties that had been prepared, make a perfect plate, and enjoy the food in unison. It gave me anxiety the first few times I attended a barbecue in this garden, and I realized that it was because I never really knew how a family eats, because mine had been so small and unromantic about food that I had to study and replicate the carefully choreographed meals that Ina Garten and Martha Stewart made on TV. I felt anxious, not because people were eating the grilled veggies before the steaks were ready, but because I was inexperienced in how to truly be part of a brood, and I was scared to be found out. Alix would pass me a baby to hold while she opened a bottle of wine, and I would panic in silence, feeling like an actor, burning and sweating under the stage lights, my lines out of reach. Here in the garden I was just a cog in the machine of a beautiful evening, and though it made me nervous, I loved it and needed it.

I'd dreamt my whole life of living this way, of being one of many. I had spent hundreds of thousands of dollars and years attempting to create it at Brucie, but it is challenging to make the scene convincing if you've never lived in the place in which you are writing about. I wanted to be with David, but I also wanted so badly to be a part of this family. To live as part of a pack that ate grilled meats straight off the barbecue, and argued, and made up, and shared inside jokes, and had each other's backs. I wanted to be David's partner, and Alix's sister and Arty's daughter-in-law.

I ended up staying six weeks on that visit in 2019, and while we reestablished and deepened our friendship, I began an outright campaign to get him to be in love with me, which only made him pull further away from romantic entanglement. The accident had provided me with a distinctive boldness when it came to taking chances. When you have a true near-death experience, it makes you realize how superfluous it is to be precious about your desires, but one must be careful when maneuvering a newfound superpower. The balance comes in realizing that not everyone has had a brush with death, and thus does not necessarily share the same sense of urgency. My exigency made me say *fuck it* to everything. Life is short, there is no time to mince words, there is no time to waste.

But this is a mirrored way of thinking, and relationships should be a window. You are meant to see how your own desires affect not only you, but also the other person. I was looking at myself in the mirror saying, *This is it, this is what I want,* and I kept saying it over and over, hoping the repetition would give way to reciprocity. But in a window, you can see yourself as well as the other person. If I could have really seen David, I would have noticed that he was struggling to find joy, and was in no position to be in a relationship. He had a way of hiding this behind that beautiful gap-toothed smile, witty humor, and matchless charm. Had I looked at him through the window, I would have seen it better, but the mirror made me believe that I was simply not enough, or maybe too much, or simply fucking cursed and haunted.

. . .

A YEAR PASSED. IN the summer of 2020, I was walking twenty-five miles a day around the ghost town of New York City, and though we still spoke regularly, the romantic part of my relationship with David still felt pretty much one-sided. And then one day, without warning or explanation, he started flirting with me in one of our morning chats, and the flirting turned to more than that. What started as a seemingly innocent conversation about sharks became very provocative by nightfall.

I called my friend Mary. *I think David is, like, sexting me.*

I couldn't really believe it, but I felt like I was floating back to my apartment from the corner store, like I was a bird aloft on the breeze. A bird whom someone loved. I felt like I could finally put down a huge boulder I had been carrying around my whole life. I wondered if we had been face to face, if we would have begun the life I had wanted since we had met, or if this was an intimacy he was only capable of with so much wind and water and earth between us. I wondered why now, why had it taken so long for him to find me here, but I never asked. I didn't want to spoil it or come back down to earth.

This new phase of our relationship was so alive, and for a few months that summer it made me feel galvanic. But even though I had gotten what I had wanted for so long, I was still waiting for the right moment to ask for more. I wanted to be together for real, no matter how impractical that may have been at the time. He didn't want things to change, and I wanted to move to Italy. *I love you, and this is our only life, and we have something so special, and you are missing it,* I'd say. *Wake up, you're missing everything.*

I can't be in a relationship right now, I am too consumed with looking after Arty, he would rebut.

And this was fair, as Arty was now tragically in the throes of a very ugly battle with dementia. David, who had never learned to drive, was left alone to care for him for over a year, literally trapped in paradise. But it wasn't just Arty, it was his fear of intimacy and my codependence. Every time it seemed like we had a chance of circumventing the obstacle that he claimed stood in the way of our relationship, he would move the finish line farther away, until I became tired and frozen in place, like the pipes in the old house on top of the hill. We would fall out of touch for a few cold months, and then one of us would call, and we would remember how life was better with the sound of each other's voices, and things would thaw again.

. . .

DAVID AND I OSCILLATED between deeply emotional friendship and noncommunication for the better part of a year, and the next time we saw each other we hadn't spoken in six months. I took a solo trip to Puglia in the early summer of 2022, then drove eight hours up to the house on the hill. I was all stomach knots and heart tangles as I pulled into the gravel driveway, but as soon as I saw his face and felt the weight of his hug, I was exactly where I needed to be. We had a barbecue in the garden the day after I arrived. Alix's husband, Levi, and I made dough, and we all baked delicious pizzas topped with local cheeses and vegetables in the wood oven. We drank what felt like hundreds of bottles of wine, and when Alix and Levi's girls went to bed, we smoked Marlboros and told dirty jokes around the fire as we were eaten alive by mosquitoes. David and I were always the last two to go to bed, and this night was no different, except this night he grabbed me by the waist and kissed me.

I remember many kisses before and after with many other men, but this would be the one I would ask to be buried with. We stayed there for a long time in the garden, tangled up in each other like twisted vines, and then he took me into his part of the house for the first time. It was damp and mildewy, and filled with beautiful paintings, ceramics, and artifacts from his parents' past lives, when the family was operating in all its glory. Even in the middle of the night it was evident that at one time this part of the house had been filled with air and sunshine, and now it was not because that memory was too painful for him. It now felt like a wing of a museum that was closed for renovations, with a thick layer of dust caked on anything that was a reminder of the air that once flowed through so freely. There was a single bed surrounded by hundreds of books and trinkets and statues from his years living in India and China growing up. We pushed aside the dirty clothes on the edge of the bed, and finally, after five very long years, we had sex without an ocean between us.

For the next three weeks David and I were as close to a couple as we would ever be. We took long drives and had picnics in olive groves, eating fat sandwiches of tuna and mozzarella hugged between spongy focaccia and soaked in vinegar and local olive oil. We had epic barbecues in the garden surrounded by friends and family. We crudely chopped vegetables and drowned them in olive oil and salt and watched them blacken in all the right places on the grill, his hand on the small of my back and my heart in the pocket of his wrinkly shirt. If gravity worked the way it was supposed to, I could have stayed in these moments forever, having him feed me little bits of pecorino ginepro with pickled onion on top as I flipped the steaks.

There are some foods, like panzanella, that hurt my throat because of the lump that forms in it when I remember eating them with him. David loves food, and I thought that if I could make the most delicious thing he had ever eaten, we could stay stuck to the ground in the garden forever, together, rooted in happiness like the centurion pines from which the owls watched us kissing and laughing in the wee hours of the night. Much like the freezer at my father's house that I packed with "don't die yet" food, there had to be a way I could fix the unfixable with my cooking. A perfectly composed radicchio salad with anchovies and parmigiano could unscramble the realities of who we were and who we were not. The surprising addition of mint would change the fact that he has a complicated relationship with happiness, and my grilled tomato sauce will take away my propensity to snuff out the flickering flames of love with my anxiety. We convince ourselves of these things to try to bargain with reality, with gravity, with free will and damaged hearts. There is no tiramisu that can close the gap in the Atlantic, or bring someone's beloved mother back from a sudden death, or reverse dementia, or change attachment styles, not even mine, which I make with ricotta in place of mascarpone, and is really quite delicious.

Two nights before I left, we went for a cookout at David's best friend Alberto's house. Alberto is a charming and jovial Tuscan man who lives with his beautiful partner, Azzura, in the countryside on a sprawling plot of land, with acres of Sangiovese vines that he would harvest in the late summer to make his own wine. His ancestors had built a giant outdoor fireplace that he used to cook everything from whole pigs to coils of freshly made sausage to charred bulbs of fennel and sweet red onions.

I was bringing with me a pot of white beans that I had sweated over all day. I often make things the quick way, but I had made these beans with attention to every last detail. I browned fat chunks of pancetta and then added coarsely chopped onions and whole smashed cloves of garlic. I made a bouquet of thyme, rosemary, and sage from the garden at David and Alix's house. I added the soaked beans, homemade chicken stock, and a healthy glug of local olive oil and covered the pot, stirring every twenty minutes or so until the beans were creamy and tender.

It's funny because I always know exactly how to make food turn out the way I want it to. You could make the point that if you do steps A–Z in a recipe, it will turn out perfectly, but it's more than that. You can learn a recipe, and perfect it, but if you do not have an inherent sense for the integrity of a bean, that perfect dish will remain elusive. The same can be said about cultivating healthy love. To get it right, you have to really understand the mechanism of it and at this point I was still very much a student of love, but I was more secure in my grasp of the beans.

I was terribly nervous to bring my food to the party, more nervous than I had ever been for someone to eat a dish that I cooked, and I had once made spaghetti and meatballs for Cameron Diaz. Alberto and the rest of David's friends in attendance were real Tuscans, and Tuscans, like most Italians, are deeply protective of their regional specialties. Even one too many thyme sprigs could be called into serious question. I once made the mistake of putting apple agrodolce atop a porchetta and am yet to hear the end of it.

We drove the winding twenty minutes to meet Alix, Levi, and the girls at Alberto's house with the red oval Le Creuset at David's feet. The sun was still strong in the early evening, and the smoke of the roaring fire filled the air like a fog coming off a lake at dawn. We drank wine from mismatched cups and the girls ran around in the yard, their golden blond hair catching the sun like a spider's web. Alberto's sister emerged from the house with a large pot filled with pappa al pomodoro, and we all waited patiently for steaming bowls to be passed around. I scooped the thick tomato and bread stew into my mouth, realizing that I could never properly re-create it, even if I meticulously followed her recipe. You had to have been on a first-name basis with the local tomatoes and finished the dish with bitter, peppery olive oil that was pressed just down the road. This comforted me, knowing that some things are only alive in one place, and to enjoy them you have to know how to get there.

We cleaned our bowls with tears of crusty, unsalted Tuscan

bread, and then it was time for dinner. Alberto's famous juicy pork ribs that had been seasoned with only salt and olive oil and set just out of reach of the flames, perfectly charred and running with hot fat. Sausages roughly cut to reveal pungent garlic and parmigiano and flecks of rosemary, simple and rustic like the land and the breeze pulsing through the olive trees. I sheepishly removed my pot of beans from the corner of the outdoor hearth and placed them on the dinner table for inspection. *Looks-a very-a-Tuscan-a,* said Alberto, then turned to David and added something in Italian, which I made out to be, *You have a good one here, David.*

I am good, I promise. Listen to your friends, tell me not to go. I reached under the table and squeezed David's leg, and he looked over and smiled at me.

Alberto took a scoop of beans. *Buono,* he said, and I knew I will never again need another compliment.

We finished our meal and stacked the dishes and poured more wine. There was sadness in this moment because I knew how long I had waited to get here, and that soon it would be over, with no guarantee that I would ever come back. How would I go about regular life, trying to convince people of what I had seen. Like someone who had been abducted by a UFO, or rescued by a mermaid. *I swear it was real.* The group thinned as it got later and later, and David and his friends rolled a few joints and attempted to teach me to play poker, as we took turns changing the soundtrack. I thought they were just about the coolest people I had ever met, and they thought I was funny even though they could only half understand what I was saying. I would try to better explain myself in broken Italian, and David would come to my rescue and then everyone would laugh.

We left somewhere around two a.m., and made our way backward across the winding roads and sharp turns to Moncioni. I was driving slowly around a curve, Brian Eno's "Spinning Away" playing. David was singing along with his hand on my knee, and as I glanced over to look at him, a small deer ran in front of the car, and I hit it straight-on. We came to a screeching halt, but we were unharmed. The deer ran off into the night, the front bumper of the rental was dented, and the pot of beans that David had placed on the backseat had exploded its leftover contents as if the *Challenger* had been made of cannellinis.

Are you okay? he asked, gripping my face and staring past my eyes and into my heart, into the little-girl version of me that had been waiting her whole life to hear someone she loved ask this with such conviction.

I am, are you? I replied. For some reason, my first thought was that he would be upset with me, although that kind of reaction is not in his nature. I thought, *Please be okay now, and forevermore. Please let this shock change us both. This deer was the reincarnation of our dead parents, demanding that we stop and realize who we are to one another. That life is short and it could end at any moment and we should be living it together.* We kissed each other hard, with stray beans stuck to the sides of our faces, the only two humans awake for miles. The only two people in the whole wide world.

Everything that had happened between us up until that point had felt slightly askew, but in that moment we were two soft baby deer happy to be alive, totally in love under the ancient Etruscan moon. We arrived at the house and got into his single bed and had sex and then fell asleep naked, sweating under the thin sheets as we held on to each other and this fleeting love for dear life, like two people on a lifeboat who had just escaped a shipwreck. Morning came, and we met Alix and Levi upstairs in their part of the house to tell them what had happened with the deer, and with every passing word, the miraculousness of the event began to lose its power. Ghost stories are perhaps more true when we don't share them.

Two days later, I had to fly back to New York. My flight left at ten a.m., which meant that I had to leave the house in Moncioni at three in the morning to drive the three hours to Fiumicino. I woke David up, crying, and picked a fight because I knew it would never be this way again, us together, because I felt I had reached my limit for the haunted nature of our love. I knew that I needed to be with someone whom I could grab on to, and who could also grab me back. I had grown tired of my hands slipping through him and trying to convince my loved ones of what I had seen. But before I left, I needed to wail and bang my fists on the casket like a bereaved Italian grandmother. I was unsatisfied with a hug and kiss and *call when you get to the airport*. I did not wish to call when I got to the airport, I wished that the airport would disappear, and the roads would turn to rivers, and planes to rubber.

Home? Was my six-hundred-square-foot apartment in Carroll Gardens still my home? How could anywhere on this earth where we were apart be home? I had loved my apartment more than anything in this world, but it now seemed like a dungeon I was being banished to after living in a glorious castle, so I picked a fight. I said things to break my own heart and his. I said, *You don't care that I am leaving. We won't see each other again for at least a year, and I will just meet someone else and then this will all be over, because I am ready for the real thing, and when I meet that person, I will never come back to you.* I wish this had been true, that I would have met someone I could have really loved, and who would have made it easier to be away from him. I wish that our love didn't feel like it was merely a dream. It was and still is the best love I have ever felt, because it came from someone that I truly believe in, celebrate, and admire.

After that visit, I gave up the dream that we would ever be together in an effort to be awake in my own life. I stopped thinking of how we would parent our future children, or how cute Alix's girls would be as older cousins. I stopped contacting him altogether. I regrouped, and after a few months, I realized that I missed my friend. When I went back to Italy a year later, we began to patch up our friendship, leaving our romantic past in the shuttered parts of the house on the hill. It was hard to see him and not kiss him because my heart was, and forever will be, in some way spellbound, but we had managed to salvage a real friendship from the miles of yarn we had spun, and it felt worth protecting. We spent the days laughing and joking and shopping for groceries and having coffee and pastries, and it was healing to remember where this had all begun and why.

It may not have been the romance that saved my life, but of course it wasn't, because the romance that is meant to save my life is the one with myself. David may not have wound up as my husband, but he did have the hard conversations with me over and over, as many times as we needed to, always with grace and respect, and that is real love, no matter what shape it takes. For all the missteps we took together, he was always delicate and thoughtful. He never once dismissed a single feeling I had, or made me feel small. Even when we pushed each other to our absolute limits, we were always on each other's sides. He may not have been able to show up as a partner, but he set a metric for altruism and kindness that anyone I choose to love in the future must meet, and I am so lucky to have a scale like that to reference. Real love, all-terrain love, gets stuck between gears sometimes when it's shifting, but it gets you where you need to be, pulling you up the hill, to a special place with a beautiful view.

. . .

I HAD A TERRIBLE and emotionally abusive relationship a few months after David and I ended things in 2022. I know, you're thinking, *I thought you just said that he gave you a metric for good relationships, what happened to the metric, Zahra?* And he did, but I just had one more painful lesson to learn before I could accept these truths. I had to fall hard to reset my bones properly.

After I broke up with the guy I got involved with after him, David really showed up for me while I was desperately struggling to scoop up the pieces of my smashed heart. I was at the point where I hated my heart. I spent months waiting for it to dry up and fall out the leg of my pants. I would be happy to be rid of it, this ridiculous blob that always got me into so much trouble. I couldn't trust it. But David would call, and as I listened to his words on the other end of the phone, they sounded like us laughing as we climbed on stone walls and picked ripe figs. They sounded like the squeaky wheels of the shopping cart as we pushed it around the Coop supermarket in Montevarchi, filling it with fresh vegetables, fancy cheeses, big steaks, and tall bottles of salty beer for dinner, giggling like little kids pretending to be adults for an afternoon. I heard the pebbles crunching underneath his feet as he walked beside me on our way to have an adventure off in some old medieval town. I heard the first thing he ever said to me—*Hello there, let me get that for you, you must be exhausted*—and realized that benevolent gesture never stopped existing for one single second. I had met someone across the world who would, no matter what, always help me carry what was too heavy to hold. And slowly but surely, I started to hate my heart less and less. It did not dry up and fall out of my pant leg, it started to grow back and fill with blood and become squishy and warm.

You have a good heart, Z, David said in his beautiful, deep voice, *please don't forget that.*

You too, D.

What I had wanted from Leonardo DiCaprio and all subsequent lovers was a teammate, someone who I could trade poems with. I don't know how the story of David and me ever ends. Maybe it doesn't, and we live again a hundred times eating tuna sandwiches, singing at the top of our lungs to our favorite songs and catching each other's tears like big wooden buckets. Or maybe we will become ghosts who float among the wild juniper, or lovers, or grandparents. But we are, and always will be, the one thing I had wished for since I knew how to wish: best friends.

Almost Tuscan Beans

THIS IS A LOVELY POT OF BEANS, PERFECT FOR A CHILLY NIGHT, or paired with grilled meats for an Italian-style summer barbecue. No matter how delicious, beans seem to have a way of being left over at the end of a meal, but fear not, legume lovers! Heat them up in a frying pan and crack a few eggs in for a special breakfast the next morning, serve warmed over sourdough toast, or whip them in the food processor for a luscious bean dip.

SERVES 10 TO 12

1 pound dried cannellini beans, soaked overnight and drained
1½ tablespoons salt, plus more for cooking the beans
½ cup extra-virgin olive oil, plus more to taste
½ pound diced pancetta
4 ribs celery, cut into 1-inch pieces
2 large leeks, white and green parts, cleaned and cut into 1-inch pieces
1 medium fennel bulb, sliced into ¼-inch-thick pieces
6 garlic cloves, smashed
2 bay leaves (fresh if possible)
2 large sprigs rosemary
6 to 8 thyme sprigs
8 sage leaves
4 cups chicken stock

2 rinds of parmigiano
Coarsely ground black pepper
Finely grated zest and juice of 1 lemon

Preheat the oven to 375°F.

Boil the soaked beans in a large pot of salted water for about 45 minutes, then drain and set aside.

In a large Dutch oven, brown the pancetta in 3 tablespoons of the olive oil over medium heat for 4 to 5 minutes. Once browned, remove from the pan and set aside.

Add the rest of the olive oil, the celery, leeks, fennel, and garlic and sauté for 2 minutes. Tie the herbs together in a little bundle with kitchen twine, then add them to the pot along with the reserved beans, chicken stock, parm rinds, salt, and pepper to taste. Cover the pot and simmer over medium-low heat for 20 minutes, then uncover and transfer to the oven for 30 minutes.

Remove the pot from the oven and discard the herbs and parm rinds. Stir in the lemon zest and juice, the reserved crisped pancetta, and then drizzle with additional olive oil to taste. You want the beans to be creamy and starting to break down, but not total mush. If they seem too firm, but the liquid has evaporated, add a little water to loosen them and put it back into the oven until they reach the desired texture. Once the beans are nice and soft, you can mush them up a bit with the back of your mixing spoon. Check the seasoning and adjust accordingly.

LAZAGNA

LASAGNA IS WHAT YOU MAKE FOR SOMEONE WHEN THEIR parent dies, or for a person whom you are falling in love with. Lasagna is what you prepare at Christmastime, when a friend has had a baby, or when the cold turns unkind and you need to get warm. Lasagna is a project. It is intentional. It is exertional. It is emotional. There is something about the repetition in the layering of pasta, sauce, and cheese that is like a mantra being repeated over and over, simple and heartfelt: *I care about you.* There are no bad lasagnas, not even ones that are too wet or raw in the middle, too salty or not salty enough, because lasagna is not about the what, it is about the why. And the why of lasagna is almost always love.

I made my first lasagna when I was twenty-one for a boy whom I loved who did not love me back. I invited him over for dinner at my studio apartment on 106th Street. I bought all the best ingredients that I could find, which left me completely broke for the rest of the month, and spent the entire day making sauce and pulling magma-hot noodles from the boiling water, burning every exposed inch of skin in the process (a reason I now only use uncooked fresh pasta sheets, which are not only far less dangerous, but also far more delicious). I set the finished casserole in the oven, and as it began to cook and bubble, my three-hundred-square-foot apartment filled with smoke, setting off the alarm and annoying all of my neighbors. As you may have guessed, the boy who did not love me back never showed up, and after I finished crying for seven hundred hours, I had a piece, and it was really quite delicious, or maybe it wasn't, but I enjoyed it, and although the *what* had hurt my little heart, the *why* was left to find a more deserving audience for all that effort.

. . .

BRUCIE WAS IN COBBLE HILL, Brooklyn, which is divided from its more Italian next-door neighbor, Carroll Gardens, by the ironically named Union Street. I moved to Carroll Gardens in 2018, two years after I closed Brucie, once I had begun to recover financially from bankruptcy, and emotionally from the stomach punch of my father's death. When I found my apartment, I was at the lowest point of my life. I thought for sure that my bankruptcy would disqualify me, and I would have to live in the spare bedroom at my mother's house at least until I went through menopause. But I still booked an appointment to view it, just in case.

Just in case are three powerful little words. They are free of toxic positivity. They don't promote getting your hopes up, but they do invite you to try. *Fuck it, why not.* Why not give the cute person at the restaurant your phone number (or have your friend do it for you, duh)? Why not audition for a role or submit an essay or apply for a cool-sounding job that you don't think you're qualified for? No one is watching if you happen to fail in your pursuit, and if they are, even better, they could learn something about the importance of sticking one's neck out in this life.

I walked through the apartment on a chilly day in mid-April, and all I could think about was a quote from Basquiat that I had picked up somewhere along the way: *Happiness will find you when you stop hiding.* I had literally been hiding under a dog-puke-stained comforter that had been in my mother's linen closet since before cars came with seatbelts, all day every day for two months, only emerging to smoke and text my friends to forget about me. It was hard to stop hiding. My trying muscles were atrophied. I felt like a starving, cranky bear with clumps of fur falling out after a long winter's nap. It was hard to stop being a tired, crabby bear, but I am glad that I did, because by some miracle, happiness found me that day and I officially became a resident of the neighborhood that I held so dear. I have never felt so lucky as I did that first day walking down my new block. No matter how dark the world's shadow feels, everything becomes dayglow as soon as I walk down my street, heading home to my little space in the world where I can just be me.

There are so many beloved small businesses that line Court Street and the surrounding area, like Court Pastry Shop, which is open three hundred and sixty-five days a year. This means that my Christmas-morning loneliness dissipates as soon as I sink my teeth into one of their shatteringly crisp sfogliatelle. Their homemade Italian ices are as quintessentially New York summertime as a burst fire hydrant. If you spend enough time talking to a neighbor who has lived in Carroll Gardens for more than five years, the conversation always leads to which bakery has the better lard bread, Caputo's or Mazzola's. I think both versions of the salumi-and-provolone-packed loaf have their strengths—Mazzola's has slightly bigger chunks of salami; Caputo's is heavier on the coarsely ground black pepper, which I count as a plus—and I would take either one as a part of my last meal. But I almost always get mine from Caputo's because that is *my* bakery.

Caputo's bakery is classic, and perfectly unmodern. The only thing that has changed in the past seventy-five years is the addition of a new and very talented baker who started making the best sourdough baguettes, croissants, and bialys that I have ever had. Older women from the neighborhood stand behind the counter packing up boxes of marzipan-rich rainbow cookies and bagging pillow-stuffed, cracker-crisp-coated, sesame-seeded Italian breads, sourdough fougasse generously coated with crunchy sea salt, and focaccia so fluffy that it would blow away like dandelion seeds if you held it to the wind. Caputo's bakery is totally perfect, and is only surpassed in my heart by Caputo's Fine Foods (strangely of no relation), just down Court Street.

At Caputo's, freshly made pastas fill the display refrigerators, and a never-ending influx of locals come to get their daily goods, almost all of whom make sure to include the tender house-made mozzarella in their order. Caputo's was opened in 1973 by Giuseppe and Flora Caputo. Their son Frank still works at the shop, grinding pecorino to order and making lasagna sheets, alongside his sons Franco and Joseph, who are determined to keep the much beloved shop serving its lovingly prepared food to its loyal regulars for decades to come. When I walk into these places, the people behind the counter say, *Hey Zahra, how are you?* Being greeted by name, and doing so in return, is one of the many things that makes a neighborhood so special.

Carroll Gardens and Cobble Hill sit side by side, nestled amid Red Hook, Brooklyn Heights, and the East River. While the boundaries are invisible to the average person, people from the neighborhood are well aware of the borders, even as gentrification tries its hardest to homogenize all of New York City into one unrecognizable lump brought to you by tech-bro coffee shops.

Cobble Hill, in comparison, is more posh, and has been gentrified for longer. The Italian influence is not as strong, but the small-town vibes are still alive at Cobble Hill Cinemas, KC Arts, Staubitz and Paisanos butcher shops, Hibino, Fish Tales seafood market, Shelsky's Appetizing, Brooklyn Wine Exchange, and of course Sam's Pizza, which is like walking into the set of *Goodfellas*. I think they have the best plain pie in the city, and it's only made more delicious by how safely protected it is from changing tastes. Brucie was right next door to Sam's, and while it only lasted for six years, I know that for many people it felt like a neighborhood institution, and that was its greatest accomplishment. Being a part of the community and feeding people who lived in it was hugely important to us, and while there were many ways in which I missed the mark at Brucie, I succeeded in enmeshing it into the fabric of the neighborhood ecosystem.

South of Union is Carroll Gardens, and that is where things start getting very Italian. Private, unmarked social clubs, bakeries and delis where people order in slang that always ends in a vowel, and the guy who lies out shirtless in a lawn chair in front of his flower shop from which people are not actually allowed to buy flowers, every day from sunup till sundown when the temperature is above seventy degrees. There are dozens of single-family brownstones with a Madonna and child statue out front, and old folks who sit in their front gardens all day, judging the new neighbors and passing the hours until it's time to walk to their bakery of choice for a loaf of seeded. Rising costs and changing tastes might have pushed out Esposito's pork store and forced out most of the old-school restaurants, but my neighbor Albert and his septuagenarian crew still sit out in front of D'Amico coffee shop each afternoon and say things like *fa shkeeve* when a cockroach crawls by in the summer.

My local pizzeria Lucali may have become famous, rocketing the owner, Mark Iacono, to A-list celebrity status, but he is and always will be a shy, sweet guy from the block. He has told me stories about what it was like when he was growing up in the seventies and eighties, about how each block had its own social club, and they were essentially like mini gangs who fought each other at night after days spent playing pinochle and eating *prushiot* and *mozzarell sanguitches*. People wait in line for three-plus hours for his pizza, but I'm here for the stories and the friendship shared over Marlboro Reds and Manhattan Specials. But if you do get a table, don't miss the calzone.

When you walk down any given street in Carroll Gardens, you're likely to hear one lady in her sixties telling her friend about her mother's skin condition. *Madone, that's horrible. I'll ask Father Giolitti to pray for her. I brought a ziti with some tomatez from the garden with fresh mootz, so at least youz don't have to worry about dinner tonight.* My neighbor Albert and his brothers have lived in the brownstone next door since they were babies. His lawn is immaculate and adorned with several miniature American flags. We do not align politically, and I don't care that he busts my balls and calls me *gagootz,* because I know that he would do almost anything to help me if I needed it. These kinds of relationships, ones that are built upon something more primitive and human, are deeply important to me. Underneath all of the collections of attributes and ideals that we layer ourselves with is a synonymous core, a kindred beating heart that pumps the exact same sticky red liquid. That nucleus is what makes a community. That is the gestalt that I live by, and the one that has saved me from the worst that life has sent in my direction.

As a young person, the mythos of New York City was like a sacred text scrawled between the margins of the East and Hudson rivers, and in the twenty-plus years I have spent in this venerable metropolis, it has become the only church I chose to pray at because it delivered tenfold on the promise of salvation. I was redeemed by its vastness and unparalleled abundance of different kinds of people, cultures, cuisines, and ideologies. I was delivered by the intimacy that can be found with perfect strangers. I am filled with fervor, a true believer, because while it can sometimes be wicked and rotten on the outside, it has the most vibrant and magical core. I love the slice at Joe's for the same reason I love lasagna and New York—very good sauce, and plenty of it. This place is all sauce and it is more delicious than I could have imagined all those years ago, and even when it burns my heart, I love it all the same.

We did a thing at Brucie, a lasagna service of sorts, where you could bring in your pan from home, and we would bake a fabulous lasagna in it for you. As cutesy as this may have been, it wasn't a gimmick; it was meant to help create personal connections with our customers, and it did just that. As one of the most emotionally charged dishes that I can think of, lasagna naturally helped forge a heartfelt bond with the people we prepared it for. We made dozens of types of lasagna over the years at Brucie, from our classic with red sauce, with house-made mozzarella and ricotta, provolone, and tons of Pecorino Romano, to a summertime special with heirloom tomatoes, sweet corn, and goat's milk cheese, to wild creations like rabbit ragù layered between bright orange sheets of carrot and tumeric pasta.

A few months after opening Brucie, I was invited to be a guest on Martha Stewart's TV show to make lasagna with her. I passed away upon hearing this news and was reanimated in the green room several weeks later, and somehow managed to pull myself together and attempt to *teach* the domestic goddess herself how to make a lasagna. She was very kind, and I managed not to make a complete idiot out of myself, and a little birdie told me that she actually took the leftovers home for dinner. My mother is not the celebrity-worshipping type, but I think that seeing the same daughter who she had assumed for many years might not really make it standing next to Martha, cracking jokes and tearing mozzarella, made her feel like she had done at least a few things right, which was true. To this day, every time I meet a new guy, she tells me on the first date to show him my *Martha Stewart tape*.

. . .

I AM VERY LUCKY to have an apartment that I love because I spent a great deal of time stuck in it during a very dodgy and frightening time in 2020 and 2021 that I chose not to refer to by name for fear of summoning it back to life like the Candyman. After Brucie I had picked up the pieces by starting a boutique catering business, and quickly realized how little people need catering when society begins to collapse.

My neighborhood was nervous and still. People avoided each other like the plague, because there was a plague. No more bopping up to Frankie's to yuck it up with Nicky and Betty. No more cheeseburgers and martinis and local gossip at Henry Public with Marty and Christian. Rest in peace to the olive bar at Sahadi's. I actually missed the line of tourists and Carroll Gardens sojournists wrapping around the block for Lucali. I missed everything, but mostly what I had taken for granted, despite how important it was to me, was my community. I missed bumping into my beloved Brucie regulars like Sam and Sarah and giving them big hugs. I had never considered how wide six feet was, and how deeply it impacted one's ability to connect with others.

Here in New York City, we tangle with each other like seaweed in a tide, moving with the cluster so we are never too far out to sea all alone. This time made us all into lonely strands of seaweed, with no real idea of when the tide would come in and bring back the rhythm. But though New York may slow, it never truly stops, and in a few months' time, the water began to move in and out and I went with it.

I had never thought of opening another restaurant. Brucie had not only burned me out, but more importantly illuminated the ways in which I no longer wished to be. Owning a restaurant doesn't inherently make one dysfunctional, but it tempted the rabid dog inside me with bloody meat every day. Also, I have no desire to run out of my bed at three in the morning because a porter's key breaks off in the door, or deal with the New York City Department of Health and Mental Hygiene.

One time in 2013, the health department came right before service for one of their lovely surprise inspections. A visit from the DOH is kind of like having an unplanned colonoscopy but more inconvenient and uncomfortable. During the inspection, the inspector found a few mouse droppings in a far-off corner, way behind the walk-in. Brucie was sparklingly clean, but almost every restaurant in the entire city has the occasional mouse. That doesn't mean that they were backstroking through the vodka sauce, just visiting occasionally, and realizing the place was sealed up better than Fort Knox before moving along. Regardless, the guy found mouse poop, and I immediately told him it was not mouse poop, it was black rice. I picked it up and told him I would eat it to prove it was, indeed, rice. Just before I got the literal mouse shit into my human mouth, the health inspector violently swatted my hand, sending the rice/poop to the floor, and scolding me: *MA'AM! YOU ARE ABOUT TO EAT MOUSE POOP, I CANNOT LET YOU DO THAT. GET A HOLD OF YOURSELF!*

Mouse droppings carry with them a roughly two-thousand-dollar fine, and almost certainly a B grade, which makes people think your place is a sloppy mess and decide to eat next door at the restaurant that happened to vacuum their mouse shit right before DOH stopped in. This is why I had never considered opening another restaurant: too dangerous to *my* health and mental hygiene. But during the dark days, chefs started doing pop-ups, and I realized that this might just be a viable way to check all of the boxes of what I loved about Brucie, without the outrageous stress, constant financial instability, and pressure to ingest animal excrement.

By late 2020, I had reached my threshold for loneliness. I wanted to be back in the world, and for the world to exist again in a way that I knew how to be a part of. I walked the same streets that had brought so much effortless joy ever since I had been in the neighborhood, and while they were still just as beautiful, there was emptiness and silence in the air that used to be filled with living. I had wanted Brucie back in some way since the day I walked out the door for the last time, even though I knew the relationship was toxic. What I missed, as with any bygone relationship, were the highs. The inside jokes that went on for days. The passion that I once had in making food for the masses, and the ability to be a part of an industry that was definitely fractured, but also fabulous and vital to the rolling thunder that is this great city. Restaurants may be problematic, but they are also fucking incredible. They are time capsules for the most rich, complicated, and romantic moments in our lives, the backdrop for the pivotal scenes and the celebrations, and the shitty days that can only be made better by French fries and a stiff drink at the bar surrounded by strangers. I longed to be a part of that in some small way again, and in the midst of this global crisis, I took a chance to get back in, *just in case*.

After Brucie closed, I had continued to make lasagnas for anyone who asked when I had the time. When there was a cause or organization that I wanted to raise money for, I would bake a few dozen and donate the profits. So I decided to try doing a lasagna-based pop-up, and called it Zaza, after the short-lived business that my parents had in the eighties that ultimately led to their bankruptcy and divorce. One could read this as a bad omen, but I thought of it as a way to pay homage to their efforts.

I enlisted the help of my two good friends and former Brucie chefs, Ryan and Steven, and Zaza Lazagna was born. We started out cooking in the basement of Shelsky's of Brooklyn, a Jewish deli run by some lovely colleagues of ours, Peter and Lewis. They let us use the space for free at night after their staff had finished working for the day. We would start at around five in the evening and finish around two in the morning, on Wednesdays and Thursdays for our Lasagna Friday pickups. From the first week we launched we were selling out, packing up over a hundred orders for people to heat and eat at home. I knew that there were still Brucie loyalists in the neighborhood, but I had underestimated just how many, and how big Zaza was going to get in such a short amount of time.

We had a small menu: classic red sauce lasagna, plus weekly specials like vodka sauce lasagna with peas and spinach, or carbonara-style with crispy guanciale and egg yolk–laced béchamel. We only made pasta dishes that were good reheated, so any classic preparation, like cacio e pepe or aglio e olio, was reimagined as a lasagna. We always had not-my-grandfather's meatballs in red sauce, a hearty soup like Italian wedding or pasta e fagioli, a classic entrée like chicken parm or pork chops with vinegar peppers or beef braciole, and sides like garlicky broccoli rabe or squash and cauliflower caponata. We served massive, size-of-your-thigh garlic breads, made on Caputo's bakery's extra-large sesame Italian loaves, slathered with Brucie's famous tomato butter. And there were desserts like ricotta tiramisu and my dad's pineapple-heavy carrot cake.

The conditions working late at night in a basement were rough, but we were happy to be making food for people, and most of all, seeing how much joy this little project was bringing to our customers' lives. We partnered up with our buddies across the street at Brooklyn Wine Exchange, offering little free glasses of white and red each week to pair with our menu. This was a time when we were collectively all going out of our minds, getting sick of the people we were trapped in the house with, worried about getting a deadly illness, losing our jobs and our hope, and missing the way the world used to work.

Zaza didn't cure the sick, but it made Friday nights better for a few hundred people each week, and it inadvertently gave my life the meaning that had been sterilized out of it with Lysol and Purell.

I loved our customers at Brucie. It was not for a second lost on me how lucky we were to have such loyal, kind, and enthusiastic people joining us night after night, and I had cared very much about them enjoying the food and their experience. But something had shifted now that I was running Zaza, not only in the obvious change of format, but in the drive behind the entire project. This was about trying to offer some type of healing to the community and city that had given me so much. At Brucie, it was all about what *the chef recommends,* and yes that is cringy, but it's true. I wanted to show off what I could do. Brucie was the *what* and Zaza was the *why*. At Brucie I was telling and at Zaza I was listening. What kind of food do people need right now in the dead of winter, trapped in their houses, worried and stressed and fed up with the endless bullshit? They wanted classic comfort, and they wanted it with a smile, and that is what we set about to give them. The meaning it gave me was life-altering because I got the opportunity to finally really get the picture, and to understand what cooking for people is really meant to be about.

We got thirty seconds to interact with our customers each week, and I was determined to make those thirty seconds as densely packed with care as I could without coming off as creepy or unhinged. People lined up around the block to pick up their brown paper bags, filled to the brim with chicken marsala and lasagna amatriciana and chocolate and butterscotch budino that three old friends had made in a tiny basement in the middle of the night. We had dozens of folks who ordered from us every week, and those thirty seconds with them was the thing that gave me hope for my own future and for my city's.

What had started as an experiment got us a *New Yorker* review and several other pieces of amazing press. I hadn't been sure after Brucie if my work would ever be recognized on that scale again, or if I even wanted it to. When I had Brucie, I felt almost addicted to the press. Getting a write-up or being on TV was like a fix that I needed to make all the other bullshit feel worth it. The sixteen-year-old me only believed she had grown up to be worth a damn when someone else was telling her so in writing. But when the *New Yorker* review of Zaza came out, I was able to appreciate it in a whole new way. It felt great to be recognized for our hard work, but I knew in my bones that we were onto something good, and what had come to matter to me more than anything was giving people a small slice of joy during a very challenging time.

Our takeaway pasta test-drive had turned into a full-blown lasagna-thon. It was such a success that after our summer hiatus in 2021, we returned in the fall for one more four-month run, still just Ryan, Steven, and me cooking, and our dear friend Ali helping out at the door. When the guys and I went our separate ways after 2022, my best friend Mary, who was on summer break from her job as a professor, did a summer run of Zaza with me, serving warm-weather fare like BBQ chicken, ribs, and giant summer salads. We had lots of at-the-door specials like biscuits, homemade ice cream, and Italian ices, and fluffy corn breads packed with blueberries and goat cheese.

By fall 2022, I had also enlisted the help of Zach, a barista from my local coffee shop. They said that they wanted to learn more about professional cooking, and while I don't know how professional I am, I told them I would teach them how to make meatballs and superglue their wounds together. We moved our operations around the corner to a huge commercial kitchen space, where we were finally able to work during the day and aboveground. We had more time to work, and so much more space, so were able to take our time and do much more creative things.

Zach soared as a cook, and is a pastry wizard and one of my favorite people I have ever had the privilege to work with. We would page through cookbooks and spot fun things we wanted to make, and they would knock it all out of the park. People lined up an hour in advance to score Zach's baked goods and my savory specialties. Zach made hundreds of hand pies filled with everything from peaches and raspberries, to creamy chicken and vegetables, to sausage and broccoli rabe. They rolled pistachio crème–filled morning buns and coated them in crunchy cardamom sugar, filled freshly fried doughnuts with blueberry jam, and spun batch after batch of ice cream and sorbet. We had sourdough Sicilian pizza and giant stromboli. We made dips and spreads galore, from house-smoked swordfish salad to classic spinach and artichoke and olive tapenade. There was always an assortment of massive cookies and tall, flaky buttermilk biscuits served with a quarter-inch-thick slab of butter. On Easter I made the Tangorra family's famous pizza rustica. We would do a Greek Week menu every month or so, paying homage to the Long Island Greek diners I grew up frequenting as a kid, and I rolled hundreds of spanakopita, just like my parents had at The Lovin Oven.

I had never in my life enjoyed the process of cooking so much, either professionally or at home, as I did in that last year of Zaza. I was truly happy, and inspired, and not bogged down by the constant stress that came with running a restaurant and managing a staff. Zach and I spent our time joking around and cooking really fun food that was unfussy and unpretentious and made people happy. I came home every night exhausted, but in the right way, from a hard day's work that I really enjoyed and felt proud of. I would have stayed there, in that moment, with those people, for the rest of my days if I could have, with spirit that felt as light as freshly whipped cream and gratitude so great it was almost too heavy to hold.

But I knew that the moment was not meant to be more than that, and had we kept it going much longer, we would have been the last one at the party. New York is fickle, and the business model that we had created, regardless of how popular it was, would eventually become less so the further we moved away from the plague. People would eventually stop planning their weekly meals the way they had during the dark days and return to their regular way of eating, and that was a good thing. You need to be able to accept when all the cocaine is finished and it's time to take yourself home and get some rest.

Zaza was supremely special to me, and I would like to think it was to a lot of other people too, and I wanted it to live on in our collective hearts as such. I made a lot of mistakes both personally and professionally during that three-year run, some that I would give anything to correct and do over, but that is what happens when you are a person, and as much as I wish that fact was not so, alas. I tried, really hard, leading with my heart, and even if it got broken, I will never regret knowing true joy and love, and also knowing when to walk away.

I also knew that as much as I loved this project with all my heart, it was meant to be a part of my life, a true chapter. I had no desire to take it to the next level. I did not wish to build a lasagna empire, or any empire of any kind; I wished to explore my creativity and passions and see what else was out there for me. Zaza was a project, similar to a film, and when a film has been shot, edited, and presented to an audience, the filmmaker goes on to make their next one, and that is how I felt about what we had done with the pop-up. It didn't mean there could never be a sequel, it just meant that I was looking for new material to sink my teeth into.

On the day of our last pickup, Ali, Zach, and I packed over a hundred orders. We set up our specials racks and tables and gave out chips and dip and Jell-O shots to the line of sweet people that stretched two full city blocks. Right before the doors opened, my agent called me to let me know that The Dial Press wanted to publish my book. I put the phone down and laughed into a hard cry at the bizarre and beautiful nature of timing, barely even being able to comprehend how lucky I was. I never saw the past and future dance together so gracefully, and I am sure I never will again, but in that moment I realized the power of surrender.

. . .

A NEIGHBORHOOD, AT ITS BEST, is a community, is a tribe, is an oasis. Cecei says, *Hi baby, how we doing today? How's your mom feeling?* when I walk into Caputo's bakery. When my neighbor Albert or his wife get sick, I make them soup. When my car is coated in ice that I can't get off because I refuse to purchase the proper tools, Mark does it for me. When I am too sad to talk to my friends and family, I walk into the coffee shop where I met Zach and shoot the breeze with the baristas, or into Brooklyn Wine Exchange to talk about weird movies with my friend Thomas, and I walk out having found my voice again. When I was at my rock bottom, I took refuge in my little apartment with a big kitchen and started my ascent upward. When I miss my father, I sit at the bar at Frankie's and talk to my friends there and eat eggplant marinara, thinking how much he liked eggplant marinara, and how good his was, and the pain shape-shifts. When I was twenty-six and totally green, people came into Brucie and ate dinner and had a nice time, and made it possible for me to find some much-needed purpose. My co-workers came through the subterranean doorway at 234 Court Street for their shifts and helped me know what it was like to have a family. This neighborhood has given me so much, more than I could ever possibly manage to repay, but I hope that with Zaza I was able to make a small dent in showing my appreciation and love for a community that has saved my life a dozen times over, layered with care and intention. With goodwill and special ingredients and served with a great deal of love.

Zaza Lazagna

LASAGNA IS A LOVE LANGUAGE, AND THIS ONE IS EASY TO SPEAK. I like to use fresh pasta sheets, unboiled, as I think it gives the finished product the perfect texture, not too runny, which can often be an issue with lasagna. No-boil dry noodles also work just fine, but if fresh is an option, go for that! The great thing about lasagna is that it can be a huge mess on the inside, but once it's baked, it will look and taste beautiful, so don't stress too much about the appearance before it goes in for a sauna. This recipe serves 8 to 10 people, but you can easily divide it in half if you have a smaller pan. If you have extra, don't sweat it! You don't have to eat lasagna all day every day for a month straight! Just toss that baby in an airtight container and freeze for up to three months!

SERVES 8 TO 10

2 tablespoons extra-virgin olive oil
1 cup water
1 pound (8 sheets) fresh lasagna noodles
9 cups marinara sauce (page 26)
6 cups ricotta cheese
4 cups shredded or small diced fresh mozzarella cheese
1 pound thinly sliced or shredded provolone cheese
2 cups finely grated Pecorino Romano cheese

Preheat the oven to 350°F.

Rub the olive oil around the interior of a 9 x 13–inch baking dish. Pour the water and 1 cup of the marinara on the bottom. This creates a nice base and ensures the sauce won't burn to the bottom. Don't worry if water seeps into the first layer, it's all good!

Cover the bottom of the pan with pasta sheets. Spread 2 cups of marinara evenly over the pasta, followed by one-third of the ricotta in big dollops, evenly spaced. Then sprinkle over one-third of the mozzarella, one-third of the provolone, and one-quarter of the pecorino. Repeat 3 times. The top layer will be 2 cups of sauce and ½ cup pecorino.

Cover with a layer of parchment paper, then tightly seal with foil. Place the baking dish on a sheet pan to catch any drips, place in the oven, and bake for 1 hour. Remove the foil and return to the oven for 25 minutes. Allow to cool 20 minutes before serving (if you can wait that long!) for best results when slicing.

Enjoy every last bite, and don't forget to lick the plate!

SPAGHETTI MARINARA

As a chef, I am often asked what my last meal would be, or what my favorite food is. There is an expectation here that the answer will be either very fancy or super iconic: Doritos or caviar, or perhaps even a combination of the two.

When I started getting asked this question regularly, my answer was always bread and butter. This was honest for the most part, but also provocative in its simplicity and timeless grace and appeal. This response made me feel like someone who wears linen pants in the summer and has an expensive couch, and a special wicker basket that I take to the farmers market, but also smokes a cheeky cigarette once in a while. A woman who does not wake up with searing anxiety, and feels naturally radiant without makeup. Someone whose joy is effortless and who has been blessed with an above-average metabolism. I do not wear linen because it gets too wrinkly and makes me feel like a scarecrow, even if I am able to channel Diane Keaton for about forty-five seconds whenever I try. My couch was reasonably priced and purchased with a promo code from my favorite podcast, and I often forget to bring my own bag to the farmers market and end up walking home with loose potatoes falling through the cracks of my elbows and into a dirty puddle.

I love bread and butter. It is the greatest food combination that mankind has managed to come up with, and I place its significance in my life alongside that of my parents, but this is an answer that I *wish* to be true. An answer that makes me a different woman with less anxiety, more discipline, and a more breathable wardrobe.

. . .

A TRUER ANSWER WOULD be peanut butter. More specifically, peanut butter eaten directly from the jar. I like it salted creamy, room temperature, with maple syrup drizzled in, and a hefty pinch of flaky sea salt to finish. I assemble my mise en place and add streams of syrup and sprinklings of salt, bite by bite, until I have eaten a quarter of the jar. Sometimes I skip the syrup and salt and let the peanut butter speak for itself, and for this preparation I typically abandon the spoon, implementing nature's utensil, the fingers, or a carrot or celery stick if the contents of the jar are too low to scoop. Sometimes I get out the raspberry jelly and make little perfect bites and shovel them into my mouth. Whenever I eat peanut butter, I say out loud to myself, *MMM, I love peanut butter.* This is odd, but the words do make their way from my lips each and every time I imbibe.

Eating peanut butter from the jar is a personal experience, one you can only have at home, typically alone. It is not served in restaurants. It is not practical to eat while walking down the street. Friends do not serve it at dinner parties. It is a private pleasure like taking a bath or masturbating. Eating peanut butter from a jar is like my version of a black leather couch, or a *Scarface* poster: a totem of my rugged independence. There is a power in embracing the things you wish would not define you but follow like a shadow.

This is also how I feel about being single. I am very good at it, but I wish it did not feel forced upon me. I wish that when I walked around my neighborhood alone, I didn't imagine people wondering what on earth could be wrong with me that I am always roaming the streets unattended to. I must be *one of those women.* The kind that is too intense, or dramatic, or fucked up to be doing errands with a loving partner. *She must have pushed him away. She must have loved him too much. She must be crazy.* And maybe this is all true, or half of it, or none of it, but the *people* judging me for this are all living in my brain, and to get them to shut the fuck up, I dance alone in the mirror in my underwear, stay up late watching nineties action movies every night before bed, and eat peanut butter from the jar with my fingers. *Ha!* I say. *I bet you boring, miserable relationship people wish you could taste freedom like this!* Freedom tastes like peanut butter. Making a batch of hearty, nourishing vegetable soup that could fortify my body with vitamins and minerals for the whole week is giving up. I'd rather buy the vegetables and watch them wither while I remain in control of the narrative of my life.

But my actual favorite food is spaghetti with marinara sauce, heaps of pecorino cheese, and a hefty glug of good olive oil. Spaghetti is the only pasta that emotionally affects me. As far as I am concerned, you can take every other pasta shape and give it back to L'Artusi. I will eat almost anything, but as far as a food that would hurt my soul to live without, the sultry slurp of spaghetti strands is the only shape that would truly break my heart should it tell me it's over.

As a child, my mother would make me spaghetti with Prego jarred tomato sauce that she would add a spoonful of sugar to. When I was around seven, I had a meltdown on the school bus one day, crying and refusing to ride home on it, while the other children made fun of me, fueling my panic into a full-blown hysterics. Someone from the school took me off the bus and waited with me until my mother was able to come and pick me up in her silver Subaru. When she arrived, I clung to her, digging my little nails into her back, burying my face in her mess of curly black hair. We drove the twenty minutes to our house, me reacclimating to the air and the trees and the feeling of the ground beneath me. I was still alive.

My mother sweetly asked me what I wanted for dinner. *You can have anything you want,* she said, because she wanted my pain to go away. Sometimes, when I squeeze my brain, I remember her this way, and to be fair, these moments were not as rare as my trauma wills me to believe.

Through a clogged nose, I replied, *Spaghetti and tomato sauce, the way you make it with a little sugar.*

When we got home, I curled up in the brown corduroy loveseat in our living room to watch television, and a short while later she brought me a big, steaming hot bowl of sweeter-than-average spaghetti with tomato sauce and heaps of grated pecorino and olive oil, and I was safe.

When I was in my twenties, I made spaghetti for my best friends Alexis, Kyle, Nert, and Alison and sometimes other random stragglers at our weekly Sunday night dinners. We ate it out of a big pot placed in the center of the table. We would finish the portions on our plates and go for seconds by plunging our forks directly into the pot, then thirds as we pinched strands of pasta with our fingers and dangled them into our mouths. We drank bad wine that made us feel good. We told jokes and smoked pot and laughed because while we were around this table, we were free. I made the sauce from scratch, and I put a little extra sugar in it, and everyone thought it was delicious. I didn't think of my mother or the crying on the bus, but those moments were with me, in my watering eyes as I minced the onions and tossed them into the pot to soften. I was present in these times, which was something I had often struggled with. But here, I was present for the delight of the twirling of warm noodles in my mouth, reminding me what is important: friendship, laughter, pleasure. I was present for the precious company I was in, and isn't that the whole thing about a last meal?

Your last meal is not only your favorite food, it is the most important one. What would you eat to feel happy one last time? What edible matter made you feel love in your life? How did it make you love back, and who, and where were you when this all happened? What could you eat in your final moments with a beating heart that could bring you back to the best times, the times before everything became such a mess? Almost everyone has a favorite food no matter how complicated this life has been. Something that transports them to a moment of unencumbered pleasure.

I love bread and butter, but it will not bring me back to my mother and her most loving moments, or being weightless around the table with my favorite people, or make linen fall on my hips the way it does Diane Keaton's. My eyes roll back in delight when I eat peanut butter, but I would not crave standing in my underwear in an open refrigerator, fingering a jar of peanut butter in place of dinner because I am too depressed to buy real groceries. Take me to my mother, the version of her who adored me and held me. Take me to Bamonte's on Christmas Eve, with a room filled with families who have all left their pain and troubles in the car for a few hours. Take me to the Amalfi Coast, sitting on a slab of rock looking onto the sparkling sea, feeling the day's worth of sunshine radiating from the ground as my best friend Michael and I inhale spaghetti vongole and say over and over how this is the best time we have ever had in our entire lives. Take me to Sunday dinner with my friends and let me eat from the pot until I am too full to move, and curl up on the couch to drift to sleep in front of the fire.

My favorite food is belonging. Twisted and twirled up, in love and being loved. Piping hot, prepared with intention and eaten with gusto. The last thing I would want to eat would make me think of my friendships, which kept me alive when I felt too sad for this world, or of my favorite restaurants, which gave me something to truly look forward to: a temple of laughter and too many negronis and just the right amount of ambient candle light, a Rorschach of red wine stains on the tablecloth. Spaghetti is my favorite because it makes me feel close to my mother, so close I can feel the exact temperature of her skin, and smell her hair, and I need something that can bring her back to me exactly that way, because it reminds me that it wasn't all bad.

Spaghetti is messy, and so am I. Too messy for linen pants or a nice couch, and I prefer it that way. I was not born to be bread and butter, or an oyster, or a stack of pancakes. Those are lovely things, lovely ways to be. I know oysters and they are graceful, and I envy that in them. I didn't try an oyster until I was twenty or so, and for me this means it could never truly be my favorite. Spaghetti makes me six years old, and I sometimes need a time machine to bring me back to such purity, the days before I knew too much. Every time I eat it, I can be that little person again, if only for a few slurps.

Painful memories have a way of eclipsing every other thing that ever happened in our lives, leaving us to believe that we are a jar of half-eaten peanut butter rather than a warm bowl of something delicious and special. There is magic tangled in a plate of spaghetti, in knowing that sometimes we were held and loved, and there is something we can touch that becomes a hearth when we need warming.

My last meal would be spaghetti marinara, or a steamed lobster and corn on the cob, drowned in butter, with my mother, watching her suck the guts out like a hungry seal. Or it would be my father's pizza rustica, but only if he made it with his big smushy, sausage-fingered hands. Those hands are now gray powder, so maybe instead it would be the meatballs and creamy polenta left in the steam tray after dinner service at Brucie, which we would all swarm around, dipping in our giant spoons for big bites after a long night of hard work, washing it down with gulps of silky Maule Masieri Garganega. Or maybe a roast chicken with a beloved, while things were good, before it all broke in half. Because this is all about love and how to unbreak it. Love is like a wishbone made of need and desire, which snaps apart again and again throughout a life, and my very last wish would be the ability to glue it back together somehow. Maybe with my grandmother's matzah balls, or ribs from Bobby Rubino's on my seventh birthday. Maybe I could die happy if I could remember the flavor.

What moment do you want to live in forever, and what does it taste like? What does it smell like? Who is there with you? In my life, love has often been an enigma, a word on the tip of my tongue that I cannot seem to find when I need it. Four simple letters that I am no good at spelling. But I know I can give it. I can give it like air to a fire. If I never receive the love I desire, I know that I have at least given that love to someone, and I hope they could taste it.

Love is never giving up on an answerless question. Love is trying your best to say soft phrases when things feel hard. Love is hoping it gets better, and knowing you are in the moment when it finally does, even if that moment goes out like a candle at the end of a very nice dinner. May we all be illuminated if only for as long as it takes to eat a good meal and laugh over great stories. Love is trying to get to the point, and it is the point, and the point is fixed and also fluid, so drink it up because there might be a drought. Love is running around until you can stand still. Love is a sweetness and a call to indulge. Love is why I do everything, and also why I seem to do nothing at all. Why my savings account is empty. Why I write. Why I breathe. Why I lie awake and why I dream about him every night, no matter what, always. If love made sense to me, I would be rich, but I'm not because I have poured all my earnings into figuring it out. If love made sense to me, I would know what to order before it was all over. Like David Lynch said, *Keep your eye on the doughnut, not the hole.* So maybe a doughnut. Maybe a bagel. Maybe just something to remind me what was instead of what wasn't. When I felt love, when I gave love, when I could touch and taste it.

APPLE STRUDEL

THERE WAS THE ROAD, AND THEN IN AN INSTANT, THERE WAS not.

There was dry desert littered with thorny cacti. There was a still and silent December night, completely indifferent to the panic and the screams that echoed through the canyon. There were chevron floors and a thick red velvet curtain, and I saw figures moving and heard voices whispering behind it, and though I was tempted to see what lay beyond, I took my blood-soaked body and went out the door instead.

In the scramble to hold on to my life, I thought of absolutely nothing except the inches I could manage to see in front of my face. I thought of nothing but survival, no time to remind myself what I was surviving for. Everything was tight and narrow. I have never been more present, and I hope to never be again in such a violent manner, but I do search for it in meditation, trying to dial into that focus from the safety of my couch. It's not the same, and neither am I. I am better at living today than I was before I almost died. It wasn't easy, but it happened. I took the long way, but I got to see the leaves change. I stayed alive to taste my mother's apple strudel a hundred more times. I had not eaten enough of it before my first and only visit to El Centro, California, and I had not told her how much I loved it, and her. I had to live to get to know her, to give her the chance to say she was sorry, and to eat the warm flaky strudel that my grandmother had taught her to make. I had to live to see the sky get bigger, to learn that country roads lead to superhighways, and back again, to trails in thick forests with tall trees that are centuries old. I had to become the auteur behind the lens of my own life, and make peace with love, and both the lack of it and the wealth of it.

I have made a mess of a great many things in my travels from there to here, and I am lucky to have had the chance to do so. And I have also made amends, and friends, and delicious food that I hope helped to turn some bad days good for some people, sometimes. I saw fire and brimstone after the bus was pulled back down to the earth, but what I could not make out was that the road had actually come to a junction, and though the stretch I traveled down may have lacked pavement, it did have promise. In my memory, the crash was silent, everything as quiet as fresh snow. I know there was brutality in the quiet, which broke glass and bone, ripped skin and burned metal. It ruptured the inertia within me that saved my precious life. I was forced to learn that when you are scared, you are not meant to hold on, you are meant to let go.

It takes immense courage to unfasten the grip around the story of ourselves. We do it by loving, and allowing ourselves to be loved. By being vulnerable, and finding strength within our fragility. I don't know who I will be if I am not the girl who got into a horrible bus accident, if I stop writing this on my name tag and instead just put *Zahra*. If I stop believing that the only interesting or valuable thing about me is that I cheated death so I could make lasagna. If my first word was not really spanakopita. If I stop believing, finally, that I am unlovable. I have been afraid to pry my fingers from the edges of this narrative because letting it go is a freefall, and I am dizzy from falling, but I do love the view.

Letting go is a high practice, one that comes with years of repetition and many stumbles. It is making a fool of yourself and having your heart broken, because those things only ever happen when we become one with the tide. Letting go is not antithetical to fighting for what you want or believe in, it is essential to the possibility that those things can become true. When I was at my most despairing, my mother said, *Ask yourself: What can I hold on to so that I can let go?* I hold on to my humor, and to my friends. I let go of people who couldn't show up to love me or be loved by me, who aim to keep me outside of the locked door. I hold on to my spirit, because I know that while my body might slow and shrink, my spirit is evergreen and ever growing. Letting go is not the absence of fear, it is admitting, like my aunt Flo always used to say, that *fear is not a stop sign.*

. . .

I BOUGHT AN OLD rotary phone a few years after my father died at Yesterday's News, the beloved antique shop on Court Street near my house. I had seen a feature on the CBS Sunday morning program about a person who had set up a phone attached to a giant old tree in the redwood forest so that bereaved people could pick it up and talk to their loved ones who have passed away. Mine is beige with a number dial and a curly cord connecting the receiver and base, and it sits on a glass side table next to the squishy gray couch in my living room.

The last voicemail that my father left me was on New Year's Day 2018, exactly one month before he died. *It's me. I'm calling to wish you a happy New Year. Happy New Year! Um if you call back and I don't answer, that's because I'm still in my funk. F-U-N-K. And um I'm up I'm down, I'm awake I'm not. But I did want to wish you a happy 2018, and I hope everything, or most everything, or some things work out for you, and I know they will. I love you buddy, you take care, happy New Year, bye!*

The phone is not plugged into anything, but when you put it to your ear you can hear a static. Maybe this is true of all old rotary phones, but I choose to believe it is John, the twinkling reminiscence of his soul, at the ready to take my calls. I pick up the phone on days when I wish he were here the most. Christmas, Halloween, his birthday and mine, and of course, the first day of every New Year. I say, *I miss you Daddy, I wish you could come back. If you can hear me, please make the lights blink. Make your wind chimes clank together on the fire escape so I know you haven't left me for good.* I say, *Merry Christmas.* I tell him I have a broken heart and ask if he can please help to mend it. *There was a line two city blocks long for the last Zaza pop-up! I'm going to Italy tomorrow! I saw a shark today as I was leaving the beach.*

I don't bring up the last time we went to the beach together because I don't want to embarrass him, but I remember it. A few years before he died, he wanted me to take him to Jones Beach, where he had spent his summers as a kid splashing in the waves and doing tricky things under the boardwalk. He had a very hard time walking, and his flip-flops wouldn't stay on, and the hot sand burned his big, swollen feet. When we finally stopped, he tried to sit in his chair, but it collapsed beneath him. His newly purchased swim trunks fell down, and we had to turn around and get back to the car almost as soon as we had arrived at the water's edge. This is a memory that has made my heart turn to gasoline every time I think of it. How sad it was that this was the last time he got to see the ocean before being thrown into it as a pile of gray dust a few years later.

But I change my mind, and I say into the phone, *Remember when we went to the beach and you mooned everyone,* and I laugh, and I swear I can hear him laughing too through the static, the faint crashing of waves in the background. *Comedy = tragedy + time,* the only equation worth remembering. I tell John I am writing a book, that I am scared because I don't know if I can find the words, and if I do, how could I ever manage to make sense of them? *Help me find the words. Who was I to you? Who were you to me?* That honest wish, for *some things to work out,* that is how I have come to see the time between sunrise and sunset. A little bit of hope for a little bit of joy, and a reasonable prayer into the void, into the static beyond the beige receiver, for some great big love, for the breakdown and the come up, and the wish that it all works out.

I love you buddy, take care.

I will, I promise.

. . .

OUR LIVES ARE MORE than a series of superlative moments. More than just a highlight reel. They're the moments we don't remember. The day-to-day, the routine of how we prepare ourselves for sleep. The laundry, the drive to work, the breeze. The plainness, when things were steady. The meat of it. But the punctuations—the effervescent love affairs and the fractures that bore down to the marrow, and the mascara stains running down your cheeks like paths of moving glaciers, the wine stains on the table, and the smell of someone irreplaceable—that is the sauce, and I will take as much of it as I can until the pot is scraped dry.

When it does come time for me to watch the slideshow at the end of my life, I will see the moments when I asked for more, and lapped it up, unafraid of judgment or an impending stomachache. I will see the wound and the suture. I will see the fights I had with my mother, and the map that led us to find the buried treasure we hid long ago. I will see my father's grin spread from the corners of his eyes across his undulating lips when he listened to Charlie Parker play the saxophone, and smell his pea soup, hoping that if we are set to meet again, he will greet me with a steaming hot bowl. I will see him again through watery eyes the first time I see Brad's face and feel his incredibly familiar hug. I will see the times I held my heart between my outstretched palms, knowing it could possibly become smashed, but glad that I kept my hands open, because one day someone will gently take it into theirs and I will be glad I was not precious with it.

I will see my friends who made me laugh until my ribs hurt, thousands of times, and proved that being perfect wasn't necessary, or possible, or the point. Becky, Dan, Mary, Catherine, and I sitting around the pool in the summer, cracking jokes and doing handstands in the water like we did when we were children, drinking O'Malley Specials, equal parts bourbon and Fresca with a splash of lime, eating Carvel Flying Saucers—the world spinning to the reverberations of our joy. Floating in waters off the Amalfi Coast with my dear friend Michael, splashing the aquamarine sea at one another.

This is the best day of my life!

Me too!

The first time I saw *Jurassic Park* in a freezing cold movie theater. The sound of the beach. The smell of autumn. The view from the plane as it touches down in Rome. My lips on the back of David's neck. Interlocked fingers and very long kisses. I will see the bitter things, the scars and harsh words. Swollen eyelids in the morning. *I hate you. It's over. Please don't go.* Finding the strength to go forward back in New York over a plate of chicken parm with a side of spaghetti. A baked potato with sour cream and butter. A tomato sandwich in late August. A tall pile of nachos. Extra lemon. Too many negronis. I will see myself on a bench in Central Park with a tuna sandwich on rye from Barney Greengrass, and at Henry Public eating a burger, hot fat and red juices running down my wrists, dripping onto my copy of *Jaws.* Dancing in the kitchen with my mom and Rob to Talking Heads. My father playing me his favorite song: *You can't always get what you want, but if you try sometimes, you just might find, you get what you need.*

This is what it's all about, buddy, he tells me.

I will feel freedom from my physical being, knowing that nothing I have ever done in my life really mattered besides how and when I decided to use my heart. Our hearts are our legacy, everything else is melting ice. I will see my young body, with so much to learn, so many mistakes still left to make, go sailing through the air over a cliff, determined to live, grateful I did, and finally, all these years later, ready for a new story to tell.

Cue "Dream Baby Dream" . . .

Apple Strudel

WHEN I ASKED MY MOTHER FOR HER CHOCOLATE MOUSSE RECIPE, she said, *What chapter is the chocolate mousse going with?*

I replied, *Your chapter, of course!* and she was upset. I can tell when Bobbie is disappointed because there is a long, chilly pause that hangs in the air like a storm cloud. *I thought I would be apple strudel. I feel much more attached to apple strudel than chocolate mousse.*

Then I paused, and saw the version of me that up until recently would have become incredibly offended by this. I would have taken it to mean she didn't understand or care about me, and all of the effort I had made trying to put to words the way I love her, and that I couldn't just go back and rethink my whole concept for her chapter simply because she needed to be represented by a dessert she preferred. I would have started a fight and ended up saying things that hurt us both. But instead I simply said, *I'm sorry Mama, I have already written it, and I hope you like it when you read it. I did the best I could. I love you.* I was worried when I finished writing this book that perhaps I wasn't qualified to do so, because maybe I hadn't really grown enough to share my story. But in that moment, I knew that I believed I had.

SERVES 8 TO 10

FILLING:

5 pounds Granny Smith apples, peeled, cored, and thinly sliced (2 quarts when sliced)
4 tablespoons unsalted butter, melted
Finely grated zest and juice of 1 large lemon
1 cup brown sugar
⅓ cup all-purpose flour
2 teaspoons ground cinnamon
¼ teaspoon grated nutmeg
½ teaspoon ground cardamom
1 teaspoon kosher salt

NUT MIXTURE:

2 cups finely ground walnuts, hazelnuts, or pecans, or a mixture of all or any!
1 cup granulated sugar
1 teaspoon salt
1 tablespoon ground cinnamon

STRUDEL:

1 (1-pound) package phyllo dough, defrosted in the refrigerator
2 sticks (½ pound) salted butter, melted

Preheat the oven to 350°F.

Make the filling: In a large bowl, combine the apples, melted butter, lemon zest and juice, brown sugar, flour, cinnamon, nutmeg, cardamom, and salt and mix together until thoroughly combined. Set aside.

Make the nut mixture: Combine the nuts, sugar, salt, and cinnamon in a medium bowl and set aside.

Line a cutting board with parchment paper. Lay out two sheets of phyllo aligned horizontally and brush them generously with melted butter, then sprinkle evenly with one-third of the nut mixture. Repeat this 5 times, so that you have a stack of 10 total sheets of phyllo. Allow your last layer to be dry on top. Gently press down on the phyllo stack.

Working horizontally from the bottom of the dough, fold over a roughly 3-inch section of the phyllo stack on top of itself. Arrange the apple mixture as evenly as possible on top of this doubled-up portion of dough. Try to leave behind any extra juice when you scoop the apple mixture out of the bowl so that your pastry doesn't get too soggy.

Carefully roll the strudel up into a log and arrange it so that the doubled-up part of phyllo is on the bottom.

Use a knife to score the top with three small slits, roughly ½ inch each. Brush the top with the remaining melted butter.

Transfer the parchment with the phyllo to a baking sheet and bake for 30 minutes.

Cool on the counter for at least 1 hour for best results.

Enjoy, and cheers to Bobbie before you dig in!

ACKNOWLEDGMENTS

OH MY, WHERE TO START. THIS BOOK WAS MADE POSSIBLE BY a great many people, and I would like to take this opportunity to thank as many of them as I can in the allotted pages. To the pit orchestra, please do not play me off the stage.

I would like to begin by thanking my incredible literary agent, Jamie Carr. Jamie, I could not have done this without your endless support and expert guidance. You are the perfect mix of pragmatist and pixie, and it has been such a joy to work with and learn from you. Thank you for taking a chance on me, and to everyone at The Book Group, thank you for welcoming me into the fold.

To my sweet, wise, brilliant editor Clio Seraphim at The Dial Press, I am forever grateful for having you as a co-pilot in this process. Writing a memoir can be emotionally draining at times. There were things about my life that I would have preferred to forget rather than share with the world. Thank you for encouraging me to be brave and attempt to describe what often felt indescribable, and for laughing at the same strange parts that I did. You really made this experience so positive and empowering, and I couldn't have done it without you.

A ginormous thank you to the whole team at The Dial Press, especially Whitney Frick, for making me a part of the

Dial family. Whit, you are an incredible leader and I am humbled and honored to have a seat at the Dial table alongside such accomplished and talented authors. Thank you for believing in me and giving me this life-changing opportunity. Thank you to the lovely Leila Tejani for all your dedication and attention to detail throughout this process. And a huge thank you to everyone at Dial and Random House who worked on this book. To Donna Cheng and Alicia Tatone, who designed the beautiful cover of my dreams, and all the folks working behind the scenes in every job, from maintenance people to copy editors, your work is deeply important and I appreciate you.

Thank you to the incomparable Dana Cowin for giving me my first big writing break in your wonderful zine, *Speaking Broadly*. You do so much to help others shine, and I am so blessed to have had your mentorship and friendship. You are a spectacular person.

Greg Mollica, if I could afford a plane to skywrite THANK YOU I would, but I cannot, so I will say it here: THANK YOU!!!

Every time I have a question about basically anything in life, I ask my dear friend Liz Milch, because she is savvy and smart and she has all the answers. Thank you for your friendship, advice, limitless capacity for brainstorming, and enormous heart!

Nick freaking Fauchald, you are a stellar human. Thank you for always going out of your way to help me sparkle. I hope you feel the same about me even though I had food poisoning whilst catering your wedding.

To John Cassavetes, Spike Lee, Nora Ephron, David Lynch, Frank Capra, Akira Kurosawa, Alfred Hitchcock, Stanley Kubrick, Robert Altman, Francis Ford Coppola, Sergio Leone, Tony Scott, Ridley Scott, the Coen brothers, Mike Nichols,

Steven Spielberg, Brian De Palma, Howard Hawks, Ingmar Bergman, Joe Dante, Martin Scorsese, Paul Thomas Anderson, Sidney Lumet, Federico Fellini, Paul Schrader, John Carpenter, Wong Kar-wai, William Friedkin, Noah Baumbach, Richard Linklater, Wes Anderson, Rob Reiner, Nancy Meyers, Greta Gerwig, John Waters, Paul Verhoeven, Billy Wilder, Albert Brooks, Gena Rowlands, Denzel Washington, Jimmy Stewart, Bette Davis, Toshiro Mifune, Tom Hanks, Diane Keaton, Philip Seymour Hoffman, John Cusack, Marlon Brando, Gene Hackman, Harrison Ford, Sidney Poitier, Laura Dern, Arnold Schwarzenegger, Carrie Fisher, Charles Bronson, Michael Douglas, Steve Martin, Chevy Chase, Kevin Costner, Brad Pitt, Bruce Willis, John Candy, Joe Don Baker, George C. Scott, Martin Short, Pam Grier, Nicolas Cage, Elaine May, Meg Ryan, Mink Stole, Robin Williams, Keith David, Paul Reubens, Divine, Samuel L. Jackson, Kurt Russell, Julia Roberts, Jack Nicholson, Susan Sarandon, Paul Newman, Leo, De Niro, Pacino, Travolta, Christopher Walken, Warren Oates, Cher, Whoopi, Keanu, Winona, Swayze, Robert Redford, and most of all TOM CRUISE (plus countless others), for filling my life with movie magic. From an early age, I was able to decode life's most difficult puzzles through film. I learned to write from watching movies, by seeing how many infinite ways there are to tell the same story. It is almost always about love, just shot from different angles. While I may not be a religious person, I do pray daily at the church of cinema.

To my beloved Brucie crew, each and every one of you who I was fortunate enough to work alongside, thank you for your hard work and dedication. Thank you for teaching me and sticking by me even when I may not have deserved it. Thank you for inside jokes and bits that went on for days. I have never laughed so hard. Restaurants are chaotic and wild. You get burned and cut. You get drunk, you shoot the moon. But at their best they are so much more than that. They are little nooks in a great big world where you intersect with random people and find commonality in the strangest parts of yourselves. You guys made my life rich, meaningful, and extremely fun! Some of the best times I ever had were spent cooking and laughing at 234 Court Street, and I could not have done any of it without you all. This Bud's for you!

Thank you to Ryan, Steven, Zach, Ali, Herman, Mary, and Michelle for making Zaza possible. And to the lovely Cobble Hill/Carroll Gardens community of patrons and small business owners for supporting both Brucie and Zaza all these years. I hope you enjoyed your meals. And to the woman whose head I spilled spaghetti on, I am very, very sorry.

AD and Guy, you make even the most grueling of catering gigs feel whimsical and joyous! Thank you for that and also for continuing to teach me about how to best help our neighbors and our world.

Oh, Jennie Lupo, you goddess you. I have already written you a love letter, I hope you liked it. You're a real class act, J, the best of the best, a perfect ten. You are grace personified and I love you dearly.

Mary, Becky, Dan, I combine you, not because you are the same, you are wildly different and uniquely special to me, but because to me we will always be a group. We may not all be in close physical proximity to each other these days, but in my heart we all live in the O'Malley family's backyard, cooking breakfast over the fire and spending the day making each other laugh while splashing around in the pool. I really don't know who or what I would be today without you guys. There have been times in the past fifteen years since we all met that I have really struggled to find joy and purpose, but even when it is hard to see, I can always make out your shapes. Friendship is a flashlight, and yours has guided me through the darkest nights. I love you all from the bottom to the top of my heart.

Lex and Kyle, the formative experiences that I had with you are the load-bearing walls of my existence. Nothing that has been built since would stay in place without the solid framework you helped me form. I love you so.

Thomas, I love talking about movies with you, and you might just be the funniest person I know, don't tell the others. What you might not know is that there were times over these past few years that your friendship helped to keep my head above water. Even in the darkest of times you remind me how much fun life can be.

Janet, you're the sun!

Kira, you're the moon!

Catherine, you're the stars!

Preston, you are a sweet bean. Your determination to remain joyful is an inspiration.

To all the sweet babes in Italy who have made me feel at home halfway across the globe, grazie mille! Al, Levi, and the girls, thank you for sharing your home, hearts, and countless epic barbecues. The memories I have with you guys are somehow even sweeter than the figs from that big tree in your garden. To Alberto, Azzura, Neste, Blerina, Giulia, Simone, Jennifer, Callie, and Jane, thank you for showing me the ropes, taking me to sagras, hidden bars, and locals-only restaurants, and making your corner of Tuscany feel like *Cheers*. I could never put into words how beautiful it is there, or how much you have all meant to me.

To Jeffrey Haynes, you literally saved my life. I'm not sure thank you even scratches the surface of my gratitude, but thank you nevertheless. And thank you for inviting me on tour all those years ago. It certainly didn't turn out as planned, but I guess that is the moral of this story. I'm glad that I went, though, and that we made it and that I know you. Love you buddy, always.

David, you silly goose, you. No matter the weather, I will always see you in the sunshine with that big smile of yours, listening to Penny and the Quarters sing "You and Me," the rolling hills of the Tuscan countryside in the background. When I am sad, I listen for the roar of your laughter and feel the magnitude of your hug. Thank you for teaching me about true love.

Rob, you are such a gentle and warm person. Thank you for all your support and for always being at the ready to help me fix anything and everything. Thank you for always helping me find solutions, and for your bottomless well of patience. We have come such a long way in our relationship and you have become a dear friend and an outstanding and ever-supportive father. Love you, Rob-O.

Dad, I wrote a book. I wish you were here to read it. I think you would be proud, but I am also not convinced you would have the emotional strength to get through it, seeing as you die in the end. You were with me while I was writing it, though, and many other times too. I miss you very much, Daddy-O, catch you on the flip side.

Mama, I wrote and rewrote this part a hundred times because it is impossible to summarize in a few sentences, or a thousand pages even, what you mean to me. Thank you is a kindness, but not totally sufficient for someone whom I literally owe my existence to. But it's far more than that, and while I am deeply grateful for the air in my lungs and the blood in my veins, I am more so for the head on my shoulders, which has not always been screwed on straight, but always filled with interesting ideas, esoteric concepts, good jokes, and bright colors, and also for my heart, which I hope to be a fraction as big as yours someday, but mostly for all the incredible '90s hand-me-down clothing that garners me tons of compliments, but more importantly, makes me feel like you—something I have always wanted to be, even when I tried my hardest to hide it. I am your greatest admirer and your number one fan, forevermore. Here's to being best friends in this lifetime and the next.

And finally to all of you out there, thank you for taking the time to read this. In this wild and weird journey of living, may you hold on tight to your joy; it's a life raft. Be good to yourselves and each other, and may you all have the best time.

Cin cin!

ABOUT THE AUTHOR

ZAHRA TANGORRA is a chef, restaurant consultant, and writer living in Brooklyn, New York. She is the chef and owner behind the cult favorite Italian American pop-up Zaza Lazagna and also the beloved former Cobble Hill restaurant Brucie. Brucie and Zaza have been featured in multiple publications and TV shows including *The New Yorker*, *The New York Times*, *The Village Voice*, *Time*, *The Daily News*, *Women Chefs of New York*, *Eater*, *Grub Street*, *Brooklyn Magazine*, *Mass Appeal*, *Glamour*, MTV, *The Martha Stewart Show*, and ABC News. Zahra's writing has been featured in *New York Magazine*, *Lenny Letter*, *Speaking Broadly Zine*, *DVEIGHT Magazine*, and *Epicurious*.

ABOUT THE TYPE

This book was set in Dante, a typeface designed by Giovanni Mardersteig (1892–1977). Conceived as a private type for the Officina Bodoni in Verona, Italy, Dante was originally cut only for hand composition by Charles Malin, the famous Parisian punch cutter, between 1946 and 1952. Its first use was in an edition of Boccaccio's *Trattatello in laude di Dante* that appeared in 1954. The Monotype Corporation's version of Dante followed in 1957. Though modeled on the Aldine type used for Pietro Cardinal Bembo's treatise *De Aetna* in 1495, Dante is a thoroughly modern interpretation of that venerable face.